Surveying Christianity's African Roots
Second Edition

"... *Christian intellect apparently found a richer thought environment in Africa than elsewhere. It discovered itself in the intellectual centers of Africa before Europe had produced such centers. Eventually it offered its rich wisdom to the cultures of the northern side of the Mediterranean ...*"

Dr. Thomas C. Oden
Professor of Theology and Ethics at Drew University 1980-2016

© 2019, 2022 by Jimmie Davis Compton, Jr.

First edition published 2019. Second edition 2022.
Published by Jimmie D. Compton, Jr.
Printed in the United States of America

All rights reserved. Except for brief quotes in printed reviews, no part of this publication may be reproduced, stored, or transmitted in any form or by any means without the written consent of the author.

Publisher's Cataloging-in-Publication Data

Compton, Jimmie Davis, Jr., 1951-

Surveying Christianity's African roots / Jimmie D. Compton, Jr.

    p. cm.
Includes bibliographic references and notes.
Paperback - ISBN 978-0-940123-05-2
Spiral bound - ISBN 978-0-940123-06-9

Survey of the rational, organized, thriving, scripturally informed and Holy Spirit-inspired roots of indigenous Christianity in Africa. Christian faith communities there had existed centuries before the First Council of Nicaea, before Rome adopted Christianity, before the Byzantine Empire, and before King James commissioned a compilation of the Bible. African Christians' faith in Jesus Christ, perseverance, suffering, sacrifice, exegetical principles, theological dogma, and canonical processes were instrumental to the foundation and institutions of Western Christianity. This survey helps to balance existing mainstream church history resources.

    1. Christianity—Africa, North. 2. Church history—Berbers. 3. Church history—Persecution—Africa, North. 4. Church history—Martyrs—Africa, North. 5. Church history.
I. Compton, Jimmie Davis II. Title.

BR 190. C 2022

276—dc23

Cover photo © titoOnz (modified)/Shutterstock
In-text photo, page 11 © bible-history.com
In-text photo, page 12 © dikobraziy
In-text photo, page 13 © Charles Schulz
In-text photo, page 16 © Nabaten
In-text photo, page 23 © Jimmie Compton
In-text photo, page 38 © worldmap1.com
In-text photo, page 48 © Jimmie Compton
In-text photo, page 60 © anthrogenica.com
In-text photo, page 62 © numisology.com
In-text photo, page 65 © anthrogenica.com
In-text photo, page 89 © Drew Montgomery
In-text photo, page 95 © Jimmie Compton
In-text photo, page 98 © en.wikipedia.org
In-text photo, page 126 © wordpress download content
In-text photo, page 145 © JeroMe Matiyas
In-text photo, page 159 © Encyclopedia Britannica
In-text photo, page 180 © unknown (modified)
In-text photo, page 181 © JoaoLeitao.com

All Scripture quotations, except those noted otherwise, are from the Holy Bible, NEW INTERNATIONAL VERSION®, NIV® Copyright © 1973, 1978, 1984, 2011 by Biblica, Inc.® Used by permission. All rights reserved worldwide.

Thanks to Carolyn Drew for inquiring about this subject for her Youth Church teachers and their students. Her query sparked the academic expedition that resulted in this book.

To my wife Nancy, who stepped into my office often as I worked during weird hours and shook your head then quietly walked out: Thanks for peace and for understanding my obsession.

Without the editorial, linguistic, and theological expertise of Dr. Barbara Joyce Brooks, this work would have fallen far short of God's intended purpose. Having said that, I must add that any flaws or inconsistencies found are a result of my vain exercise of author prerogative, against her better judgment.

In memory of the late Deacon Jackie Cooper, Jr., the first to inform my African consciousness and who taught me wisdom from the Scriptures.

Table of Contents

First Century A.D. Map of the Roman Empire 10
Map of Africa 12
Introduction 15
Chronological Perspective 21
    Dates of Significant Historic Events 21
    How to Use This Book and Other Resources 22
Chapter 1: What the Bible and Its Era's History Reveal 23
    Hamito-Semitic Language Expanse Across North Africa 23
    Migration of Hamito-Semitic Speaking People into North Africa before Jesus' Birth 24
    Preservation of Hebrew History Between the Testaments 26
    Jason of Cyrene 26
    Preparation for the "Set Time to Come" Was Complete 27
    Early African Missionaries 28
    Simon of Cyrene 28
    Libyan and Egyptian Believers of the Upper Room 29
    Libyans Take the Gospel to Gentiles Prior to Apostle Paul 30
    African Spiritual Leaders in the Church at Antioch 30
    What the Epistles Reveal About Early Believers 31
    What the History of This Era Reveals About Early Missionaries 32
Chapter 2: Egypt 37
    Mark's Ministry Challenges in Egypt 38
    Apollos of Alexandria 38
    Hebrews in Egyptian Bondage Again 39
    Yet, the Gospel Flourished 39
Chapter 3: Persecution of Christians Begins in Rome 41
    Persecution of Christians in Rome 41
    The Cause 41
    Suspicion about Christians 42
Chapter 4: Cyrene 45
    African Hebrews of Cyrene 45
    Romans and the African Hebrews of Cyrene 46
    Impact of Jesus' Jerusalem Prophecy Upon Cyrene 46
    Northwest Migration of Messianic Hebrews of Cyrene and Egypt 48
Chapter 5: Sacred Texts and Truth Teaching 51
    Septuagint Text 51
    Catechetical School in Alexandria, Egypt 51
    Old African Text 52
    Methodology for Identifying Right Teaching of Scripture 52
    Use of the Term "Catholic" 53
    The Early Church by the End of the 2nd Century A.D. 56
    What the Early African Church Understood and Practiced 57
Chapter 6: North Africa's Proconsularis, Numidia, and Mauretania 59
    Africa Proconsularis 59
    Leptis Magna Evangelists into Numidia 62
    Ancient Numidian Kingdom 62
    First African Church Council 63
    Mauretania 64
    General Perceptions of Christians by Roman Writers 64
    Earliest Record of the Persecution of African Christians 65
    Namphanio 66
    Africans Persecuted for Bringing Africans to Christ 67
    Speratus and His Pupils 67

    Pope Victor I 69
    Persecution: Emperor Severus' Edict of 202 A.D. 70
    Perpetua and Felicitas... 70
    Church Life under Emperor Severus 71
    Unique Expression of Early African Christian Faith.. 71
    The Martyrdom Perspective in the Region.. 72

Chapter 7: African Church Fathers (pre-Nicene)... 75
    Clement of Alexandria 76
    Tertullian.. 77
    Origen of Alexandria 79
    Cyprian of Carthage 81
    Arnobius of Sicca 83

Chapter 8: Persecuted for Not Sacrificing to Roman Gods,   Part 1................... 87
    Roman Emperor Decius' Edict of 250 A.D. 87
    End of Favor from Rome... 87
    Africanus and 40 Companions 88
    Isidore of Chios 89
    Church Life under Emperor Decius 89
    Peculiar Nature of Persecution in Africa 89
    James, Marian, and Friends.. 90
    Anthony the Great 91
    The Crisis within the Roman Empire 92

Chapter 9: Persecuted for Not Sacrificing to Roman Gods,   Part 2................... 95
    Roman Emperor Diocletian's Persecutions and Tetrarchy 95
    Africa Gave the Tetrarchy Most of Its Martyrs 96
    Persecution, Martyrs, Events, and Church Leaders During the Tetrarchy 98
    Marcellus the Centurion.. 98
    Cassian the Stenographer 99
    Arcadius of Mauretania 99
    Victor the Moor 100
    Salsa.. 101
    Typasii the Veteran 101
    Maurice the African, Roman General... 102
    Lucius Caecilius Firmianus Lactantius 104
    Maximilian of Tebessa 105
    Crispina.. 105
    Felix the Bishop of Thibiuca 106
    Victoria of Albitina 107
    Saturninus, His Children, and Companions 108
    Maxima, Donatilla, and Secunda of Tuburga 109
    Martyrs of Milevis... 110
    Alleged Betrayal by Bishop of Carthage and His Deacon 110
    Theodore of Cyrene 111
    The Deacon Arius... 112
    Timothy the Church Reader and His Wife Maura 113
    Alexandrian Christians Detest Diocletian 113
    Rais of Alexandria 115
    Theodora (and Didymus) 116
    Catherine of Alexandria.. 117
    Church Life under the Tetrarchy 117
    Dichotomies Rippling Through Time and Cultures... 119
    Biblical Anticipation of African Martyrs 119

Chapter 10: Dissenting African Congregations 125

    Origin of Their Dissent... 125
    The Dispute.. 125
    Dissenting Congregations Categorized as Donatists 126

Chapter 11: Rome Ends Its Persecution of Christians.. **129**
    An Abrupt Loss of Roman Emperors Shakes Up the Tetrarchy............................. 129
    Pope Miltiades (a.k.a. Melchiades the African)... 130
    The Edict of Milan in 313 A.D. 130
    Emperor Constantine Reunites with Lactantinus.. 131
    Constantine's Aggression Against Donatists After the Edict of Milan 131
    Alexander of Alexandria.. 133
    Athanasius.. 134
    The First Council of Nicaea.. 136
    Some Outcomes from the First Council of Nicaea 137
    Dueling Congregations... 138
    Didymus the Blind 141

Chapter 12: Ethiopia **145**
    Aksumite Emperor Ezana's Conversion... 145
    Earliest Illustrated Christian Bible... 146

Chapter 13: Rome Adopts Christianity as Its State Religion................................. **149**
    Donatists' Apprehension Confirmed... 149
    Gildo's Coup in Rome's African Territories 150
    Catholic-Imperialist Repression of Donatists.. 151
    Differentiating Between Donatists and Catholics.. 152

Chapter 14: Africa's Hardening of Christian Philosophy....................................... **155**
    Aurelius of Carthage.. 155
    Augustine of Hippo 157
    Evidence of Augustine's African Consciousness 159
    Desert Fathers: Founders of Monastic Living 160
    Moses the Black 161

Chapter 15: Africa's Hardening of Christian Ecclesiology **165**
    Code of Canons from Africa-Specific Church Councils 165
    On Doctrine, Jurisdiction, Religious Pride, and Closed Canon.............................. 165
    African Canons as the Gold Standard Throughout Christendom 166
    Primacy and Influence... 167

Chapter 16: Arian Invaders Persecute Donatists and Catholics............................ **171**
    Huneric's Deceptive Oath Given to African Bishops... 173
    Enormous Devastation to the Early African Church... 173
    Dionysia of Africa 174
    Pope Gelasius I 175
    King Masuna 176

Chapter 17: Nubia **179**
    Location of Nubia 180
    Gradual Christianization of Nubia 180
    Inscription Evidence of Gradual Christianization 181
    Artifact Evidence of Gradual Christianization... 182

Chapter 18: Decline of Christianity in Northwest Africa... **185**
    What Happened to Donatists and Nicaeans?.. 185
    Reflections on the Decline of Christianity in Northwest Africa 185
    Africa's Eastern Coast Stronghold... 186

Africa's Prominence in Church History at a Glance **189**
Bibliography.. **192**
About the Author.. **206**

First Century A.D. Map of the Roman Empire

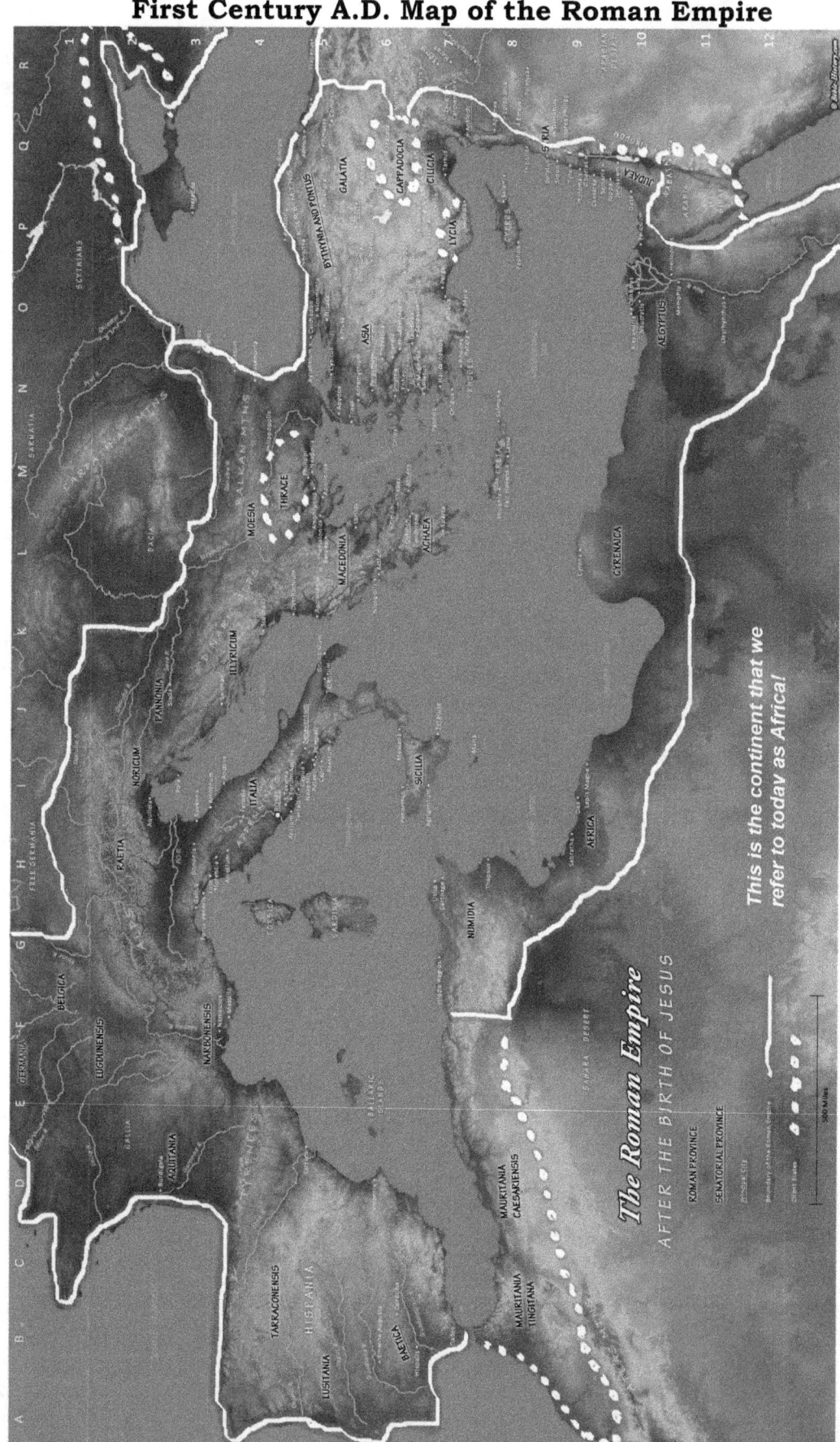

View this in better contrast through the QR Code at the end of the Chronological Perspective chapter

Outlined on the map in solid white on the previous page is the boundary of the Roman Empire, as it encompasses the Mediterranean Sea. This was nearly four hundred years before Rome adopted Christianity as its state religion. The white dotted outlines are Rome's client states. Those were territories economically, politically, or militarily subordinate to Rome in international affairs; and whose leaders were made subservient to Rome.

Notice the first century A.D. African Roman territories of Mauretania, Numidia, Carthage, Hippo Regus, Leptis Magna, Cyrene, and Alexandria, Egypt that existed at the birth of Jesus Christ. This survey will delve into the lives of African Christians, places, and the faith challenges that generally do not make it into mainstream Christian resources.

African Christians worshipped Jesus Christ within the Roman Empire. To summarize a PBS documentary "The Roman Empire in the First Century: Roman Gods," Rome's worship was twofold: (a) private, where families worshipped specific individual spirits, and (b) public, whereby the Roman state honored many gods. Romans were religious. They believed that many gods (with human characteristics) had taken part in the founding of Rome. Therefore, the emperors and statesmen consulted and honored them in order to ensure that its political and social actions met divine approval. For the next three hundred years, the tension between African Christians and Rome grew fierce.

Map of Africa

African territories under discussion in this book are within these ▬▬▬▬

Deficiencies in Mainstream Church History Resources

Charles Schulz's September 4, 1975 Peanuts comic strip aptly reflects the narrow and truncated approach in the study of Church History. It compelled me to reflect back twenty-five years ago to my first Church History course in seminary. While thumbing through the Early Church section of the two-volume textbook, I came across a table that contained key historic entries. In its header were four columns: Emperors, Bishops of Rome, Authors and Documents, and Events. Listed in each row under its respective header were the names of people, the duration in years, writings, and key events in chronological order. Another section in the textbook had a similar chronological table. Noted at the bottom of one table was a footnote stating that only the most important rulers and popes were listed. After a careful perusal, I found only a handful of entries of key persons of African descent or early church events in Africa.

The vast majority of the tables' details were centered on Rome. Not unlike the Peanuts cartoon, those tables will easily mislead the reader. One could easily assume that the origin of Christianity and significant contributions to the Church throughout history came from Rome. Below are several reasons why such an impression is misleading:

- The first 280 years or so after the resurrection of Jesus Christ and while gospel missionary activity swept across North Africa, the state of Rome cruelly put Christians to death for not embracing its pagan gods (particularly in Africa). Then for the 67 years after Rome had outlawed the persecution of Christians, it still had not embraced Christianity for itself.

- As a political state, Rome was not Christian for the 347 years after the resurrection of Jesus Christ; nor was it Christian while Christian doctrine, worship, and ecclesiology formally emerged. It was not Christian while the principles for textual analysis, criticism and interpretation of Scripture were established.

- The first Christian church was not in Rome. Prior to those Rome-centered events that are detailed in my church history textbook:

- - Missionaries from Cyrene (Africa) and Cyprus had already planted the Antioch church (Acts 11:20-21). This was before Saul used his Roman name Paul and before his first missionary journey (Acts 13:2-4).
  - Mark had already planted the church in Alexandria, Egypt.
  - While Rome's state religion was pagan as it persecuted Christians, Africa had been the first and most profound intellectual center of the Church before Europe.[1]
- When the state of Rome eventually embraced Christianity, it was not the first political state to do so. The Ethiopian Empire and Armenian Empire had already established Christianity as their state religion.

So why do mainstream Christian resources and teaching institutions in the West promulgate a Rome-centered prominence in church history?

Grace, truth, redemption and eternal life through Christ as the "Way" came first from Judea, but the Church's ecclesiology, doctrine, penance, creed, and liturgy were forged primarily in Africa (Numidian, Carthage, and Egyptian regions). This survey brings some balance to discussions about church history. It provides nearly 400 proofs of Africa's profound contributions to church history and the Christian religion during the first 500 years after the resurrection of Jesus Christ.

For the sake of Africa's identity and that of her children of the diaspora, it is imperative that the foundation she has laid for the Christian Church be given its due visibility. That is the objective and divine burden upon this author of Berber ancestry himself.

---

[1] Thomas C. Oden, *How Africa Shaped the Christian Mind* (Downers Grove, IL: InterVarsity Press, 2007), 95.

Introduction

After Jesus' betrayal, suffering, death, burial, and resurrection, He met his eleven disciples at a previously agreed upon location (Matthew 26:32, 28:16). Once there, He told them

> All authority in heaven and on earth has been given to me. Therefore go and make disciples of all nations, baptizing them in the name of the Father and of the Son and of the Holy Spirit, and teaching them to obey everything I have commanded you. And surely I am with you always, to the very end of the age. (Matthew 28:18-20)

<u>The Perspective</u>

God's plan is for people from all nations to hear the good news of divine reconciliation through Jesus Christ. This was not to be a religion, but the restoration of the broken relationship between humanity and God that occurred as a result of Adam and Eve's disobedience.

Within the first century A.D. the eleven disciples, endowed by the Holy Spirit with miraculous signs and abilities, accomplished this mission as the Lord commanded.[2] After the gospel had been spread far and wide, the power of God's Word, along with the work of the Holy Spirit, required nothing else to propagate itself throughout souls in foreign lands. In fact, self-replication is implied by Jesus' command above. From the Day of Pentecost in the upper room, the early African missionaries realized that being a disciple required them to make other disciples. It has been a never-ending process that continues into our day.

Transport along the Maghreb and Nile waterways of the Mediterranean Sea's coastline (now Morocco, Algeria, Tunisia, Libya, and Egypt) significantly expedited this process of making disciples throughout North and east Africa. Port cities where diverse cultures converged for trade and commerce provided an idea point of connection for spreading the gospel. People gathered there to sell, exchange, eat, rest, or restock supplies before moving on. Whether it is intentional or not, port cities create ideal occasions for different ideas and beliefs to also be exchanged. Early African gospel missionaries undoubtedly seized the opportunity to do so.

In support of a few assertions about Africa's contribution to Christianity, this survey will include some ancient history about people and places around the Mediterranean Sea. This history will serve as a backdrop to Africa's contributions from the first through the mid-sixth centuries A.D. Her contributions to foundational Christian institutions, doctrine, sacraments and ecclesiology establishes Africa's identify as a major contributor to the formulation of Christianity as a religion. In this survey you will discover what Africa had contributed long before the Nicene Council, Rome adopting Christianity as its official religion, the emergence of Byzantine Christianity, Arab conquests, the origin of Islam and King James' compilation of the Bible.

You won't get too far into this book before realizing that these African Christians were not only intellectual scholars in theology, science, apologetics, and monasticism (who read the Gospels, Apostle Paul's letters and the Old Testament), but they also aided Rome's first "Christian" emperor as he accommodated Christians within the empire. The faith of these Africans had been well established long before Roman Catholicism. The taproot of Western Christianity is firmly planted in Africa.

The People and Their Language

The indigenous people of the Maghreb (North Africa) were referred to as "Berber" people. The map below shows the geographic area where their language was predominately spoken around the fifth century B.C.[3]

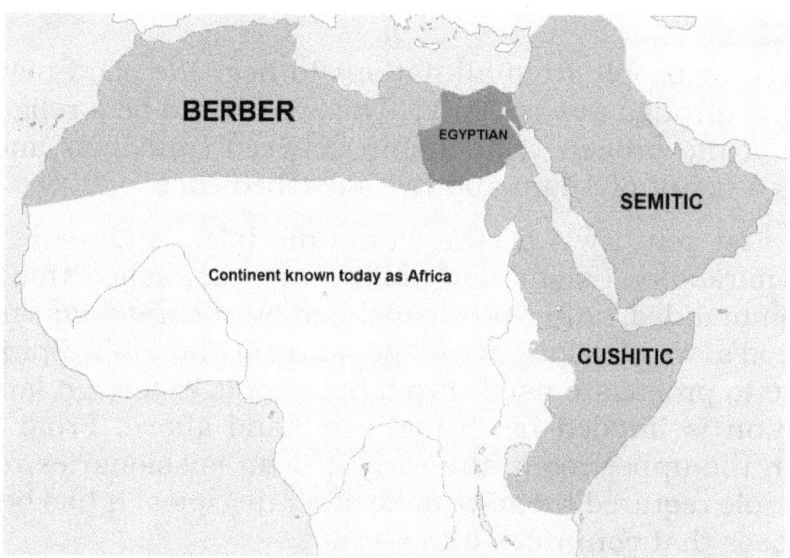

Scholarly research suggests that the Hamito-Semitic languages (Berber, Egyptian, Semitic and Cushitic) were derived from a single language that had been spoken thousands of years prior. For reasons lost to oblivion (perhaps a polarizing dispute, a catastrophic event, migration, etc.), this geographically dispersed singular language evolved independently into these separate distinct languages.[4]

Actually, the term "berber" was a name that the Greeks and Romans assigned the people (no earlier than the fourth century B.C.) It meant "barbarian". Originally, the term was used as an onomatopoeia (formulation of a word to imitate the sound made by its referent): "bar-bar." That was a mockery of how the people there sounded to the unfamiliar Greek and Roman ear. To them, it was mere rude and harsh speech. But after the Greco-Persian wars in the first half of the fifth century B.C., the term also acquired the sense of rudeness and brutal behavior.[5] Nevertheless, I'll continue using the term since it has been socialized by historians to designate a particular people (who themselves also embrace the term today). Out of respect for the Berber people, I will defer to the historian Herodotus, who names the individual Berber tribes: Adyrmachidae, Gilligammae, Asbytae, Auschisae, Cabalians, Nasamonians, Numidians, Psylli, Garamantians, Macae, Gindanes, Lolophagi, Machlyans, Auseans, Troglodytes, Zavecians, Gyzantians, Atarantians, and the Atlantes. Moors initially descended from the Berber indigenous people of the Maghreb. Then the name "Moor" was later also applied to Arabs.[6] It has been said that they were all descendants of Noah's son Ham.[7]

As for the ancestors of these Berber-speaking tribes, due to their oral tradition, not much of their history survived. Though limited by his Roman-centric perspective, there is a surviving account by the first century B.C. Roman historian Sallust.[8] He sheds some light about their ancestors that obviously predates the arrival of Christianity into the region (by at least two centuries). Sallust describes the indigenous inhabitants of North Africa as the Getulians and Libyans, both nomadic hunting and gathering cultures. He goes on to say that their culture later mixed with a wave of sea migrants [Canaanites/Phoenicians]. The new mixed cultures then began trade contacts with the Iberian Peninsula and became ancestors of the historic Mauri (Moors) and Numidians.[9]

Their descendants today are the Amazigh, the Mozabite, and the Tuarega, who live in scattered communities across Morocco, Algeria, Tunisia, Libya, Egypt, Mali, Niger, and Mauretania. They speak various Amazigh languages belonging to the Hamito-Semitic family related to ancient Egyptian and the African Great Lakes region. Amazigh (plural, Imazigen) means "free and noble men."[10] They have been present in these territories since ancient times, according to historian Malika Hachid. Their presence in the region dates back more than 10,000 years, and "Berber as an identity and culture was forged in the lands of North Africa and nowhere else."[11]

In the reprint of her 1927 book, Steuart Erskine describes the indigenous Berber people of Africa as follows:

> "The most curious feature of this people is certainly persistency. [They] lived in villages often built over the ruins of the more powerful nations, speaking the same language that they spoke three thousand years ago and having an alphabet peculiar to themselves."

> "The Berbers were an intensely strong, hardy race; they died in battle or from the attack of some wild animal; seldom from any illness. They were willing and patient, and kept a word once given ..."[12]

A People Described as Black, Dark Brown, Ethiopian

While browsing through historical references that describe the original Berber-speaking people, I discovered that they were never described as anything else but black, dark brown, Ethiopian, or something similar. That is, until the twelfth century A.D. One explanation for the discrepancies between the pre-twelfth century A.D. and today's descriptions of the people of North Africa involves the famous nineteenth-century A.D. German explorer of Africa, Heinrich Barth. In his written observations, he described the inhabitants as "a mixed race of blacks and whites." He goes on to say that "the whites were Berbers and Arabs."[13] Yet, before the twelfth century A.D., the Berber people were described as dark skinned.[14] The social presuppositions and ethnocentric ideas during Barth's and his colleagues' day likely precluded them from attributing advanced civilization and critical thinking to any race except the "white" race. I believe this to be the case because a few decades prior, Barth's own distinguished contemporary and countryman, the physician Johann Friedrich Blumenbach, included North Africans in his classification of Caucasians (the white race). Even though his mistaken classification is well-known and documented, it is often ignored.[15]

However, genetics provide a more accurate set of facts. It is unlikely that the Berber gene pool originated from north of the Mediterranean Sea (Europe), but rather, from deeper south (further into Africa). A May 5, 2004 article in the *American Journal of Human Genetics* bears this out. Though there has been gene flow into North Africa from the surrounding regions, some areas have experienced long periods of genetic isolation. This would allow a distinctive genetic marker to proliferate among some populations in the region, particularly amongst isolated Berber people. Haplogroup E is the most prevalent haplogroup amongst the Berbers, accounting for up to 87 percent of Y-chromosomes in some Berber populations.[16] This haplogroup is thought to have emerged from East Africa, and later dispersed into North Africa and West Asia. The parent marker originated in East Africa. It has been affectionately named the Berber marker (or Maghrebi marker) for its prevalence among Mozabite, Middle Atlas Mountains, and other Berber speaking groups and is quite common among other North African groups.[17]

Their Proclamations

Members of these Berber speaking people of Africa made early and lasting contributions to the Christian faith. In addition to the many unnamed Berbers who have been martyred, were other notable Christian Berbers such as Namphanio, Tertullian, Cyprian, Maximilian of Tebessa, Arnobius of Sicca, Marcellus of Tangier, Majorinus, Donatus Magnus, Lactantius, Arius, Gildo, Maximian (Bishop of Carthage), Augustine of Hippo, and King Masuna. The reach of influence of Berber-speaking people is demonstrated through the success of even a Berber Roman Emperor, Septimius Severus.

This survey will profile many African Early Church Fathers of Berber descent prior to the First Nicene Council in 325 A.D., as well as those thereafter. One marked difference between the pre and post-Nicene Church Fathers is the situation of life to which (and from which) they wrote, taught, and preached. The writings of the pre-Nicene African Church Fathers had more to do with how to live the Christian life. They explained to outsiders what Christians believed, or contrasted the tenets of a false teaching with what their Christian faith community believed. On the other hand, the post-Nicene African Church Fathers were more concerned with defining precise points of right teaching and structure for the church. This distinction is important because otherwise, our tendency would be to expect to see the technical precision of post-Nicene Church

Fathers in the theological concepts used by pre-Nicene Church Fathers. We must understand that the latter understood right teaching in terms of general concepts about living a Christ-honoring life, not by using meticulous theological definitions. Pre-Nicene writers were primarily concerned with how Christians should live. With centuries of writings that establish how Christians are to live, the task of post-Nicene writers was to institutionalize "how to live as a Christian" into teachable, defendable, and repeatable doctrinal terminology and concepts for future believers. This post-Nicene perspective was invaluable as the African Church Fathers assisted Rome's first Christian emperor, Constantine.

I would be remiss if I did not say a bit about heretics. In the early church, most of the men who had been deemed heretics held positions of influence in the church long before they were labeled as such. Unfortunately, a consensus on the recognizable body of right teaching was still in the process of being established. As a result, one might find himself on the list of heretics, but later be taken off the list. Through the scholarly work of understanding scriptural meaning and interpretation, early African Church Fathers hammered out the tenets of the Christian faith. A recognizable body of right teaching emerged as its elements were debated. Let it suffice to say that these scholars made passionate efforts to set forth truth. Though some of them fell short (and were deemed heretics), it demonstrates the African Church's sincere grappling with establishing what was to be accepted as true and scripturally consistent about the nature of God, Christ, and the virtues of His redemptive work on the Cross.

The Prospect

As you will read, copies of the Gospels, Apostle Paul's letters, and the Old Testament Scriptures existed throughout North Africa by the second century A.D. But for the most part, those copies were written in the languages of the authors and in Latin. Unfortunately, they had not been translated into the native languages of Berber, Punic and Old Nubian, as they had been in Egypt and Ethiopia. Had they been translated into those native tongues, along with documenting their worship practices infused with some elements from their local culture, it is quite possible that Christianity would have flourished much longer and more pervasively throughout North Africa, Nubia, and perhaps beyond. Nevertheless, the faith in Jesus Christ, perseverance, and sacrifices of each African Christian in this survey (and an unknown number of others) helped to establish the philosophy, teachings, and religious institutions of Western Christianity for centuries to come.

The resurgence of Christianity throughout the continent of Africa since the mid-twentieth century honors the sacrifices and contributions of the African Christians of the early church. African Christians today can eat the fruit from trees that their ancestral countrymen and countrywomen planted and watered with their blood millenniums ago. In fact, Christians anywhere would benefit from their fitting example of genuine spirituality, Christian living, and faith in Christ.

Introduction Notes

[2] Mark 16:17-20; Acts 2:1-4; Acts 3:1-7; Mark 16:20, Colossians 1:23; Romans 16:26.

[3] Wikipedia Contributors, s.v. "Afroasiatic Urheimat," Wikipedia, The Free Encyclopedia, November 7, 2019, https://en.wikipedia.org/wiki/Afroasiatic_Urheimat#cite_note-1.

[4] Ibid; Catherine Miller, s.v. "Nubien, berbère et beja : notes sur trois langues vernaculaires non arabes de l'Égypte contemporaine," *Égypte/Monde arabe, Première série*, 1996, November 10, 2019, https://journals.openedition.org/ema/1960#article-1960.

[5] Merrill F. Unger and William White Jr., eds., *Vine's Expository Dictionary of Biblical Words*, s.v. "Barbarian," (Nashville: Thomas Nelson, Inc., 1985); Wikipedia Contributors, s.v. "Barbarian," *Wikipedia, The Free Encyclopedia*, December 5, 2018, https://en.wikipedia.org/wiki/Barbarian.

[6] Wikipedia Contributors, s.v. "Moors," *Wikipedia, The Free Encyclopedia*, https://en.wikipedia.org/wiki/Moors.

[7] Rudolph R Windsor, *From Babylon to Timbuktu* (Chicago: Lushena Books, 2003), 104.

[8] He recorded this history from the perspective of a victor after the war between Rome and King Jugurtha of Numidia.

[9] Sallust, *The Jugurthine War*, ed. John S. Watson (New York and London: Harper & Brothers, 1899), in the Perseus Digital Library, http://www.perseus.tufts.edu/hopper/text?doc=Perseus%3Atext%3A1999.02.0126%3Achapter%3D18.

[10] Peter Prengaman, "Morocco's Berbers Battle to Keep from Losing Their Culture," *San Francisco Chronicle*, March 16, 2001, http://www.sfgate.com/news/article/Morocco-s-Berbers-Battle-to-Keep-From-Losing-2941557.php.

[11] "Indigenous Peoples in Algeria," IWGIA, 2016, http://www.iwgia.org/regions/africa/algeria.

[12] Steuart Erskine, *Vanished Cities of Northern Africa* (London: FB & Ltd, Dalton House, 2018), 16-17.

[13] Heinrich Barth, *Travels and Discoveries in North and Central Africa: Being a Journal of an Expedition,* vol. 5 (New York: Harper & Brothers, 1857), 486.

[14] Dana Marniche, "African Moors: The Appearance of the Original Berbers According to European Perceptions," Rasta Livewire (blog), September 12, 2008, http://www.africaresource.com/rasta/sesostris-the-great-the-egyptian-hercules/the-appearance-of-the-original-berbers-according-to-european-perceptions-by-dana-marniche/.

[15] Race Project, "Early Classification of Nature," American Anthropological Association, 2007, accessed May 15, 2017, http://www.understandingrace.org/history/science/early_class.html; Race Project, "Caucasian," American Anthropological Association, 2007, accessed June 5, 2019, http://www.understandingrace.org/#c.

[16] A *haplotype* is a group of genes in a living being that are inherited together from a single parent, and a *haplogroup* is a group of similar haplotypes that share a common ancestor.

[17] Fulvio Cruciani, et al., "Phylogeographic Analysis of Haplogroup E3b (E-M215) Y Chromosomes Reveals Multiple Migratory Events Within and Out of Africa," *American Journal of Human Genetics* 74, no. 5, 2004, http://www.sciencedirect.com/science/article/pii/S0002929707643651.

Chronological Perspective

Dates of Significant Historic Events

Understanding the sequence of events is essential for gaining an appreciation for how profound it is that passionate, rational, and devout African believers took bold stances of Christian faith from the first through the sixth centuries A.D., not to mention their scholarly role in shaping Christian thinking in the west. Tracking each event or person against the dates on the table below helps one grasp the depth and profoundness of their faith. Keep in mind that the religions in their region at the time were either of a pagan variety or Hebrew. Also noteworthy is that paganism was the pervasive religion of Rome's imperial power over the North African regions where Christianity was spreading until the fifth century.

A.D.	Dates of Significant Historic Events
33	Jesus' resurrection, Great Commission and Ascension
*64	First organized persecution against Christians by Rome
*70	Fall of Jerusalem and the destruction of the Second Temple by Roman General Titus
*73	Fall of Masada to the Romans
*278	Anthony the Great practices monastic living in the Egyptian desert
*312	Roman Emperor Constantine's vision in his dream about Christianity
313	Rome ends its persecution of Christians
325	First Nicene Council
380	Rome adopts Christianity as its state religion
395	Rise of the Byzantine Empire (new Rome in Constantinople)
476	Fall of Rome
529	First monastic practice in the West by Benedict of Nursia
570	Birth of Muhammad, the prophet and founder of Islam
1054	Universal Church splits into East (Orthodox) & West (Roman Catholic)[18]
1095	First Roman Catholic Crusade
1440	Invention of the printing press in Rome
1441	Europe kidnaps people from Africa as permanently owned property
1490	Europe sends Christian missionaries to Africa
1611	Europe's King James Bible compilation completed
1880s	Europe divides and exploits Africa for its natural resources
1881	Europe establishes Christian colonies in Africa

*This is the duration of state organized persecution against Christians by Rome.

How to Use This Book and Other Resources

Under each chapter heading is the time span (as close as possible) within which the events described in the chapter occurred. Each chapter details one to five types of content categories:
- PROFILE OF EARLY CHRISTIANITY IN AN AFRICAN TERRITORY
- PROFILE OF AN AFRICAN EARLY CHRISTIAN LEADER
- PROFILE OF AN AFRICAN EARLY CHRISITAN MARTYR
- SOCIAL/POLITICAL FACTORS
- Narrative (under a descriptive subheading)

Beneath each type are details that expound on the faith and/or contributions of North African Christians. They had embraced the gospel of Jesus Christ centuries before the Roman Empire adopted Christianity as its state religion, and before Rome used it for political advantage. Pinpoint the date (or date range) of a particular event. Then find where it occurs in the table on the previous page. You'll develop a clearer perspective about the leadership of Africa and Africans in church history.

Research Assignment – Chronological Perspective

Use your preferred internet search tool to find information about the following:

a. Ancient Berber people prior to the second century A.D.

b. Berber DNA haplogroup marker

Too Busy to Read?

Listen to narrations about key people and events in *Early African Church History*, while you drive, wait in line, sit in a waiting room, or on a break (you can even watch the illustrations in the video narration). Just scan this QR code from your smartphone or tablet to access the low-cost 18 video narration course.[19] Also, reach out to us if you are interested in being certified as a teacher of this body of knowledge.

---

[18] Justo L. Gonzalez, *The Story of Christianity,* vol. 1, *The Early Church to the Dawn of Reformation* (New York: HarperSanFrancisco, 1984), 251-252.

[19] Or enter the URL https://hopeinstitute.teachable.com/p/scar-book-companion into a web browser.

Chapter 1: What the Bible and Its Era's History Reveal
(9th Century B.C. through 1st Century A.D.)

This chapter opens with a survey of events that were occurring elsewhere, while many Old Testament events took place. Centuries later, they had a significant impact on the Early Church in Africa.

Hamito-Semitic Language Expanse Across North Africa

Canaanite civilization (2500 B.C. to 539 B.C.) gave the world the alphabet. Their seafaring traders of Tyre, Sidon and Byblos dominated the Mediterranean Sea from around 1200 B.C. to 800 B.C., long before the founding of Rome.[20] Isaiah 23:1-12 and Ezekiel 27:3, 8 provide vivid portrayals of their dominance at sea and in trade. In Jeremiah 25:22, Jeremiah refers to them as "the kings of the coastlands across the sea." Also, trees from their cedar forests provided an excellent source of timber for their skillful craftsmen to build ships (2 Samuel 5:11, 1 Kings 5:6, 1 Chronicles 22:4, Ezra 3:7). The Greeks would later referred to the Canaanites as Phoenicians. Below, notice the locations of their city-states on the rightmost side of the map. The dotted lines denote trade routes.

Their Canaanite language was a part of the Hamito-Semitic language family, which also included Hebrew.[21] In addition to being the dominate trade merchants around the Mediterranean Sea, this gave them the advantage when negotiating an acquisition. In the interest of commerce, learning the language of trade was an advantage. As a result, the comprehension of Hamito-Semitic dialects rapidly spread amongst people in port cities throughout the Mediterranean as a way of mitigating the advantages of their peers. The map below is a graphic depiction of this spread. The dark areas on the map represent areas where the Canaanites' Hamito-Semitic dialect was understood, even if it was not spoken as a second language.

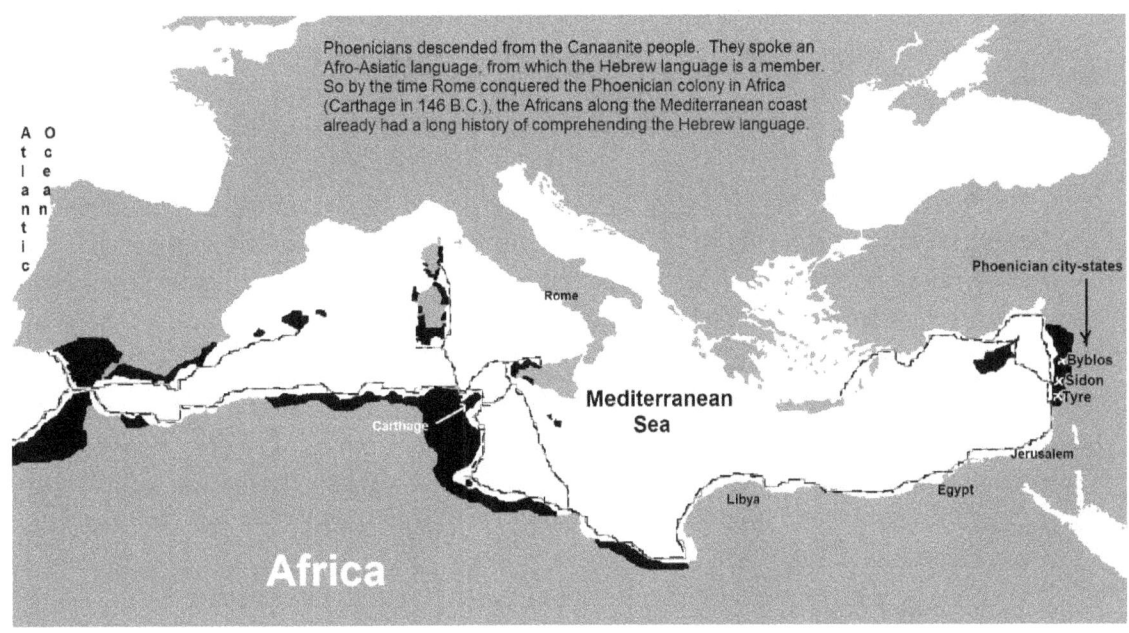

Migration of Hamito-Semitic Speaking People into North Africa before Jesus' Birth

Hebrew communities existed in North Africa (the Maghreb) as far back as just prior to Israel's divided kingdom. Moroccan, Tunisian, Libyan, and Egyptian Hebrews constitute the second largest Hebrew diaspora group. The following are timelines and brief descriptions about their migration and relationship with the indigenous Berber population of Africa.[22]

814-146 B.C. The Tunisian Hebrew community (also known as Carthaginians) is no doubt the oldest in the Maghreb. Just for some perspective, their history was concurrent with the reign of Israel's evil King Jehoahaz (2 Kings 13:1-9). Below is the Tunisian's explanation of how their Canaanite ancestors acquired control over some coastal regions of Berber territory. Also explained, is how the population of their Canaanite ancestors increased after successive waves of immigration and proselytism.[23]

> In 814 B.C., over eight hundred years before the birth of Christ, a Canaanite woman of royalty named Elissa of Tyre fled westward by sea into North Africa. A loyal following (including military commanders) and a hoard of the king's gold went with her. Elissa had been joint heir to the throne of Tyre with her brother, but fled out of fear for her life. The indigenous Berber people of Africa called her *Dido*, which means "wanderer." Her first task was to acquire land from the Berber King Larbas.[24] That she did with wisdom and intrigue. She founded the port city of Carthage along the Mediterranean Sea, long before the city of Rome was founded.

> During the era when the Phoenicians had circumnavigated the continent of Africa, Carthage became one of the leading commercial centers of the West Mediterranean region.[25] Carthage continued to grow in military power and nautical prowess. Not even Rome could match its technological and engineering superiority. But Carthage's progress had dramatically impacted the indigenous population. The Berber civilization there was already at a stage in which its agriculture, manufacturing, trade, and political organization supported several regions. Trade links between Carthage and the Berbers in the interior grew, but territorial expansion resulted in the enslavement or military enlistment of some Berbers and in the removal of trade from others. Carthage soon became the pre-eminent sea power in the western Mediterranean.

> By the mid-second century B.C., the Roman navy had discovered an abandoned Carthaginian military ship. After reverse-engineering its design, they created a superior fleet. With its newly designed fleet, Rome was finally able to subdue the Carthaginian navy, totally destroying the city and killing a significant number of its inhabitants.[26]

Being strategically located and having a port that was an engineering marvel, Rome decided to rebuild the city and resettle a colony there. The rebuilding of Carthage was a huge undertaking. An assessment by the historian Herodian gauges the magnitude of the effort: "Carthage vied with Alexandria for second place in the Roman empire."[27] By the first century B.C., Carthage had grown to the second largest city in the western half of the Roman Empire, with a peak population of 500,000. It was the center of the Roman province of Africa, which was a major breadbasket of the empire.[28]

In terms of language, archaeologist and historian Nahum Slouschz was convinced that the language of Carthage was Hebrew, with an Aramaic-Phoenician variant.[29] Archaeologist Alexander Graham reported that the "primitive inhabitants" there spoke Libyan (probably a euphemism for a language of one of the Berber people), and the "educated" Carthaginians spoke Greek.[30] The Romans referred to the Carthaginians' language as Punic, but introduced Latin into its colony.

587 B.C. Oral tradition reports that Moroccan Hebrews migrated to this area after the destruction of the First Temple in Jerusalem (2 Kings 25:8-9 and Lamentations 2) and settled among the Berbers.[31]

539 B.C. The Persian Empire extended westward to territories in Cyrene, Libya (that would include Alexandria, Egypt), then eastward to India (Esther 1:1). This was the year that Persia's King Cyprus conquered Babylon, ended Judah's seventy years of captivity there, and then allowed the Hebrews to return to Jerusalem if they desired (Ezra 1:1-4).

A blending with the Persian culture, its Zoroastrian beliefs and its goddess Anhita[32] undoubtedly would have occurred.

In his 2003 article entitled "St Mark, the Apostle and Beholder of God," Dr. Medhat Ibrahim of Theological College in El-Mina, Egypt states, "In Alexandria there were Greek philosophers and scholars, Jewish scholars and teachers of Scriptures, and Persian wise men."[33]

By the 3rd Century B.C. - Libyan Hebrews extend back to the third century B.C., at the least, when Cyrenaica was under Greek rule. The Hebrew population of Libya was a part of the Berber Hebrew community. In 250 B.C., Cyrenaica became part of the Ptolemaic empire (Ptolemy I Soter was the Greek general who succeeded Alexander the Great) controlled from Alexandria, Egypt. It became Roman territory in 96 B.C. when Ptolemy Apion bequeathed it to Rome. In 74 B.C., the territory was formally transformed into a Roman province. Biblical references to Alexander the Great can be found in Daniel 8:4-5, 8, 20-22; 10:2-11:4.[34]

Preservation of Hebrew History Between the Testaments

Sometime after 167 B.C., the Cyrenaican Hebrew Jason is credited for preserving the continuity of Hebrew history. After war, some of the sacred books of Israel had been lost. But it was Jason who gathered and reconstructed the lost books.

Before the Birth of Jesus Christ

Jason of Cyrene

Key Location	Cyrene, Libya
Modern-Day Name	Same
When	• After the events described in the last book of the Old Testament • After the Maccabees' revolt against the Seleucid Empire (167-160 B.C.) • Before the Judaism of the gospels (~57 B.C.)[35]
What	The Cyrenaican Hebrew Jason is credited for preserving the continuity of Hebrew history during the violent and sacrilegious period after 167 B.C. As a result of the war, some of the sacred books of Israel had been lost. But it was Jason who gathered and reconstructed the lost books.[36]
Related Event(s)	Using Jason's library as the basis, the writer of Second Maccabees credits Jason of Cyrene as the source of his material.
	He writes, "All this, already in five books by Jason of Cyrene, we shall attempt to condense into a single work." (2 Maccabees 2:23)[37]
	The Judaic system (rabbis, priesthood, sacrifices, worship, Sanhedrin, and application of Mosaic Law) in the Gospels that shaped Jesus' upbringing, and often opposed Him, was based on derivatives from Jason's library in Cyrene (an African city in what we know today as Libya).

Note: About the terms *Cyrene* and *Libya*: By the fifth century B.C., all of what we call "Africa" today was referred to as *Libya*. Up to the late third century A.D., only the peoples living west of Egypt (Cyrene included) were referred to as *Libyans*. Thereafter, the territory that we know today as Libya (which includes Cyrene) was established as a formal State.[38]

In 132 B.C., the Greek translation of the Hebrew Old Testament was completed in Alexandria, Egypt. It is called the Septuagint or LXX.

In 40 B.C., the Numidian King Arabio (a Berber) died and western Numidia and Cirta became the Roman province of Africa Nova. Remnants of the great Berber kingdom survived until 24 A.D., when its territory was annexed to the Roman Empire.

Between 24 B.C. and 21 B.C., the Roman General Petronius attempted to subdue Nubia and seize control of the gold trade. The Nubian army, led by Queen Amanirenas, defeated the Roman forces at Aswan, Philae, and Elephantine.[39]

Preparation for the "Set Time to Come" Was Complete

This section of the chapter surveys historic events after the birth of Jesus, as they relate to the Early Church in Africa.

Believed to be providentially orchestrated, there had been some seemingly stage-setting conditions that have occurred around the Mediterranean region. These conditions were in place at the birth of Christ, and would later prove to be instrumental in the advancement of the gospel of Jesus Christ into Africa.

Already in place were:

- Seafaring transportation infrastructure
- Over 1,300 years of Hamito-Semitic dialects (Hebrew, Phoenician, Punic, etc.)
- The Greek language flourishing in the region for the past 325 years
- Port cities where merchants and traders from diverse cultures aggregated for commerce
- Multi-linguistic populations across North Africa that understood variants of Hebrew and Greek
- The Old Testament was in circulation (in Hebrew and Greek)
- Multitudes of Hebrews who had migrated into North Africa and anticipated their Messiah
- The Roman Empire had begun experiencing a period of unprecedented stability and prosperity, where the Latin language (derived from Etruscan and Greek) was spoken throughout its western provinces.
- Vast and paved Roman roads between Africa and Jerusalem upon which to travel

As suggested in Galatians 4:4-5, an unspecified preparation was necessary before the birth of Jesus. The wording in the passage suggests that such preparation needed to be fully completed, as a precondition for God's redemptive plan. In retrospect, this survey has deemed the conditions listed above as essential facilitators to Messianic Hebrew missionaries of African descent. They took advantage of this preparation to spread the good news of Jesus Christ and the Way into their homeland.

Early African Missionaries

The Libyan Hebrew Synagogue in Jerusalem

The fact that Jason, a Hebrew from Cyrene in Africa, had the resources and perspective to make such a contribution sheds more light on the existence of a Cyrenaican Hebrew community in Jerusalem. For over a century of travel, before the birth of Jesus, African Hebrews from Cyrene and Egypt had established familiar routes into Jerusalem (for religious and other purposes). This allowed ease of travel and accommodations when Joseph, Mary, and the boy Jesus fled into Africa for Egypt.[40] Scripture also reveals African Hebrews in Jerusalem. By the time of the Apostles, these Africans had their own synagogue in Jerusalem and performed other evangelic activity (Mark 15:21; Acts 2:10; 6:9; 11:19-21; 13:1).[41]

Before Jesus' Crucifixion

Simon of Cyrene

Key Location	Jerusalem
Modern-Day Name	Same
When	As Jesus carried the cross to the place called Golgotha. ~30-33 A.D.[42]
What	Only Mark's gospel mentions Simon's sons Rufus and Alexander (Mark 15:21-22).[43]
	For Simon to have been identified by the names of his sons might suggest that while he might not have been personally known to Mark's messianic faith community, his sons were. Possibly, if they were Cyrenaican, Alexander and Rufus may have had a broader reputation in the faith community than their father who had carried Jesus' cross.
Related Event(s)	In Romans 16, the Apostle Paul sent greetings to Rufus (v 13, assuming it was the same individual) and Rufus' mother. He also sent greetings from his ministry partner Lucius (v 21, who may have been the Lucius of Cyrene with him in Acts 13:1). These may suggest broader missionary fields worked by early first century Cyrenaicans than what has generally been attributed to them.

Research Assignment 1.1

Use your preferred internet search tool to find information about the following:

a. Hebrews in Cyrene, Libya from 200 B.C. to 75 A.D.
b. Jason of Cyrene

At the Birth of the Church

Libyan and Egyptian Believers of the Upper Room

Key Location	Jerusalem
Modern-Day Name	Same
When	During the Hebrew feast of Pentecost ~30-33 A.D.
	This was after the risen Christ ascended to God the Father, and after Matthias was added to the eleven apostles.
What	God-fearing African believers (Libyans and Egyptians) were among those gathered in the upper room of the house. Then ...
	"Suddenly a sound like the blowing of a violent wind came from heaven and filled the whole house where they were sitting. They saw what seemed to be tongues of fire that separated and came to rest on each of them. All of them were filled with the Holy Spirit and began to speak in other tongues as the Spirit enabled them." (Acts 2:2-4)
Related Event(s)	The Holy Spirit enabled the Cyrenaicans and Egyptians to hear other ethnicities speak in their indigenous language.
	God the Spirit worked through various indigenous languages, descending as tongues of fire upon His early believers. This allowed Jesus' worldwide mission for the church to be immediately grasped. Through these unknown tongues, believers from every nation would realize that this gospel must go everywhere.[44] That moment included African languages from voices of those who had become disciples of Christ. The devout Cyrenaicans and Egyptians were filled with the Holy Spirit and took the good news to their homeland.
	Note: 33-65 A.D. was the period of the earliest oral tradition of Christian teaching in Africa.[45]

After the Birth of the Church
After Peter Preached the Gospel to Cornelius' Household
Libyans Take the Gospel to Gentiles Prior to Apostle Paul

Key Location	Antioch
Modern-Day Name	Same
When	Around 40 A.D., after Apostle Peter shared the good news of Jesus Christ with the family of Cornelius (an Italian military officer) and then explained why to his Hebrew peers (read Acts 10 and 11).
What	Messianic Hebrews from Libya and Cyprus planted the church of Antioch (Acts 11:19-21).
Related Event(s)	As a follow-up to the Libyans' ministry, Barnabas was sent to Antioch to assist them with growing the Antioch church. But before arriving there, he went to Tarsus to get Saul to assist him (around 43 A.D.). For a whole year, both of them taught great numbers of people in the Antioch church.
	It was at that church where believers were first referred to as Christians—*little Christs* (Acts 11:25-26).

After the Antioch Church Had Been Planted
In the Planting of the Antioch Church
African Spiritual Leaders in the Church at Antioch

Key Location	Antioch
Modern-Day Name	Same
When	One year after Barnabas and Saul's teaching ministry in the Antioch church, about 45 A.D.
What	The Holy Spirit spoke to Antioch church leaders (from Libya, Niger and others) commanding them to set Saul and Barnabas apart for a special service (missionary work).
	The church leadership fasted and prayed over them, laid hands upon both of them, and then sent them off (Acts 13:1-3).
Related Event(s)	The events above occurred before
	• Saul was referred to as Paul • His first missionary journey (about 46 A.D.) • His first church was planted • His first epistle was written (about 49 A.D.)

What the Epistles Reveal About Early Believers

How did the early church reconcile its Hebrew past? How could members enjoy newness in Christ while still honoring their Jewish past? How much of the Jewish way of life should be expected of Gentile believers? This would become a major issue in the early church—one that was addressed at the very first council of the Christian church in Acts 15. But this was but one of many issues facing the early church. The apostles' earliest epistles reveal that even after their missionary work, local churches were still weak and unstable organizationally, morally, and theologically.

- Epistles to the churches in Corinth, Galatia, Ephesus, and throughout Asia Minor indicate that believers were still yielding to their flesh.
- Churches were infected with false teachers – Acts 20:28-30; 2 Timothy 4:3-4; Titus 1:6-16; 2 Peter 1:12-21; 2:1-22; 3:14-18; 1 John 4:1-6.
    - The greatest false teaching during this period was Gnosticism, a movement whose advocates claimed to have a fuller, secret, and deeper spiritual knowledge that made them uniquely special. They denied the value of history and the physical world. They claimed to be the true church that had the message of Jesus Christ.
    - The value of the role of the church bishop grew out of this confusion. Individual Christians who might have been confused by all the voices around them were urged to consult their local "heavy" (bishop) for right teaching about truth.
    - Bishops in the early church bore little similarity to the bishops today. In the early church, he was the mature preaching/teaching pastor in a single locale but did not preside over several churches, as is the case today. Unfortunately, much later in church history, the perception of bishops became one that suggested they could not fail because they were in apostolic succession. In the early church, the bishop was the one with the tried-and-true teachings of the church.[46]
- Christians were defecting from the faith – Acts 5:1-11; 1 Timothy 1:19-20; 2 Timothy 2:17; 4:10; Titus 1:16; 2 Peter 2:1-3; Revelation 2:20-22.

Out of this context emerged apologists, the first group to defend the Christian faith against false teaching. They refuted the claims of rabbis and pagan philosophers that Christianity was ridiculous. Apologists contrasted the truth about Christianity with the false claims of paganism.[47]

Use of Scripture, Writings, and Translations Brought Stability

As previously explained, by this time the Old Testament books already existed (and were in circulation) in both the Greek and Hebrew languages (read more about it in Chapter 5).

Most scholars will agree that it was in the first century that a brief and anonymous early Christian exposition referred to as the Didache, also known as "The Teaching of the Twelve Apostles," was in circulation. Its first line is "The teaching of the Lord to the Gentiles (or Nations) by the twelve apostles." Parts of it constitute the oldest surviving written catechism. Its three main sections deal with Christian ethics, rituals (such as baptism and the Lord's Supper), and church organization. The Didache is considered the first example of Church Orders, revealing how Hebrew Christians saw themselves and how they adapted their practice for Gentile Christians.[48]

As early as 100 A.D., the mature Christian men and women recognized the voice of the Father in all four gospels and ten of Paul's epistles and widely distributed them throughout Christendom. In Africa, these were included in a collection of manuscripts referred to as "Old African" or "Old Latin." Today it is called the Vetus Latina (see Chapter 5 for more details). Also, other books had been regionally accepted.[49]

By 200 A.D. all of the New Testament had been widely circulated with some books still uncertain: James, Jude, 2 Peter, 2 John, 3 John, and Hebrews.[50]

What the History of This Era Reveals About Early Missionaries

The world in which Jesus promised to build His church was twofold: There was the Hebrew world (Judaism), which had shaped the lives of Jesus and His disciples, and the larger Greco-Roman world which encompassed the Hebrew world. These two worlds co-existed, with Hebrews accounting for about twenty percent of the Roman Empire.

Judaism itself can be characterized as comprising Hebrews of two temperaments:

- Judaism amongst Hebrews in Palestine as reflected in the New Testament
- Judaism for those Hebrews scattered throughout the Roman Empire, known as the diaspora

The Hebrews of the diaspora were immersed into pagan cultures. Those in the coastal regions like Cyrene (and Libya's other port cities) interacted with people from diverse cultures due to merchant ships and caravans coming and going for the purpose of commerce. Such exposure afforded them an understanding of diverse languages and ideas, as well as a better grasp of the pagan mind. They were more accustomed to Jewish life outside of Palestine. Consequently, they tended to be more flexible and adaptable to the Roman world than the Hebrews in Palestine. Hebrews of the diaspora were uniquely effective at converting other people to Judaism. But more significant to our survey, it also afforded Messianic Hebrews the necessary insight for reaching other Hebrews and non-Hebrews with the gospel of salvation.

The Impact of Rome's Political Philosophy on Making Disciples

Rome generally allowed conquered territories to maintain their original form of government as well as the local customs, as long as Rome received taxes and maintained control. Since most of the cultures that Rome conquered were polytheistic, the Romans normally requested that the culture add Roman deities to cultic worship, particularly emperor worship (syncretism). However, Hebrews were monotheistic worshippers of the One God of Scripture. They refused this demand of the conquering Romans. So rather than continually fighting these zealous protestors who refused to submit, the Romans exempted Hebrews from this policy. Rome also allowed Hebrews throughout the empire to pay the annual temple tax for the temple in Jerusalem (in support of the temple and priestly system). Ordinarily, the Romans forbade this kind of activity, as it prevented money from flowing into Rome. However, the Romans exempted the Hebrews on account of their zealous insistence (granting them special privileges).

These exemptions and the relative favoritism created a stable and content environment for the Hebrews. It was this political setting into which Jesus of Nazareth was born and began His earthly ministry. Most of the Pharisees, Sadducees, and priests were content to live under this Roman system. The Zealots, who hoped for freedom from Rome's rule, were a part of this world.

This was also the world in which the new sect of *The Way* (outsiders called them Christians) was born. From its onset it had to figure out how to relate to Judaism and how to relate to the larger Roman world.[51]

Newness in Christ in a Roman World

Rome saw itself as the civilized world and viewed everyone else as barbarians to whom Rome would bring learning, law, and equitable administration of the law to the people. Then came Christians with the huge task of convincing people that, through newness in Christ, greater insight into truth could be acquired—insight that Greek and Roman philosophers hadn't already gained.

Roman citizens had grown disenchanted with Rome's imperialism, whereby the emperor was all-powerful, and began looking for spiritual satisfaction in new Egyptian or Persian religions. Judaism was very attractive and spread because it went all the way back to the beginning of the world (to Genesis 1:1). It was thereby viewed to be the most genuine of all religions.[52] So, like the Apostle Paul, Christians used Judaism as a powerful missionary resource.

Christian missionaries demonstrated that the gospel of Jesus Christ was all that Judaism awaited—a sequel of sorts. Then it, too, began to spread rapidly. Since Jesus had been alive just a few decades earlier, the gospel message had the task of proving His connection to the antiquity of Genesis 1:1. The apostles and missionaries gained credibility with their audiences by quoting Old Testament Scriptures and pointing out themes, foreshadows, and pre-incarnate types of Christ. They appealed to the people on the basis that they were living in the great fulfillment of the promised Messiah.

Chapter 1 Notes

[20] Study.com, "The Phoenicians: History, Religion & Civilization," Chapter 1/Lesson 22 2019, https://study.com/academy/lesson/the-phoenicians-history-religion-civilization.html.

[21] Igor M. Diakonoff, *Semito-Hamitic Languages: An Essay in Classification* (Moscow: Nauka Publishing House, 1965), 9-12; Glenn Markoe, *Phoenicians* (Berkley: University of California Press, 2000), 108.

[22] Wikipedia Contributors, s.v. "Maghrebi Jews," *Wikipedia, The Free Encyclopedia,* January 27, 2019, https://en.wikipedia.org/wiki/Maghrebi_Jews; C. L. Campbell et al., "North African Jewish and non-Jewish Populations Form Distinctive, Orthogonal Clusters," PNAS: Proceedings of the National Academy of Sciences, August 21, 2012, https://www.pnas.org/content/109/34/13865.

[23] Wikipedia Contributors, s.v. "Punics," *Wikipedia, The Free Encyclopedia*, January 2, 2019, https://en.wikipedia.org/wiki/Punics; Wikipedia Contributors, s.v. "Jewish Ethnic Divisions," *Wikipedia, The Free Encyclopedia*, January 24, 2019, https://en.wikipedia.org/wiki/Jewish_ethnic_divisions#North_Africa.

[24] Mark Cartwright, "Dido," in *Ancient History Encyclopedia*, 2016, https://www.ancient.eu/Dido/. The account of how Dido acquired the land from the Berbers is full of intrigue, math and wit. Her application of isoperimetrics still baffles mathematicians today.

[25] Philip Beale and Sarah Taylor, *Sailing Close to the Wind: An Epic Voyage Recreating the First Circumnavigation of Africa by the Phoenicians in 600 BC* (Warwickshire, UK: The Lulworth Press, 2012); Wikipedia Contributors, s.v. "History of Carthage," *Wikipedia, The Free Encyclopedia*, https://en.wikipedia.org/wiki/History_of_Carthage.

[26] Tommy Rodriguez, "The World of the Ancient Carthaginians," The Ancient World, http://www.theancientworld.net/civ/carthage.html.

[27] Wikipedia Contributors, s.v. "Carthage," *Wikipedia, The Free Encyclopedia*, May 26, 2017, https://en.wikipedia.org/wiki/Carthage.

[28] Rodriguez.

[29] Rudolph R. Windsor, *From Babylon to Timbuktu* (Chicago: Lushena Books, 2003), 108.

[30] Alexander Graham, *Roman Africa: An Outline of the History of Roman Occupation of North Africa, Based Chiefly upon Inscriptions and Monumental Remains in That Country* (London: Longmans, Green, and Co., 1902), ix.

[31] Michael Frank, "In Morocco, Exploring Remnants of Jewish History," *The New York Times*, May 30, 2015, https://www.nytimes.com/2015/05/31/travel/in-morocco-exploring-remnants-of-jewish-history.html; Wikipedia Contributors, s.v. "Jewish Ethnic Divisions," *Wikipedia, The Free Encyclopedia*, January 24, 2019, https://en.wikipedia.org /wiki /Jewish_ethnic_divisions#North_Africa

[32] Medhat Ibrahim, "The History of the Coptic Church: St Mark, the Apostle and Beholder of God," *Mighty Arrows Magazine*, April 2003, http://www.suscopts.org/mightyarrows/vol3_no1/stmark.pdf, 1.

[33] Ibid.

[34] Wikipedia Contributors, s.v. "Cyrene, Libya," *Wikipedia, The Free Encyclopedia*, January 2, 2019, https://en.wikipedia.org/wiki/Cyrene,_Libya; Ibid., s.v. "Jewish Ethnic Divisions," January 24, 2019, https://en.wikipedia.org/wiki/Jewish_ethnic_divisions #North_Africa.

[35] The exact date is not clear. But according to Josephus, the first historical record of an early Sanhedrin body was during the administration of Aulus Gabinius in 57 B.C.

[36] Thomas C. Oden, *Early Libyan Christianity: Uncovering a North African Tradition* (Downers Grove, IL: InterVarsity Press, 2011), 55; Richard Gottheil and Samuel Krauss, "Jason of Cyrene," in *JewishEncyclopedia.com*, 2011, http://www.jewishencyclopedia .com/articles/8528-jason-of-cyrene; Wikisource Contributors, s.v. "Jason of Cyrene," *The New International Encyclopedia*, March 31, 2012, https://en.wikisource.org/wikiThe_New_International_Encyclop%C3%A6dia/Jason_of _Cyrene.

[37] Catholic Online, "2 Maccabees – Chapter 2," May 24, 2018, https://www.catholic .org/bible/book.php?id=21&bible_chapter=2.

[38] Ancient Names Galleria, "Names of Libya (Africa)," Accessed April 26, 2019, http://www.peiraeuspubliclibrary.com/names/libya.html.

[39] Wikipedia Contributors, s.v. "Amanirenas," *Wikipedia, The Free Encyclopedia*, September 28, 2018, https://en.wikipedia.org/wiki/Amanirenas; "Ancient Nubia," Freeman Institute, 2018, http://www.freemaninstitute.com/Gallery/nubia.htm.

[40] Oden, "*Early Libyan Christianity*," 212-213; Matthew 2:13-15.

[41] Wikipedia Contributors, s.v. "History of the Jews in Libya," *Wikipedia, The Free Encyclopedia*, April 2, 2018, https://en.wikipedia.org/wiki/History_of_the_Jews_in_Libya; William F. Albright, *The Archaeology of Palestine* (London: Penguin Books, 1949), 172.

[42] Simon of Cyrene helping Jesus foreshadowed the suffering of the African Church.

[43] Tom Powers, "A Second Look," *Biblical Archaeology Society*, September 26, 2006, https://israelpalestineguide.files.wordpress.com/2010/06/ alexander-simon-ossuary-a-second-look-from-bar.pdf.

[44] Oden, "*Early Libyan Christianity*," 213.

[45] Thomas C. Oden, *How Africa Shaped the Christian Mind* (Downers Grove, IL: InterVarsity Press, 2007), 158.

[46] *A Survey of Church History: Part 1*, "Defending the Faith," Ligonier Ministries, 2012, CD.

[47] Ibid., "Expansion of the Church."

[48] Wikipedia Contributors, s.v. "Didache," *Wikipedia, The Free Encyclopedia*, July 19, 2018, https://en.m.wikipedia.org/wiki/Didache.

[49] *A Survey of Church History: Part 1*, "The East and the West."

[50] Ibid.

[51] Ibid., "Introduction."

[52] Ibid.

Chapter 2: Egypt
(Mid-1st through 2nd Century A.D.)

PROFILE OF EARLY CHRISTIANITY IN AN AFRICAN TERRITORY

Coptic Christians of Egypt

Key Location	Alexandria
Modern-Day Name	Same
When	42 A.D.
How	Mark, who had been with Jesus, brought the gospel.
Related Event(s)	Several African traditions commemorate Mark's return home to Africa with the good news about Jesus Christ. He has been credited with founding the Coptic Christian Church there.
	Also in Alexandria, 174 years earlier, the translation of the Hebrew Old Testament Scriptures into the Greek language had been completed. The finished product was given the Latin name *Septuagint*, meaning "seventy" or LXX. (Read chapter 5 for more details.)
	Mark would have had a strong foundation for proclaiming Jesus as the promised Messiah in Scripture. However, he faced fierce opposition from Greek philosophers and scholars, Hebrew scholars (forty percent of the population was Hebrew), teachers of Scriptures, and Persian wise men.
Social, Political, or Religious Setting	Before Mark's gospel arrived in Egypt, religion there was a mixture of Greek, Roman, Persian, Syrian, and Babylonian pagan gods. The Roman Empire controlled the entire Mediterranean coast of Africa during the first century A.D.

Events and Effects

Coptic tradition asserts that the African Hebrew Mark was born in Cyrene, a city in the Pentapolis of North Africa (in the territory called Libya today). It is said that he and his brother fled after enormous troubles came upon them from the two tribes of the Berbers and Ethiopians.

But which Mark?
   a. Mark the disciple, one of the seventy-two disciples sent out by Christ (Luke 10:1)
   b. John Mark (Acts 12:12, 25; 15:37)
   c. Mark the cousin of Barnabas (Colossians 4:10)
   d. Mark the gospel writer

In his book *The African Memory of Mark*, Dr. Thomas Oden explores several African liturgical narratives about the gospel reaching them. Those narratives were commonly read in antiquity all over Africa to commemorate the event. Oden fills in the perplexing blanks in the modern Western historical memory with the African memory. The narratives identify the same John Mark who had accompanied Apostle Paul and Barnabas (Acts 12:25) as having returned to Africa with the good news of Jesus Christ. Mark is the leading apostolic figure for Africa. His missionary account has been read in both ancient and modern day African church services.53

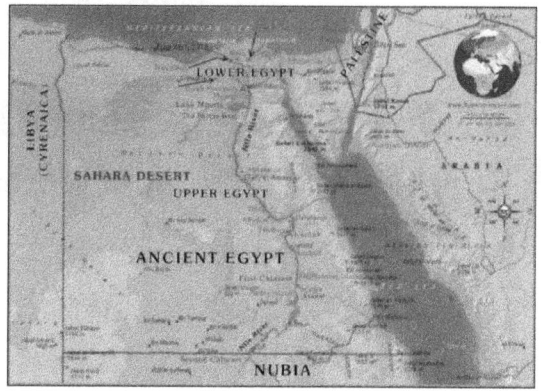

Mark's Ministry Challenges in Egypt

Upon Mark's return, he found the Egyptians still worshipping many pagan gods. Some were their state gods; others originated over the years from Greece, Rome, Persia, Syria, and Babylon. Names of some of these gods were54

> Ra: The god of the sun, considered by the pagans to be the source of light and warmth. The ancient city of Heliopolis was the center of its worship.55 It exists underneath Ain Shams today, one of the oldest districts in Cairo.
>
> Amen: The invisible god. Tibha was the center of worship for this god. Later during the Egyptian state, Amen was combined with Ra, and the combined worship came to be termed Amen Ra.
>
> Osiris: The messenger god of love and peace among the people (from Syria).
>
> Diana (Roman) or Artemis (Greek): The goddess of hunting.
>
> Khnoum: The creator god. Tibha was also the center of its worship.
>
> Anhita: A popular goddess from Persia.

Mark's first convert was a shoemaker whom he solicited for a repair. The Coptic Church holds that God used Mark to fulfill prophecy in Isaiah 19:18-19.56 According to Coptic tradition, Mark also founded a Christian community in Cyrene around 66-68 A.D., but shortly thereafter was martyred in Alexandria.57

Apollos of Alexandria

We've already examined what Scripture reveals about the Spirit falling upon the Christ-believing Hebrew Egyptians in the Upper Room. Now, let's examine some fruit from their missionary work.

Around 53 A.D., about twenty years after that Upper Room experience, an African Messianic Hebrew named Apollos arrived in the city of Ephesus. Born in Alexandria, Egypt, he is described as an educated man with a thorough knowledge of the Scriptures, who had been instructed in the way of Jesus Christ (Acts 18:24-26). Although Apollos taught the way of the Lord, he knew only of John's baptism of repentance. He didn't have an understanding of Jesus' suffering, death, burial, and resurrection for the forgiveness of sins and receiving the Holy Spirit. Yet, he spoke eloquently and boldly in the synagogue about what he understood. One explanation for Apollos' lack of knowledge about

Jesus might be related to the violent attitude that non-messianic Hebrews of Alexandria had towards the messianic Hebrews (i.e. Stephen's death twenty years prior – Acts 6:9-15; 7:58-60). To avoid being harmed themselves, Apollos' teachers may have only given him a truncated version of the events around Judea. Fortunately, while in Ephesus, he eventually received the full account of Jesus' redemptive work on the cross from Aquila and Priscilla. From there, he went on to convince non-messianic Hebrews that Jesus was the Messiah (Acts 18:26-28).

Hebrews in Egyptian Bondage Again

In 70 A.D., just as Jesus had prophesied (Mark 13:1-3) over thirty-five years prior, the Roman General Titus sieged Jerusalem in what would be the decisive event of the First Jewish-Roman War. His army burned and destroyed the Second Temple and then conquered the city.[58] Titus had the Hebrew men who had been seditious robbers put to death. Men above seventeen years old were put into bondage and shipped to work the Egyptian gold mines, or were sent to other Roman provinces. But those under seventeen years old were sold as slaves. This fulfilled Moses' prophetic warning to the Hebrews over a millennium prior (Deuteronomy 28:68). According to the 1st century Hebrew historian Flavius Josephus, when Jerusalem fell, some Hebrews were placed on ships and sent in bondage to other Roman provinces.[59] Shipping Hebrews into exile was not uncommon during this time. On two separate occasions, the Apostle Paul on his way to appeal his case in Rome, had been boarded onto a Romanized Alexandrian (Egypt) ship.[60]

Yet, the Gospel Flourished

By the second century A.D. in Egypt, Christianity had spread into rural areas, and the Gospels, Apostle Paul's letters, and the Old Testament had been translated into the local Coptic language.[61] It is believed to have spread from there westward as far as Numidia.[62] In fact, a fragment of Apostle John's gospel written in Coptic was found in Upper Egypt. Dating techniques place it in the first half of the second century A.D.[63] Also, some copies that mirror today's New Testament were found in Bahnasa, in Middle Egypt, dating back to around 200 A.D.[64]

By the beginning of the third century AD, Christians constituted the majority of Egypt's population.[65] From Egypt the ecclesiastic organization of the early church was established (its bishops, monks, priests, patriarchs, congregational prayers, liturgies of the mass, and its earliest Church Fathers).[66] Coptic Orthodox faith communities thrive in Alexandria and in other countries today. The Church of Alexandria is the oldest Christian church in Africa.

Grace, truth, redemption, and eternal life through Christ as the "Way" came first from Judea,[67] but Christianity as a religion was born in Egypt.

> Research Assignment 2.1
>
> Using the URL at its endnote, read how Jerusalem's fall in 70 A.D. was a fulfillment of Deuteronomy 28:68.

Chapter 2 Notes

[53] Thomas Oden, *The African Memory of Mark: Reassessing Early Church Tradition* (Downers Grove, IL: InterVarsity Press, 2011), 60-62.

[54] Ibrahim.

[55] This is the famous Egyptian city referred to as "On" in the Bible.

[56] Ibrahim, 2, 1.

[57] Oden, *How Africa Shaped*, 158.

[58] Wikipedia Contributors, s.v. "Siege of Jerusalem (70 CE)," *Wikipedia, The Free Encyclopedia*, February 12, 2019, https://en.wikipedia.org/wiki/Siege_of_Jerusalem_(70_CE).

[59] Flavius Josephus, *The Works of Flavius Josephus*, trans. William Whiston, Auburn and Buffalo, John E. Beardsley, 1895, in the Perseus Digital Library, http://www.perseus.tufts.edu/hopper/text?doc=urn:cts:greekLit:tlg0526.tlg004.perseus-eng1:6.9.2.

[60] Acts 27:6; 28:11

[61] Jennifer Dines, *The Septuagint* (London: T&T Clark, 2004), 11.

[62] Oden, *How Africa Shaped*, 68-69.

[63] Wikipedia Contributors, s.v. "Coptic Orthodox Church of Alexandria," *Wikipedia, The Free Encyclopedia*, June 3, 2017, https://en.wikipedia.org/wiki/Coptic_Orthodox_Church_of_Alexandria.

[64] Over 1,400 years before King James commissioned the compilation of his version of the Bible.

[65] Wikipedia Contributors, s.v. "Copts," *Wikipedia, The Free Encyclopedia*, March 16, 2019, https://en.wikipedia.org/wiki/Copts.

[66] Runoko Rashidi, *Black Star: The African Presence in Early Europe* (London, UK: Books of Africa, 2011), 17; Moses Samaan, "The Origins of the Coptic Horologion (Agpeya)," Become Orthodox, 2019, accessed May 2, 2019, http://becomeorthodox.org/prayer/the-origins-of-the-coptic-horologion-agpeya/.

[67] Throughout the Book of Acts, the phrase "the Way" was the name used to identify those who followed the teachings of the ascended Christ (see Acts 9:2, 19:9, 19:23, 22:4, 24:14 and 24:22). It appears that they referred to themselves as such based upon what Jesus told His disciples in John 14:4-6.

Chapter 3: Persecution of Christians Begins in Rome
(Mid-1st Century A.D.)

SOCIAL/POLITICAL FACTORS

Persecution of Christians in Rome

Where	Across the Mediterranean Sea in Rome, Italy
When	67 A.D.
Source	Roman Emperor Nero
What	The Great Fire of Rome in 64 A.D.

Events and Effects

Around this time period there were two other noteworthy conflicts against Hebrews and Christians. The Hebrews of Jerusalem aggressively objected to Rome's armed presence in the Holy Land and Mark's martyrdom for the gospel in Egypt. Anti-Hebrew and anti-Christian sentiment were seemingly in the air. Undoubtedly, there may have been African Christian martyrs as a result of Mark's missionary efforts. However, our research could not find African martyr stories before the second century A.D. The earliest persecution reports on record were against Christians in Rome.

A great fire destroyed much of the city of Rome (the seat of the empire). The fire began in the slums of a district south of the legendary Palatine Hill. The area's homes burned very quickly and then, fueled by high winds, the fire spread north. Heavy looting followed the chaos. The fire raged out of control for nearly three days, leaving three of Rome's fourteen districts completely burned to ruins; only four were untouched by the blaze. Hundreds of people died in the fire and many thousands were left homeless.

The Cause

Differing accounts either blamed Emperor Nero for initiating the fire or credited him with taking action to contain it and provide relief for evacuees. Roman historians Suetonius and Tacitus reported from hearsay that, in response to the public perception that he was somehow responsible for the fire, Nero blamed the devastation on the Christian community within the city. For Nero, the Christians were a perfect scapegoat, since at that time the general population hated the Christians anyway. Rome was already predisposed to suspect them of social evils. The people of Rome hated Christians mainly because they were different, and because they tried to get other people to become Christians as well. Nero arrested a group of Christians and blamed the fire on them. He continued with torturing, burning alive, and executing hundreds of Christians on the accusation that they had something to do with the fire.[68]

Suspicion about Christians

Because of the privacy of their rituals, Christians frequently aroused suspicion among the general Roman population, who were accustomed to religion being a public event. Also, beliefs had developed that Christians committed "outrageous crimes," "wickedness," and "evil deeds," particularly orgies (love feasts), cannibalism (eating the body of Christ and drinking His blood), and incest (referring to each other as brothers and sisters).[69] Christians' refusal to participate in public religion also contributed to the general hostility toward them. Much of the population believed that bad things would happen to them if their gods were not respected and worshiped properly, by all citizens. So the burning of Rome sparked the fuel of distasteful public sentiment towards Christians,[70] thereby igniting the empire's first persecution of Christians.[71]

The Effect

Nero's persecution of Christians in Rome began to shape the thoughts, perspectives, attitudes, and actions of its citizens and government officials towards Christians in other parts of the empire. Cruelties against Christians had begun to be carried out across the Roman Empire by the state and local authorities and often at the whim of local communities on a sporadic or ad hoc basis. Ironically, rather than weaken the spirit of Christians, persecution had the opposite effect: It emboldened their resolve.

- During the same period of Nero's cruelties, the apostles Paul and Peter, as well as Barnabas were put to death (but not directly related to Nero's persecution).

John Foxe's book, *Foxe's Book of Martyrs* provides a good summary of Rome's persecution of Christians throughout its empire. Below is a brief summary of significant periods of persecution prior to the first known state-ordered persecution of African Christians.[72]

<u>Persecution under Emperor Domitian in A.D. 81</u>
- He made it law, "That no Christian, once brought before the tribunal, should be exempted from punishment without renouncing his religion."
- Apostle John was boiled in oil, then banished to Patmos.
- Timothy, a disciple of Apostle Paul, was beaten to death.

<u>Persecution under Emperor Trajan in A.D. 108</u>
- Thorns were placed on the heads of Christians as they were crucified, and spears were thrust into their sides.
- A brave and successful Roman commander who, for moral reasons, refused to join in an idolatrous sacrifice to celebrate his own victories, was put to death along with his whole family.

Persecution under Emperor Marcus Aurelius Antoninus in A.D. 162

- Christians continued to be tortured, thrown to wild beasts, set afire in public, pressed to death with weights, thrown off cliffs, or beheaded for refusing to renounce Christ.

At the risk of death, faith communities located north and west of the Mediterranean Sea continued to spawn new communities far and wide. Sadly, believers from these communities continued to pay the ultimate price for their faith. Polycarp, Ignatius, Justin, and Irenaeus were a few notable defenders of the Christian faith in regions outside of Africa who were martyred for their faith stance. They were among the first Christian apologists who quieted the critique of Christian beliefs by pagans.

Decades later, south of the Mediterranean Sea, teachers and scholars began to emerge in North Africa. It's believed they were among those who had been discipled from an underground church, believed to have been originally founded by fleeing Messianic-Hebrews during late first century A.D. The African Church was the first to establish and preserve Christian orthodoxy, as we understand it today. Many members did so in the midst of persecution and martyrdom. A survey of their profiles, location, and events affecting the African Church will begin in Chapter 6.

Research Assignment 3.1

Use your preferred internet search tool to find more information about the following:

a. How the state of Rome perceived Christians
b. How Rome's general population viewed their Christian neighbors
c. The various ways Christians were persecuted

Chapter 3 Notes

[68] Gonzalez, 34-35.

[69] ReligionFacts: Just the Facts on Religion, "Persecution in the Early Church," 2016, http://www.religionfacts.com/persecution-early-church.

[70] Chris Heaton, "Nero and the Christians," UNRV History, 2017, http://www.unrv. com/early-empire/nero-christians.php.

[71] Though many citizens in Rome became Christians, its government and culture were pagan. Rome's government and culture would remain as such while persecuting Jesus' Church for over another three hundred years.

[72] John Foxe, *Foxe's Book of Martyrs*, Internet Sacred Text Archive, 2010, http://www.sacred-texts.com/chr/martyrs/.

Chapter 4: Cyrene
(Mid-1st through 2nd Century A.D.)

PROFILE OF EARLY CHRISTIANITY IN AN AFRICAN TERRITORY

Hebrews Shaped the Religious Landscape

Key Location	Cyrene, Libya
Modern-Day Name	Same
When	Sometime during the 1st century A.D.
How	Beginning with Jason, Cyrenaic Hebrew (both messianic and non-messianic) contributions and sacrifices helped shape the religious landscape of the Gospels, before, during, and after the birth of Jesus.
	They helped plant the famous Antioch church where believers were first called Christians. Then, from Antioch, the Holy Spirit spoke to them to separate Saul and Barnabas for a unique work. On each of his three missionary journeys, the Apostle Paul (formerly called Saul) departed from and reported back to the Antioch church (except his third journey where he reported back to the church at Jerusalem).
Related Event(s)	Coptic tradition holds that Mark, who return to Africa with the good news of Jesus Christ, was originally from Cyrene, Libya.[73]
Social, Political, or Religious Setting	Jewish wars against Roman oppression in Cyrene: • First Jewish-Roman War in 73 A.D. • Kitos War in 117 A.D.[74]

Events and Effects

African Hebrews of Cyrene

City of Refuge

The famous African city of Cyrene overlooked the Mediterranean Sea. Behind it to the south were the Green Mountains and vast stretches of the plains and deserts of the African continent. Its ancient ruins can still be found in the mountain clefts of Libya. From its beginning, Cyrene was a city of refugees. Since the sixth century B.C, the Greeks had been migrating to the African continent to avoid starvation. But pertinent to our survey, Hebrew refugees also lived in this African city as permanent residents for three centuries before Christianity appeared.

During the times of the Maccabees, the Hebrews of Palestine were suffering through harsh wars, population displacement, and foreign occupation. From the third century B.C. to the first century A.D., many fled to the safety of Africa (into Cyrene or Alexandria). However, they continued to faithfully keep the Mosaic covenant, which included religious visits back to the Holy Temple in Jerusalem. For generations they farmed, raised cattle, and harvested from the soil of Africa.[75]

Among the Most Multicultural African Cities

Cyrene became one of the most multicultural cities on the continent. As with other Cyrenians, the Hebrews there traded and interacted with the surrounding indigenous tribes of the Maghreb (Guarantians, Libyans, Berbers, Taureg, and others). They considered the African continent, with its cultures, commerce, and intellectual life, their home. These descendants of Hebrew refugees in Cyrene, after three centuries on the African continent, are rightly called Africans. Over time, they spoke Berber, they dressed similar to the Berbers and some Berbers, embraced their religion. By the first century A.D., any well-traveled Hebrew from Cyrenaica could easily speak Greek.

Though Cyrene was an international trading center, being an inland city, it was more indigenized to inland African ways than most other African port cities located directly on the coast. Yet, some of its Hebrew citizens were known to be actively messianic in their hopes and historical perspective (expecting the coming Messiah to fulfill God's purpose in history). The early Christians in Libya emerged from these Hebrew communities. They realized that the Messiah had already come, and His name was Jesus.[76] Having heeded the Messiah's prophetic warning, others had migrated there before the fall of Jerusalem (Luke 20:20-24).

Romans and the African Hebrews of Cyrene

As stated in Chapter 1, in 74 B.C., Cyrene was bequeathed to the Romans by the last Greek King. Under Greek authority, the Hebrew inhabitants had enjoyed equal rights. But under Roman rule, they were increasingly oppressed by the autonomous and much larger Greek population. The harsh Roman governing style may have eventually led to the Hebrews of Cyrene and Egypt building a synagogue in Jerusalem (Acts 6:9). That would have also resulted in messianic Libyan and Egyptian Hebrews being amongst the devout believers in the upper room around 30-33 A.D., as well as Mark's presence in the region with Jesus.

As stated in Chapter 2, the fall of Jerusalem in 70 A.D. was the cataclysmic event that crumbled Roman-Hebrew relations in general, especially within Cyrene. There was an influx of messianic Hebrews from Jerusalem. In order to understand the prophetic nature of this influx into Africa from Jerusalem, we must look into Roman history (not the Bible) to find the fulfillment of Jesus' prophecy.

Impact of Jesus' Jerusalem Prophecy Upon Cyrene

Upon seeing and heeding the signs that the now glorified and ascended Savior had prophesied, followers of the Way vacated Jerusalem. It was 66 A.D., the beginning of the Great Jewish Revolt. The circumstances of their exit from Jerusalem is described as follows: The Roman General Cestius Gallus marched on Judea with 30,000 troops from the north. He conquered lower Galilee as well as occupied the Judean coast. Upon turning inland to surround Jerusalem they penetrated its outer city. However, they were unable to take its Temple Mount because Jewish forces inflicted heavy losses upon his reinforcements and rearguard. After nine days, as Cestius retreated back to the coast, his troops were ambushed again and suffered additional losses and war equipment. He returned to the military's home base in shame.[77]

The surrounding of Jerusalem was the sign that Jesus had prophesied while walking among His followers about 33 years prior:

> "When you see Jerusalem being surrounded by armies, you will know that its desolation is near." Luke 21:20

Upon seeing this sign Jesus advised them to flee (while troops retreated):

> "Then let those who are in Judea flee to the mountains, let those in the city get out, and let those in the country not enter the city." Luke 21:21

> Pre-existing religious practices and relationships suggest that from the city, countryside and mountains a significant number of Jesus' followers fled westward towards Egypt and Cyrene. Within the Mediterranean coastal cities were strong messianic Hebrew communities for them to take refuge.[78]

Jesus' prophecy also described the events that would follow a few years after they had fled, during Jerusalem's actual collapse in 70 A.D. at the hand of Roman General Titus:

> "For this is the time of punishment in fulfillment of all that has been written. How dreadful it will be in those days for pregnant women and nursing mothers! There will be great distress in the land and wrath against this people. They will fall by the sword and will be taken as prisoners to all the nations. Jerusalem will be trampled on by the Gentiles until the times of the Gentiles are fulfilled." Luke 21:22-24

Continued Tension in Roman-Hebrew Relations

A few years later, tensions between the rule of Roman Emperor Vespasian and the Hebrews of Cyrene came to a head in an insurrection in 73 A.D., the First Jewish-Roman War. Tensions also continued during the Kitos War under Roman Emperor Trajan in 117 A.D. This revolt was quelled by Marcius Turbo, but not before huge numbers of civilians had been brutally massacred by the Jewish rebels.

According to historian Eusebius of Caesarea, the Hebrew rebellion left Libya so depopulated that a few years later, new colonies had to be established there just to maintain the viability of continued settlement.[79]

Due to instability and politics, much of Libya's rich Christian history is yet to be excavated, uncovered, and revealed.

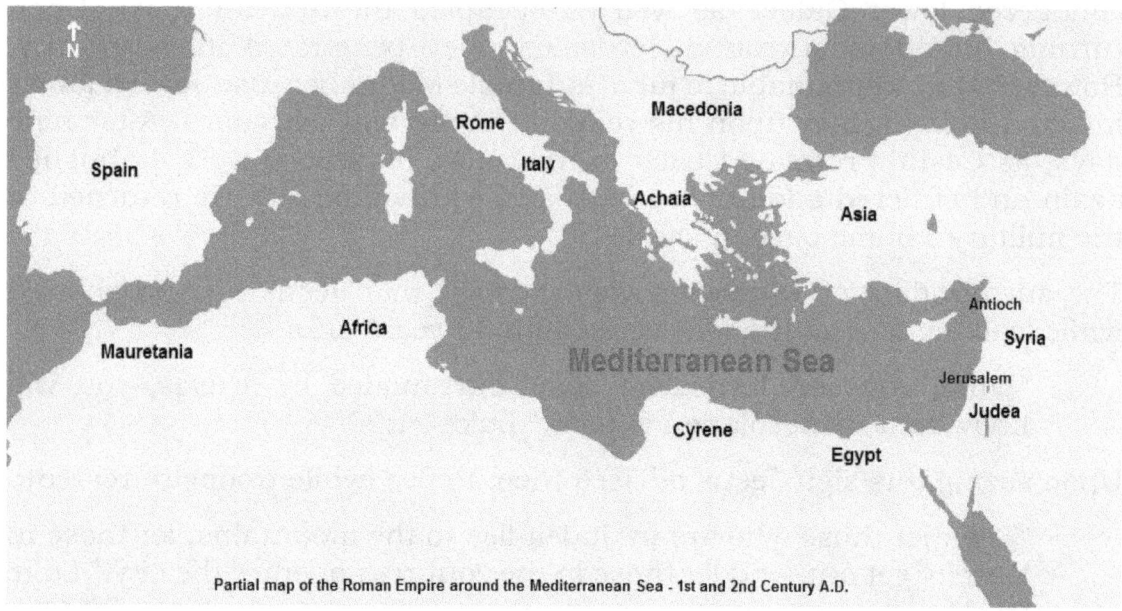

Partial map of the Roman Empire around the Mediterranean Sea - 1st and 2nd Century A.D.

Northwest Migration of Messianic Hebrews of Cyrene and Egypt

Geography, war and ruin compelled the messianic Hebrews (and others) fleeing Cyrene and Egypt to go westward along the coast towards the Africa Proconsularis, Numidia, Carthage, and Mauretania. To the north was the Mediterranean Sea, to the south was unfamiliar territory, and eastward were ruin, danger and bondage. Remember, Egypt to the east was where the Roman General Titus had Hebrew men of Jerusalem seventeen years and older put in bondage and sent to work the gold mines. Further east was Jerusalem laying in ruin, with not a stone left upon a stone (Matthew 24:2).

Research Assignment 4.1

Use your preferred internet search tool to find information about the following:

a. The Jewish-Roman Wars
b. The Libyans in Acts 2:10; 11:20; 13:1

Chapter 4 Notes

[73] Oden, *How Africa Shaped*, 158.

[74] Oden, *Early Libyan Christianity*, 213-216.

[75] Oden, *African Memory of Mark*, 17-19.

[76] Ibid.

[77] Wikipedia Contributors, s.v. "Cestius_Gallus," Wikipedia, The Free Encyclopedia, August 14, 2019, https://en.wikipedia.org/wiki/Cestius_Gallus.

[78] Implied by much activity around the holy land by messianic Hebrews from Cyrene, as well as by the presence of a Cyrenian synagogue in Jerusalem - Acts 2:10; 6:9; 11:19-24; 13:1.

[79] Wikipedia Contributors, s.v. "Cyrene, Libya," *Wikipedia, The Free Encyclopedia*, June 3, 2017, https://en.wikipedia.org/wiki/Cyrene,_Libya.

Chapter 5: Sacred Texts and Truth Teaching
(Mid-1st through 2nd Century A.D.)

Septuagint Text

In Alexandria, Egypt by 132 B.C., the Hebrew Scriptures had been translated from Hebrew/Aramaic into Greek by seventy Jewish scholars.[80] This translation is referred to as the *Septuagint*, or simply *LXX* (the Roman numeral seventy). Being nearby, the Messianic Hebrew refugees and their early converts of Cyrene and Alexandria (territories into which they fled), would have also had access to Septuagint readings. These early African Christians (underground or not), whose homelands were deemed to be part of a Roman province would have been familiar with the Greek language because it was a commercial language for trade within the Roman Empire at the time.

Manuscripts containing the Gospels and Apostle Paul's letters had been translated into Latin as well, at some point prior to the writings of second century early African Church Father Tertullian. Note that this was two centuries before the Christian west's Vulgate (the Latin translation) by Jerome. We know that the western Christian sect in Rome had not translated them into Latin because they were still using the Greek translations of these manuscripts. It definitely wasn't the state of Rome that commissioned them to be translated into Latin because they hated the Christian sect and persecuted them for their faith in Christ.

Catechetical School in Alexandria, Egypt

Christianity in Egypt was often locked in deadly struggles against the polytheistic religions of the Greco-Roman culture, Judaism, worship of Persian and Egyptian gods, and the Hellenistic movement that began in Alexandria, Egypt. In the late second and third centuries A.D., to counter the often-criticized young religion, Egypt's Christian leaders established a Catechetical School in Alexandria. This school became the heart of what then could only be called Christian philosophy. From there, scholarly Christian believers learned to battle opposition in an orderly and intellectual manner. In this university, Christianity first underwent rigorous studies that created its first theology and dogma and made the new faith accessible to all.[81] In addition to providing instruction to students attending lectures there, numerous written works were made available for individuals unable to attend the university.

Egyptian Christians also prevailed linguistically. They enlarged the Greek alphabet to include seven supplementary letters for Egyptian sounds that were not present in Greek. The resulting language and the writing system, is called "Coptic." This allowed Egyptian Christians to use the Greek alphabet for writing their spoken Egyptian language.[82] Greek, being a common language for commerce and trade, afforded broader dissemination of the Coptic Christian perspective and work products. Those work products would have resulted from exegetical interpretations, contextual criticism, and text proofing of the Old Testament, Gospels, and epistles at the Catechetical School of Alexandria. Christian orthodoxy spread rapidly throughout Lower Egypt, particularly westward along North Africa's Mediterranean port cities[83] and southward into towns along the Nile River in Upper Egypt.[84]

Old African Text

The collection of manuscripts once referred to as "Old African" or "Old Latin" is known today as the *Vetus Latina*.[85] Note that this was not a Bible, as we understand the Bible today. It was a collection of manuscript texts taken from passages in the Septuagint, Apostle Paul's letters, and very likely the Gospels, then translated into Latin. The first known reference to this collection of manuscripts was made by Tertullian who mentioned the "collected letters of Paul in Latin." Also, some scriptural quotes in Cyprian's *Heads* show evidence of its use.[86]

The faith and scriptural enlightenment of early African Christians was not based on interpretations from the colonial powers of Rome, or obviously not King James. Henri Teissier's March 2004 article "The African Roots of Latin Christianity" states, "It has been said that Africa possessed the earliest Latin versions of a certain number of books of the Bible before Jerome gives the Latin world his celebrated translation …"[87] Other French historians have made assessments similar to Teissier's:

> Pierre Maurice Bogaert: "When the need began to be felt—certainly from the mid-second century in Roman Africa—the Bible was translated from Greek into Latin … Till the opposite is proved I am for the African origin [of the translations] rather than Roman or Italian."[88]

> Louis Chevalier: "The first translations of the bible into Latin were made in Africa."[89]

> Claude Lepelle: "Western Christianity was not born in Europe, but south of the Mediterranean [North Africa]."[90]

Methodology for Identifying Right Teaching of Scripture

Christians in the regions across North Africa, Rome, Jerusalem, and Asia Minor sought to remain completely united and universal. They addressed errant beliefs about Christianity by engaging Christian teachers whose beliefs were contrary to those that were generally accepted. If the teacher demonstrated that his teachings reflected what the Scriptures taught, then his teachings were reconciled with the generally accepted beliefs. However, if the teacher's interpretation could not demonstrate its consistency with Scripture and he would not accept correction, he would be deemed a heretic and ex-communicated from the church. His teachings would then be declared heretical.

Christians who embraced the prevailing beliefs and teachings were referred to as being *catholic* (meaning "universal") and by implication "united." I'm stressing this point so readers won't confuse the first century use of the term catholic with the Roman Catholic denomination that wouldn't emerged until almost a millennium later.

Use of the Term "Catholic"

The term *catholic* comes from the Greek adjective *katholikos*, meaning "universal." It's a combination of two Greek words—one that means "according to" and another that means "the whole."[91] The early Christian church first used the term to emphasize its universal scope that encompassed all past and present believers anywhere. The earliest recorded use of the term catholic was in 107 A.D. by Ignatius of Antioch. In his letter to the Christians of Smyrna he urged them to remain closely united with their bishop. He wrote:

> Wherever the bishop shall appear, there let the multitude [of the people] also be; even as, wherever Jesus Christ is, there is the Catholic Church.[92]

The capitalization of the word *Catholic* (though in some sources it is not) in his letter was merely Ignatius' way to emphasize both, that it was Jesus' church, and that it was just as essential for believers to be unified (according to the whole) as it was for them to be the church (see Lightfoot & Hammer's 1891 translation of the letter).[93] Ignatius was not calling for a different denominational faction among Christians. We know this from his question in the section of the letter that follows the above quote. Ignatius asks,

> For if he that rises up against kings is justly held worthy of punishment, inasmuch as he dissolves public order, of how much sorer punishment, suppose ye, shall he be thought worthy, who presumes to do anything without the bishop, thus both destroying the [church's] unity, and throwing its order into confusion?[94]

At the time of his letter, persons claiming to be Christian were either a part of this universal church (also referred to as orthodox) founded by Christ, or they followed a leader who taught heresy in the name of Christianity. But the notion of a distinct Christian faction called *Catholic* did not exist until 380 A.D. That's when Roman Emperor Theodosius I reserved the use of the term (without consulting church leadership) to classify all congregations embracing the Nicene Creed. History reveals that the emperor used the term catholic as a political distinction only. Because Nicaean theology and ecclesiology, at the time, was also shared by other congregations, some who happened to be political dissenters.

Another point of clarification is needed. Theodosius I's Catholic faction mentioned above was diverse and inclusive of churches from many territories. Yet, it was not the Roman Catholic denominational faction. That faction did not exist until the churches in the west eventually split from the churches in the east in 1054 A.D.[95] over deviations from interpretations of the Nicene Creed regarding the issuance of the Holy Spirit.[96] These clarifications are necessary because the meaning of the term *catholic* is time bound. Here's how its meaning has morphed with the passage of time:

> Up to 380 A.D. the term *catholic* is to be understood to mean "universally united," unless the context refers to a distinct faction within Christendom.
>
> Thereafter, the term *catholic* refers to Nicaean Christians (see Chapter 13 for details).
>
> Around 1054 A.D. (though beyond the scope of this survey but relevant to the point), Roman Catholics emerged as a separate faction among Christian churches.

Therefore, be careful not to misinterpret the adjectival (descriptive) use of the term catholic by the early Christian Church that meant universally united. Also, do not confuse the term catholic that distinguished Nicaean Christians from Donatist Christians, in particular. Finally, do not err in believing that either of the above uses of the term catholic refers to the noun *Catholic* (which came much later) that refers to Roman Catholic as a separate Christian faction. The early African Church was not Catholic as in a separate faction. They were wholly catholic as being united under Jesus Christ with all believers, dead and alive.

Research Assignment 5.1

Use your preferred internet search tool to find information about the

a. Old African or Old Latin
b. Vetus Latina
c. LXX
d. Year Roman Catholics split as a separate denomination

This page is intentionally left blank.

The Early Church by the End of the 2nd Century A.D.[97]

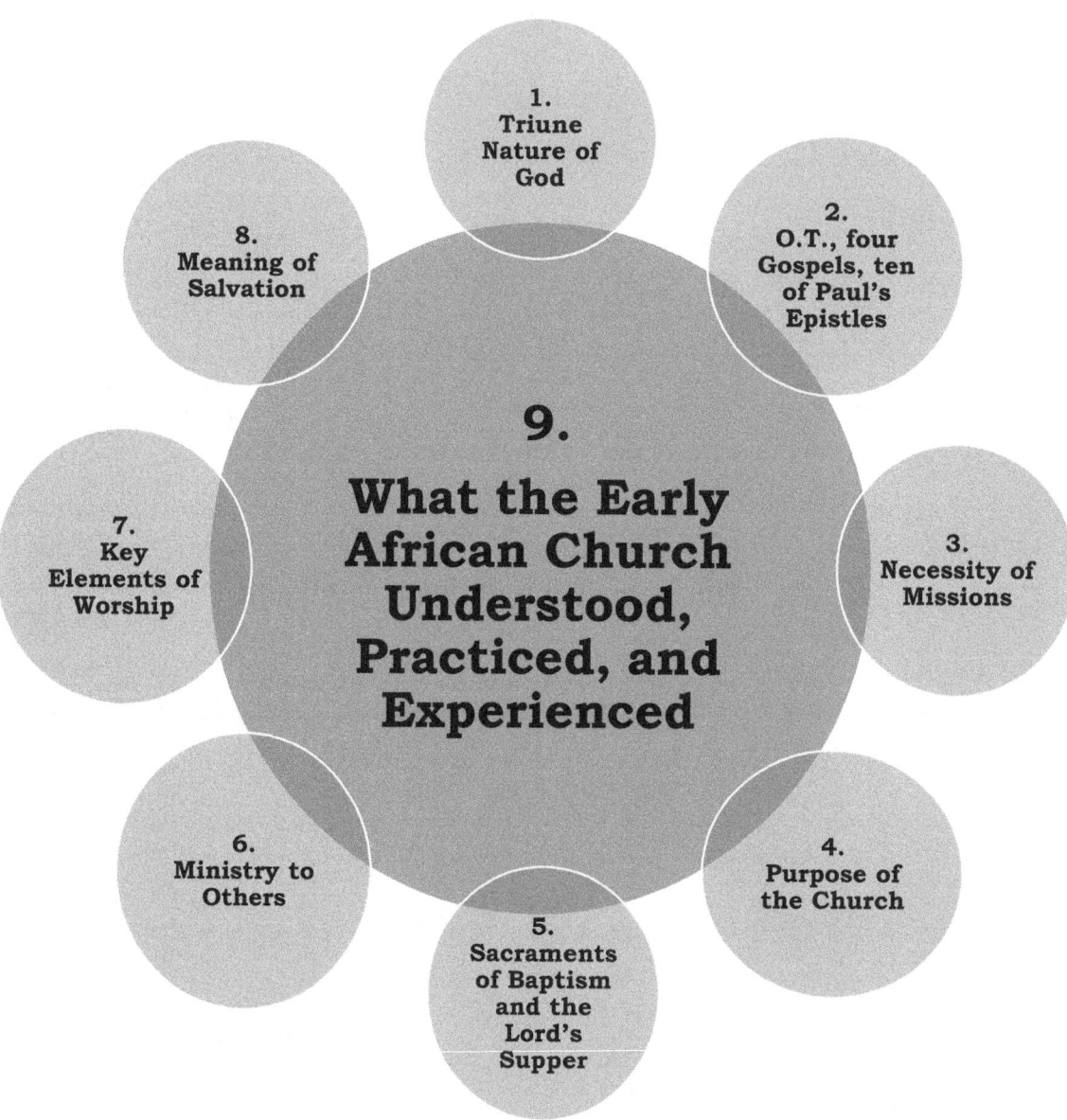

What the Early African Church Understood and Practiced

1. They understood from Scripture that the Father is God, the Son is God, and the Holy Spirit is God. An elaborate defense of this belief wasn't fully developed until the fourth century in Alexandria, Egypt.
2. Churches around the Mediterranean were united about the use of the Old Testament, the Gospels and ten of Paul's epistles. Other books in our New Testament today were also used, but their acceptance varied by region.[98]
3. The necessity of missions beginning in the upper room at Pentecost
4. The meaning and purpose of the church
5. Church Sacraments
   a. Baptism
   b. Nothing substantial supports the belief that the bread and wine of the Lord's Supper transformed into actual flesh and blood of Jesus.
   c. The Lord's Supper was celebrated as a sacrifice of thanksgiving, rather than a memorial.
6. The purpose of ministry
7. The elements of worship
   a. It consisted of Bible reading, preaching, prayers, and simple singing
   b. It was simplistic and without musical instruments.
   c. Sunday was the day of worship and recreation, but seventh-day Sabbath rest was still observed by almost all churches, because the earliest Christians were Hebrews.
8. The meaning and understanding of salvation
9. The dialogue between early African Christians and governing officials in dozens of martyr stories suggests the following:
   a. When they became Christians, they perceived themselves to have entered into an intimate union with the Lord Jesus.
   b. They severed allegiance to earthly systems and empires in order to give full allegiance to Christ long after His ascension to the Father.
   c. Although they owned property and businesses or held jobs, if ever a conflict arose with their Christian values, many followed those values in spite of the loss.
   d. They practiced their faith even at the risk of death.
   e. They were perceived as being strange, yet dangerous, because they gathered in large numbers with no identifiable leader.
   f. They viewed themselves like immigrants whose heart and sense of belonging was somewhere other than their present station in life.

Going forward in this survey, you may disagree with the early church on some points. Keep in mind that their Christian values and practices were not based on today's body of doctrine, but were based on a sense of having been immersed in the person of Jesus Christ, as revealed in Scripture.

Chapter 5 Notes

[80] Septuagint and Reliability, "Septuagint," 2016, http://www.septuagint.net/.

[81] W.H. Oliver, "The Catechetical School in Alexandria", Verbum et Ecclesia 36(1), 2015, Art. #1385, 12 pages. http://dx.doi.org/10.4102/ve.v36i1.1385.

[82] *Encyclopaedia Britannica*, s.v. "Hieroglyphic Writing," March 21, 2019, https://www.britannica.com/topic/hieroglyphic-writing/Christianity-and-the-Greek-alphabet.

[83] This is also known as the coastal territory of the Maghreb.

[84] Its progression continued into Egypt's desert regions, Ethiopia, and into Nubia.

[85] National Library of Sweden, Codex Gigas, "Translation of the Greek Text into Latin," 2015, http://www.kb.se/codex-gigas/eng/Long/texter/medeltida-bibel/translations/#Translation of the Greek text into Latin.

[86] H.A.G. Houghton, "The Latin New Testament: A Guide to Its Early History, Texts, and Manuscripts," Oxford Scholarship Online, 2016, http://www.oxfordscholarship.com /view/10.1093/acprof:oso/9780198744733.001.0001/acprof-9780198744733-chapter-1; Annette Weissenrieder, "Rethinking the Origins of the Gospel of Luke: The *Vetus Latina*," San Francisco Theological Seminary, 2016, http://sfts.edu/wp-content/uploads/2016 /03/vetuslatina.pdf.

[87] Henri Teissier, "The African Roots of Latin Christianity," *30 Days in the Church and in the World*, 2004, http://www.30giorni.it/articoli_id_3553_13 .htm?id=3553.

[88] Ibid.

[89] Louis Chevalier, *Le Problème Démographique Nord-Africain* (France: Presses Universitaires de France, 1947), 194.

[90] Teissier.

[91] Wikipedia Contributors, s.v. "Catholic (term)," *Wikipedia, The Free Encyclopedia*, June 4, 2017, https://en.wikipedia.org/wiki/Catholic_(term)#Other_second-century_uses.

[92] Ignatius, "Ignatius to the Smyrnaeans," trans. Lightfoot & Harmer, Early Christian Writings, http://www.earlychristianwritings.com/text /ignatius-smyrnaeans-lightfoot.html.

[93] Ibid.

[94] Ibid.

[95] CatholicBridge.com, "The Split of 1054 Between the Orthodox and Catholics," http://catholicbridge.com/orthodox/1054-orthodox-catholic-split.php.

[96] Ibid., "What Was Rome Thinking When It Added the Filioque?" 2018, http://catholicbridge.com/orthodox/catholic-orthodox-filioque-father-son.php.

[97] Ascertained mostly through explicit and implicit details in martyr stories and their trials, writings from that era, and details in other historical narratives regarding that time period.

[98] *A Survey of Church History: Part 1*, "The East and the West"; African Christians in the northwest had these books in hand in 180 A.D. during their trials for not worshipping the gods of Rome. If it took one generation for the socialization of Christian values to produce the number of bold faith stands and for the circulation of these books in northwest Africa, then that could mean the gospel arrived there around 150 A.D. Though in Egypt, Alexandrians credit Mark for bringing them the Gospel of Jesus Christ in 42 A.D.

Chapter 6: North Africa's Proconsularis, Numidia, and Mauretania

(Mid-2nd through Early 3rd Century A.D.)

PROFILE OF EARLY CHRISTIANITY IN AN AFRICAN TERRITORY

Africa Proconsularis

Key Location	Rome's first African territory. It includes Carthage, the former Phoenician province founded by Dido.
Modern-Day Name	Algeria and Tunisia region, but as a historic site (still lies in ruins today)
When	180 A.D. is the earliest known reference to Christians in Carthage.
How	Unlike all the other major cities under Roman control, details about the emergence of Christianity here are scarce. Some sources suggest its arrival was stealthy.
Related Event(s)	Seemingly, the Christian churches of Africa first came to the attention of Roman rule here in 180 A.D. when, according to Tertullian, the proconsul Vigellius Saturninus "first drew the sword upon us and put to death twelve Christians at Carthage."
Social, Political, or Religious Setting	Was once an independent, engineering marvel with a naval fleet that ruled the Mediterranean Sea. During this time period it was a province of the Roman Empire.

Events and Effects

This was Rome's first territory in Africa, occurring after the third Punic War in 146 B.C. This occurred thirty-seven years after the death of the Carthaginian General Hannibal. He was one of the greatest military strategists in history and one of the greatest generals of Mediterranean antiquity.

Why Rome decided to name that specific region Africa is unclear. In some form or another, our research points to the Berber people of that territory. Here's what was discovered about possible origins of its name:

1. *Afri* (singular *Afer*) was a Latin name that Romans used for the indigenous inhabitants of all the lands south of the Mediterranean (what we know today as Africa). That region was around Carthage in the second century B.C.[99]

2. It may have been derived from a Punic term for an indigenous population of the area also surrounding Carthage (as the name of the famous second century Carthaginian Berber playwright Publius Terentius Afer may suggest).[100]

3. From the Phoenician term *afar* meaning "dust." (Remember, the Phoenicians founded Carthage).[101]

4. An assertion that it stems from the Berber *ifri* (plural *ifran*) meaning "cave," in reference to cave dwellers.[102]

5. *Ifri* may be found in the name of the Banu Ifran from Algeria and Tripolitania, a Berber tribe originally from Yafran (also known as *Ifrane*) in northwestern Libya.[103]

6. The historian Flavius Josephus (born 37 A.D.) asserted that descendants of Abraham's grandson Epher (Genesis 25:4) invaded this region and gave it their own name.[104]

The map below depicts the mid-first century A.D. Africa Proconsularis:

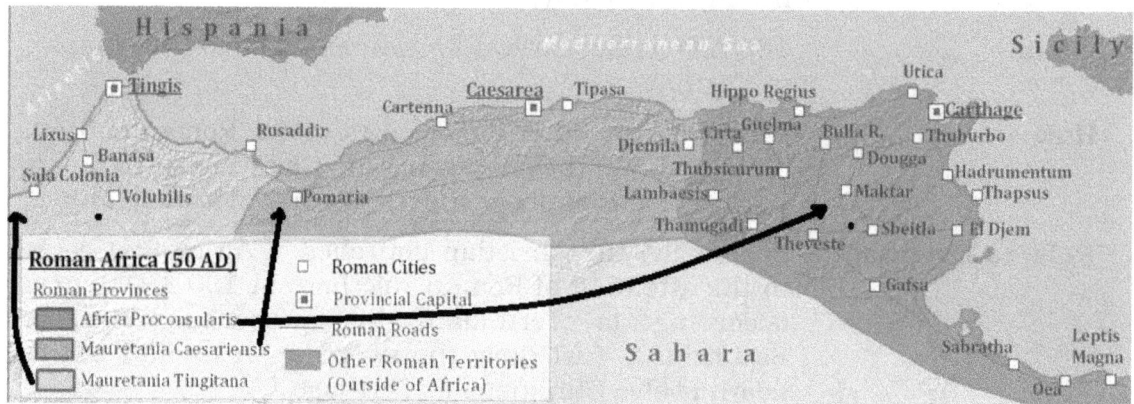

However it received the name Africa Proconsularis, there was a period of time that Berber kings around Carthage had allied with Rome (as they had with Dido). Territories surrounding Carthage were annexed and reorganized, and the city of Carthage was rebuilt. A long period of prosperity ensued; a cosmopolitan culture evolved. Trade quickened, the fields yielded their fruits.

Carthage's Relations with Its Neighbors

Numidia and Mauretania were agricultural areas west of Carthage. A great deal of their produce was exported to Italy through Carthage. The Berber people and towns around Numidia and Mauretania were much less romanized[105] than Carthage and retained their African ancestral language and customs. They viewed Rome and everything connected with it as foreign and oppressive. In Carthage, there was a strongly latinized class of landowners, merchants, and military officers who reaped more of the benefits of trade and other contacts with Italy than the indigenous Numidian and Mauretanian workers who actually raised the crops.

Settlers from across the empire had migrated there, forming a Latin-speaking ethnic mix. Carthaginian society became a mixture of native Phoenician-speaking Berbers, Phoenicians, and Berber-speaking Africans who gradually became romanized. For them, good relations with Rome and with the rest of the empire were of paramount importance. But also in Carthage and its outlying districts, there was a significant lower class whose feelings were similar to those of the Numidians and Mauretanians.[106]

As is often the case with port or cosmopolitan cities, Christianity gradually spread among the northwest coast of Africa.[107] Christianity had made significant inroads into Numidia and among the lower classes of Africa Proconsularis, and to a lesser degree, into Mauretania. This new faith of the African converts was a power even the Roman Empire could not overcome. At the same time, a smaller number of members of the romanized classes of Carthage had embraced Christianity. This brought into the Christian community some of the tensions that existed in the rest of society. Fortunately, newly converted Christians—particularly those of the upper classes—broke away from many of their social norms and contacts for the sake of church unity.[108]

Tertullian

Another great Carthaginian was Tertullian, an apologist, theologian, and one of the most skilled writers of the early church (more about him in Chapter 7). He embodied the indigenous temperament of the African Church in Carthage. After becoming a priest, his early writings stressed that "The Way" (Christianity) should be recognized as a legitimate religion by Rome. He also wrote in-depth that Christians should completely separate themselves from the world. He focused on Scripture to the exclusion of pagan philosophers.[109] Tertullian has been dubbed the Father of Latin Christianity. His writings, as well as those of others, suggest that the African expression of Christianity across North Africa had a very strong emphasis on intimacy with Christ. Particularly during the first three centuries, the life of an African Christian, whether rich or poor, strongly echoed Jesus' prayer about His people being "not of this world" (John 17:16).

Still an Illegal Religion

Despite being pious, virtuous, and scripturally based, Christianity was illegal within the Roman Empire. Every Christian realized that they could be arrested at any time.

> *Question*: Why would Christians be singled out when Rome had given Hebrews a separate exemption from worshipping Roman gods?
>
> *Answer*: Because Christians weren't seen as being a nation or ethnic group, as the Hebrews (though displaced or exported from Jerusalem).

Therefore, Christians could make no claim for special treatment as the Hebrews did. Also, Christians were accused of being atheists for denying the Roman gods. They were considered traitors for being loyal to Christ's kingdom and not Rome. They were also deemed guilty of grossly immoral acts of incest (because of scriptural references to lovefests with brothers and sisters) and cannibalism (because of scriptural references to drinking blood and eating flesh). Rome felt it needed to appease their gods in order to keep the empire intact. These accusations offended their gods. Initially, the persecution of Christians in Africa was not the seek-and-destroy variety. Rather, persecution resulted whenever empire officials became aware of a person refusing to offer incense to Rome's gods.[110]

Leptis Magna Evangelists into Numidia

Under Rome's Emperor Septimius Severus, the Numidian economy flourished. By the third century A.D., Christianity had spread very rapidly, and Numidia had become the center of a fairly sizable Christian faith community labelled as Donatists (explored in detail later in the survey).[111]

On the map, notice the proximity of Numidia and the city of Carthage. In Carthage, the sudden emergence of Christianity there suggests a stealthy underground church. Along the coast westward from Cyrene towards Carthage were the cities of Sabratha, Oea and Leptis Magna. The people in these cities, particularly the latter, were independent, self-motivated, upwardly mobile, and articulate. The earliest Christians there may have been slaves, servants, merchants, or craftsmen. Some served in the military or in a state ministry.  Regardless of how they made a living, being baptized believers, they were all potential evangelists.[112]

Ancient Numidian Kingdom

Since 40 B.C. Numidia had been ruled by the Romans, who divided it up and established provinces there. Remnants of the great African Berber kingdom survived until 24 A.D., when its territory was annexed to the Roman Empire. Like the rest of North Africa, the Numidian territories had been one of the breadbaskets of the empire, exporting cereals and other agricultural products. Substantial sacrifices and contributions to Christianity through its martyrs (men and women), great Christian scholars, and theologians of Berber descent emerged later from Numidia. Notice the location Carthage (circled). As you can see, at one time its territory was a part of the ancient kingdom of Numidia (it is now Tunisia and a smaller part of Algeria).

A second century A.D. letter from Mathetes to Diognetus describes some attributes of Christians in Carthage:

> For the Christians are distinguished from other men neither by country, nor language, nor the customs they observe. For they neither inhabit cities of their own, nor employ a peculiar form of speech, nor lead a life which is marked out by any singularity. The

course of conduct which they follow has not been devised by any speculation or deliberation of inquisitive men; nor do they, like some, proclaim themselves the advocates of any merely human doctrines. But inhabiting Greek and barbarian cities, according as the lot of each of them has determined, and following the customs of the natives in respect to clothing, food, and the rest of their ordinary conduct, they display to us their wonderful and confessedly striking method of life.[113]

Also, biblical scholar and theologian Robert McQueen Grant wrote that "The churches of [the Roman province of] Africa first came to the attention of the state in 180 A.D., when according to Tertullian, the proconsul Vigellius Saturninus 'first drew the sword upon us' and put to death twelve Christians at Carthage (discussed later in this survey)."[114]

Growth in and Around Carthage

Without church structures nor defined ecclesiastical organizations, Christianity trickled in. Districts of pastoral care were founded among the converts as the need for them arose. They were moved, possibly from place to place, and disappeared without leaving a trace of their existence.[115] The church grew rapidly in some Numidian territories. Rearranged provincial divisions by Roman authorities, mountainous regions, and the highlands of the Sahara made church growth difficult. Also, parts of Mauretania (from today's central Algeria westward to the Atlantic) remained independent, even from the Romans.

First African Church Council

From 180-203 A.D., the gospel of Jesus Christ expanded exponentially throughout North Africa. This has been confirmed through legal edicts, official persecution records, and writings of Early Church Fathers, martyrs, and church historians.[116] As with any rapid growth, conflicts and inconsistencies existed. The early African churches had their own conflicts to resolve. One conflict was the attempt to reach a consensus about what Jesus' apostles taught. The very first African Church Council was held in Carthage with sessions from 198-222 A.D. It was comprised of seventy bishops from African churches in Proconsularis, Leptis, Oea, and Sabratha. The objective of these sessions was to seek consensus on the interpretation and historical account of the apostle's teachings. The format of these council sessions formed the basis for proper decision making and consensus throughout Christendom, even to this day.[117]

PROFILE OF EARLY CHRISTIANITY IN AN AFRICAN TERRITORY

Mauretania

Key Locations	Caesariensis; Tingitana
	See map on the next few pages. Mauretania's reconfiguration that created the region of Sitifensis came much later.
Modern-Day Name	Parts of Morocco and Algeria
When	2nd Century
How	Christianity is believed to have been introduced to the region in the second century A.D., gaining converts in the towns, among slaves and among Berber farmers.[118]
Related Event(s)	In 44 A.D., Roman Emperor Claudius annexed Mauretania directly as a Roman province, under an imperial governor.[119] Later, parts of Mauretania were recaptured by Berber tribes.
Social, Political, or Religious Setting	Referred to as the land of the Moors.[120]

Events and Effects

The term "Mauretania" is derived from an adjective that means, of or pertaining to the Moors. It comes from the ancient Greek word μαυρός (*mauros*; *maurus* in Latin) meaning dark.[121] Romans called northwestern Africa Maurentania and its inhabitants *Mauri* (Moor in English).[122] Their complexion received frequent notice, as they were described as *nigri* (black) and *adusti* (scorched).[123]

For the time period of this chapter, our survey discovered two dubious inscriptions from Tipasa and Auzia suggesting evidence of Christianity in Mauretania.[124] Also for this time period, by implication, Tertullian's "An Answer to the Jews" refers to Christian believers in "the nations of the Moors."[125]

General Perceptions of Christians by Roman Writers

General descriptions of early second century Christians by Roman writers were far from complimentary. Consider their comments:

> Tacitus: "There is a group, hated for their abominations, called Christians by the people. Christus, from whom the name comes, suffered the extreme penalty during the reign of Tiberius at the hands of one of our officials, Pontius Pilate."[126]

> Suetonius: "The Christians are a class of men given to a new and wicked superstition."[127]

Celsus: "Jews and Christians alike are compared to a flock of bats, or to ants that creep forth out of their nests, or to frogs sitting around a swamp, or worms holding an assembly in a corner in the mud, and debating on the question which of them are the greatest sinners."[128]

Lucian: "The poor wretches have convinced themselves that they are going to be immortal and live for all time, by worshipping that crucified sophist and living under his laws. Therefore, they despise the things of this world, and consider them common property. They receive these doctrines by tradition, without any definite evidence."[129]

Pliny the Younger: "They were accustomed to meet on a fixed day before dawn and sing responsively a hymn to Christ as to a god, and to bind themselves by oath, not to some crime, but not to commit fraud, theft, or adultery, not falsify their trust, nor to refuse to return a trust when called upon to do so. When this was over, it was their custom to depart and to assemble again to partake of food—but ordinary and innocent food. For the contagion of this superstition has spread not only to the cities but also to the villages and farms. But it seems possible to check and cure it."[130]

Christianity was spreading so rapidly in North Africa that the Romans exercised a series of persecutions in an attempt to suppress its growth and to deter its disregard for the divinity of their emperor and the Roman gods.

Earliest Record of the Persecution of African Christians

The towns on the map below, Madauros (also known as Madaura), Scillium, and Milevis, are locations of the first and earliest African Christian martyrs. A profile of their names and circumstances of their deaths are described below the map.

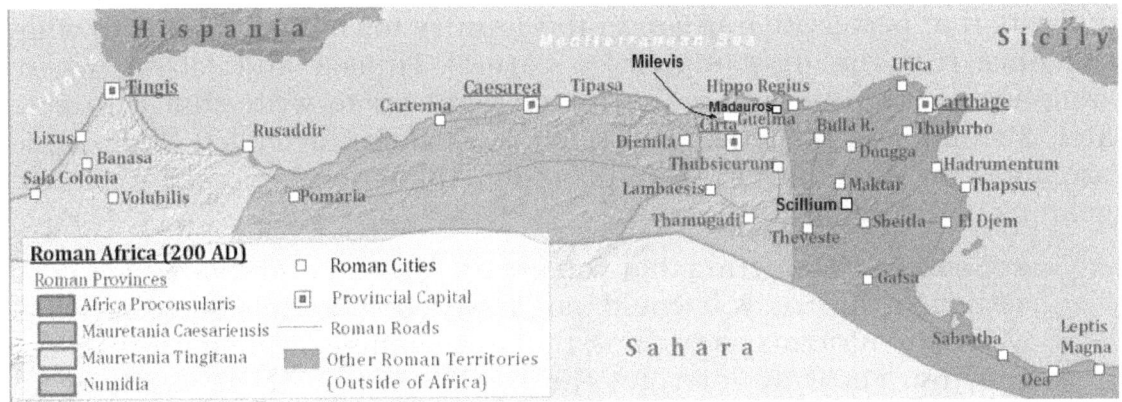

PROFILE OF AN AFRICAN EARLY CHRISITAN MARTYR

Namphanio

Ancestry or Hometown	Berber, Madauros, Numidia A town with a population of Berbers who spoke mainly Latin; located within the territories where Christianity in northwest Africa began to flourish.
Function/Status	Unknown
Stand	Unknown
Persecution Location	Madauros, Numidia
Persecution Date	Unknown, but credible sources hold him to be the first Christian martyr; sometime before the martyrdom of Speratus and his pupils
Circumstances	Unknown
Type of Death	Unknown

Namphanio's death had been absent from written history for over 200 years. The first written reference to his martyrdom was in an exchange of letters between the non-Christian African Maximus and the Numidian post-Nicene African Church Father Augustine. In 390 A.D., these letters named Namphanio as the first African to die for the Christian faith. Apparently, his death occurred around 180 A.D. by the hands of Romans, without a trial or before Rome kept official court records about persecution.

In *The Early Christian Church*, author and priest Philip Carrington suggests that persecution began in the country town of Madauros in what was once Numidia (now Algeria, a part of Tunisia and Libya), where Namphanio was a native.[131] Carrington went on to write that centuries later, Maximus, in his letter to Augustine, disdainfully called Namphanio "archimartus" (first martyr).[132] In his reply, Augustine explained the Punic meaning of the name:

> For surely, considering that you are an African, and that we are both settled in Africa, you could not have so forgotten yourself when writing to Africans as to think that Punic names were a fit theme for censure. For if we interpret the signification of these words, what else does Namphanio mean than "man of the good foot," i.e. whose coming brings with it some good fortune, as we are wont to say of one whose coming to us has been followed by some prosperous event, that he came with a lucky foot ? And if the Punic language is rejected by you, you virtually deny what has been admitted by most learned men, that many things have been wisely preserved from

oblivion in books written in the Punic tongue. Nay, you ought even to be ashamed of having been born in the country in which the cradle of this language is still warm, i.e. in which this language was originally, and until very recently, the language of the people.[133]

Africans Persecuted for Bringing Africans to Christ

The first official written record of the persecution of African Christians was also in 180 A.D. It was exacted upon the citizens of Carthage while they were in the process of converting to Christianity. According to Tertullian, that was the year in which Christians first came to the attention of the Roman officials in Carthage. They were met with the same savage persecution as the Christians in the city of Rome, as previously mentioned.[134] Following their profile below is an excerpt from the Roman transcript of the official trial.

PROFILE OF AN AFRICAN EARLY CHRISITAN MARTYR

Speratus and His Pupils

Ancestry or Hometown	Scillium, Numidia
	[Note: Placement outside of Numidia on the map on the previous page is due to changes in territorial borders between the dates of events below and the author's timeline for map topography.]
Function/Status	Teacher and his pupils
Stand	Refused to sacrifice to Roman gods
Persecution Location	Carthage
Persecution Date	180 A.D.
Circumstances	Roman proconsul ordered these twelve Christians to be brought before him and given a chance to honor the Roman gods.
Type of Death	Beheaded

These were the twelve Christians of whom Tertullian wrote to Scapula, "The Roman Proconsul first drew the sword," also known as the Scillitan Martyrs. The martyrs take their name from Scilla, a town in Numidia.

Around 180 A.D. Saturninus the proconsul ordered these twelve Christians to be brought before him. What transpired between them is detailed below:[135]

> The proconsul: You can win the clemency of our lord the Emperor, if you change your minds.
>
> Speratus:[136] We have never done ill. We have not been inclined to do wrong. We have never spoken ill. When treated wrong we have given thanks; because we pay heed to OUR EMPEROR,

The proconsul: We Romans are religious also. Our religion is simple, and we swear by the genius of our lord the Emperor, and pray for his welfare, as ye also ought to do.

Speratus: Please hear me what I have to say, I can tell you the mystery of simplicity.

The proconsul: I will not listen to you. Don't start speaking evil things about our sacred rites; but rather you need to swear by the genius of our lord the Emperor.

Speratus: The Empire of this world I know not; but rather I serve that God, whom no man has seen, nor have I've seen. I have committed no theft. If I have bought anything I pay the tax; because I know my Lord, the King of kings and Emperor of all nations.

The proconsul (to the rest): Stop letting Speratus persuade you.

Speratus: It is wrong to persuade others murder, or to speak false witness.

The proconsul: Don't partake in this man's foolishness.

Cittinus: We have none other to fear, except only our Lord God, who is in heaven.

Donata: We honor Caesar as Caesar: but fear to God.

Vestia: I am a Christian.

Secunda: What I am, that I wish to be.

The proconsul (to Speratus): Do you wish to continue being a Christian?

Speratus: I am a Christian. (And with him they all agreed.)

The proconsul: Will any of you need time to reconsider your answer?

Speratus: In all honesty, there is nothing to reconsider.

The proconsul: What are the things in your chest?

Speratus: Books and epistles [letters] of Paul, a just man.

The proconsul: Have a delay of thirty days and rethink your decision.

Speratus: I am a Christian. (And with him they all agreed.)

The proconsul read out the decree from the tablet: Speratus, Nartzalus, Cittinus, Donata, Vestia, Secunda and the rest having confessed that they live according to the Christian rite, since after opportunity offered them of returning to the custom of the Romans they have obstinately persisted, it is determined that they be put to the sword.

Speratus: We give thanks to God.

Nartzalus: Today we are martyrs in heaven; thanks be to God.

The proconsul ordered it to be declared by the herald: Speratus, Nartzalus, Cittinus, Veturius, Felix, Aquilinus, Laetantius, Januaria, Generosa, Vestia, Donata, and Secunda, I have ordered to be executed.

They all replied with, "Thanks be to God."

PROFILE OF AN AFRICAN EARLY CHRISTIAN LEADER

Pope Victor I

Lifespan	?-199 A.D.
Ancestry or Hometown	Berber; Leptis Magna or Tripolitania, Africa
Family Life	Unknown
Conversion Experience	Unknown
Contribution(s)	In 189 A.D. he became the first pope of Rome to be born in Africa, and the first pope to write in Latin.
Type of Death	Unknown
Social, Political, or Religious Setting	Victor excommunicated Theodotus of Byzantium for teaching that Christ was a mere man.
	Prior to his elevation to pope, a difference in dating the celebration of the Christian Passover/Easter between Rome and the bishops of Asia Minor had been tolerated by both the Roman and Eastern churches. However, Victor alone was intolerant of this difference. As pope he severed ties with these ancient churches and their bishops. In response, he was rebuked by Irenaeus and others.[137]

SOCIAL/POLITICAL FACTORS

Persecution: Emperor Severus' Edict of 202 A.D.

Where	Throughout the Roman Empire
When	202 A.D.
Source	Roman Emperor Septimius Severus
What	Criminalized conversion to Christianity

Events and Effects

Roman Emperor Septimius Severus (a Berber) may not have had disdain for Christians, but he sensed a threat as the church gained power through making many converts. As a result, anti-Christian feelings and persecution in Carthage, Alexandria, Rome, and Corinth were popular between 202 and 210 A.D.

In 202 A.D., Septimius enacted a law that prohibited the spread of Christianity and Judaism. This was the first universal decree of the state of Rome that criminalized conversion to Christianity. Violent persecutions broke out in Egypt and North Africa. It was during this time that Leonides, the father of Christian apologist Origen, was beheaded.

PROFILE OF AN AFRICAN EARLY CHRISITAN MARTYR

Perpetua and Felicitas

Ancestry or Hometown	Carthage
Function/Status	Perpetua: Married, wealthy, cultured and prominent woman of Carthage, said to have been 22 years old at the time of her death, and mother of an infant she was nursing.
	Felicitas: A pregnant household slave of Perpetua's[138]
Stand	Refused to worship the Roman gods
Persecution Location	Carthage
Persecution Date	202 or 203 A.D.
Circumstances	The women had converted to Christianity and received training in doctrine and discipline. Roman soldiers arrested the two young mothers and three men for becoming Christians against the emperor's edict.
Type of Death	After being imprisoned and then tried for refusing to sacrifice to the Roman gods, their sentence was death by being fed to the lions.
	When the lionesses refused to eat them, the Roman soldiers were ordered to thrust the women with swords.

Perpetua and Felicitas lived during a time of persecution of Christian converts under Emperor Septimius. Revocatus, a fellow slave who knew Felicitas, reported that at the time of their arrest they had been instructed in the faith, but had not yet been baptized.

While she was in prison, Perpetua's father, out of love for her, tried to shake her resolve to be baptized. Her reply was, "As a water pot cannot call itself by any other name, I cannot call myself by any other name than Christian." Her public faithfulness to Christ was worth the risk of death.

At the trial, the magistrate ordered the women to offer sacrifices to the Roman gods. The women refused. The magistrate had Perpetua's father (who was present) beaten, hoping it would prompt her to comply with his demand. Though grieved, she did not sacrifice to the Roman gods.

Their sentence was that both of them were to be thrown to the lions during an upcoming sports arena event. But during the event, perhaps picking up the scent of nursing females, the lionesses refused to harm Perpetua and Felicitas. So the Roman soldiers were ordered to thrust both women with swords.[139]

Church Life under Emperor Severus

According to researcher and theology professor Maureen Tilley, stories about African Christian martyrs during the aforementioned time reflect changes in their narrative about their own spiritual plight. Evidence suggests that perhaps they had been caught off guard by persecution. Then they relied upon biblical themes to re-evaluate their situation in light of the existing persecution. The intent of their re-evaluation was to determine the proper attitude towards the world, in order to frame their identity when addressing friends and enemies.[140]

Unique Expression of Early African Christian Faith

As you may have concluded, the early African expression of the Christian faith was unlike other forms, at that time and even today. But it was no less Christian. Having said that, let me caution you: Namphanio's and Speratus' early African Christianity predates the canonical process that yielded our Western expression of Christianity. Therefore, its value must be judged with respect for its pre-canonical context.

Going forward in this survey, please resist the tendency to judge early African Christians by today's western expressions of Christianity. The latter did not exist anywhere during the lifetime of these African Christians. As strange as it may seem to us, the zeal to be martyred for Jesus Christ continued for many early Africans well into the sixth century A.D. It undoubtedly had been cultivated by

- A slightly more intimate approach to Jesus' kingdom perspective (John 18:36)
- Jesus' prophecy in the Gospels (Luke 22:18)

- Paul's teachings about Jesus' return (2 Thessalonians 2:1-4)
- The destruction of the temple (Matthew 23:37-39; 24:1-2)
- Past events related to the fall of Jerusalem (Matthew 23; 24:15-16)
  - Forced and voluntary evacuation of Hebrews out of Jerusalem
  - Hebrews' stand at Masada
- Influences from the apocalyptic prophecies in the Book of Elchasai written around 114 A.D.

Christians of Africa's Numidian region interpreted these events as God's end of the Hebrew system, and the ushering in of the kingdom by the Lord Jesus Himself.

The Martyrdom Perspective in the Region

Considering their pre-canonical faith perspective and the social-political climate of Rome's imperialism, we can respect their desire for martyrdom. Consider this:

- For the reasons previously cited, these early African Christians genuinely believed that the God of the Scriptures had ended the Hebrew system, and therefore His Son Jesus' return was imminent.
  - To them, it would be foolish to renounce faith in Jesus, if in fact He was coming for His faithful in the very near future.
  - Their reasoning was perhaps: "What good would it do to renounce Jesus in order to escape Rome's punishment today, if Christ will return in a few days, weeks, or months? That brief escape from persecution would be foolish, if it costs me eternal separation in hell for renouncing the Him."
  - Rather, they may have continued to reason, "It would seem wiser to die with my faith intact, if in fact, in a few days, weeks, or months Christ will return. Then we will live again eternally with our Master in glorified bodies."
- So, we must at least respect these early African Christians for integrity to their understanding of faithfulness in Christ, albeit different from ours.

Research Assignment 6.1

a. Use your preferred internet search tool to find information about the people and politics profiled in this chapter.

b. Answer the following questions:
  1. How likely is it that an outsider would dare enter Roman territory to sway Africans to believe an "imported" Christianity?
  2. What could have convinced these African Christians to believe that death was preferable over renouncing their faith in Christ?
  3. How likely is it that the African Christian faith resulted from their own interpretation and understanding of the Scriptures?

Chapter 6 Notes

[99] *Academic Dictionaries and Encyclopedias*, s.v. "Afri," 2019, http://latin_german .deacademic.com/1644; Charlton T. Lewis, *A Latin Dictionary Lewis and Short*, s.v. "Afer," Oxford University Press, New York, 1879, 65, https://archive.org/details/in.ernet.dli .2015.147309/page/n79.

[100] Rashidi, 33-34; Wikipedia Contributors, s.v. "Terence," *Wikipedia, The Free Encyclopedia*, https://en.wikipedia.org/wiki/Terence.

[101] Daniel Johannes Venter and E. W. Neuland, *NEPAD and the African Renaissance* (Richard Havenga & Associates: Johannesburg, South Africa, 2005), 16.

[102] Michel Desfayes, "The Names of Countries: Including Some Familiar Names of Provinces or Peoples," http://michel-desfayes.org/namesofcountries.html; Geo. Babington Michell, "The Berbers," *Journal of the Royal African Society* 2, no. 6 (January 1903) (Oxford University Press, Oxford, UK, 1903), 161-194.

[103] Edward Lipinski, *Itineraria Phoenicia* (Leuven, Belgium: Peeters Publishers, 2004), 200.

[104] Crawford Howell Toy and Isaac Broydé, "Malchus (Cleodemus the Prophet)," in *JewishEncyclopedia.com*, 2011, http://www.jewishencyclopedia.com/articles/10328-malchus-cleodemus-the-prophet.

[105] Romanized in the sense that they were part of a subculture with access to the Roman Empire's basic infrastructural resources (roads, marketplace, monetary system, defense, civil laws, etc.) in their region. Note that the empire afforded these resources to every Roman citizen throughout the Mediterranean. However, these Africans used them as platforms upon which to exercise their own divinely created intellectual capacity, aptitude, and insight. The Africans highlighted in this survey are those whom we know to have used the empire's resources to profoundly shape Christian faith, ecclesiology, philosophy, and theology.

[106] Gonzalez, 155.

[107] Wikipedia Contributors, s.v. "History of Roman-era Tunisia," *Wikipedia, The Free Encyclopedia*, https://en.wikipedia.org/wiki/History_of_Roman-era_Tunisia.

[108] Gonzalez.

[109] *A Survey of Church History*, "Defending the Faith."

[110] Ibid., "The Bishop."

[111] *Encyclopaedia Britannica*, s.v. "Numidia: Ancient Region, Africa," 2018, https://www.britannica.com/place/Numidia.

[112] Oden, *Early Libyan Christianity*, 249.

[113] Mathetes, "Epistle of Mathetes to Diognetus," trans. Alexander Roberts and James Donaldson, Early Christian Writings, 2017, http://www.earlychristian writings.com/diognetus.html.

[114] Clyde C. Smith, "Speratus," in *Dictionary of African Christian Biography*, 2004, http://www.dacb.org/stories/tunisia/speratus.

[115] Wikipedia Contributors, s.v. "Early African Church," *Wikipedia, The Free Encyclopedia*, https://en.m.wikipedia.org/wiki/Early_African _Church.

[116] Oden, *Early Libyan Christianity*, 250.

[117] Ibid., 265.

[118] Wikipedia Contributors, s.v. "Mauretania," *Wikipedia, The Free Encyclopedia*, February 17, 2019, https://en.wikipedia.org/wiki/Mauretania.

[119] Ibid.

[120] Rashidi, 55-56, 60.

[121] *WordSense.eu*, s.v. "Maurus," https://www.wordsense.eu/Maurus/.

[122] Rashidi, 34.

[123] Frank M. Snowden, *Before Color Prejudice* (Cambridge, MA: Harvard University Press, 1983), 9.

[124] Roderic L. Mullen, *The Expansion of Christianity: A Gazetteer of its First Three Centuries* (Boston: Brill Leiden, 2004), 323-324.

[125] Tertullian, "An Answer to the Jews," ed. Allan Menzies, trans. S. Thelwall, in Ante-Nicene Fathers, vol. 3, Latin Christianity: Its Founder, Tertullian, Christian Classics Ethereal Library, https://www.ccel.org/ccel/schaff/anf03.iv .ix.vii.html.

[126] Cornelius Tacitus, *The Annals,* ed. Alfred John Church, William Jackson Brodribb, and Sara Bryant, in the Perseus Digital Library, http://www.perseus.tufts.edu /hopper/text?doc=Perseus%3Atext%3A1999.02.0078%3Abook%3D15%3Achapter%3D44.

[127] Suetonius [C. Suetonius Tranquillus], *Nero*, ed. Alexander Thomson, in the Perseus Digital Library, 2017, http://www.perseus.tufts.edu/hopper/text?doc=Perseus:text :1999.02.0132:life=nero:chapter=16&highlight=superstition2Csuetonius 2Cwicked.

[128] Bernhard Pick, *The Attack of Celsus on Christianity* (Oxford, UK: Oxford University Press, 1911), 239.

[129] Lucian of Samosata, "The Passing of Peregrinus," trans. Peter Kirby, Early Christian Writings, 2017, http://www.earlychristianwritings.com/text/peregrinus.html.

[130] Pliny the Younger, "Pliny the Younger to the Emperor Trajan," trans. Peter Kirby, Early Christian Writings, 2017, http://www.earlychristianwritings.com/text /pliny.html.

[131] Namphanio represents the many African Christians killed for their faith, but whose deaths were never recorded. Information about him found its way into letters from the famous Berber Augustine to Maximus.

[132] Philip Carrington, *The Early Christian Church: Volume 2, The Second Christian Century* (Cambridge, UK: University Press, 1957), 291.

[133] Augustine of Hippo, "Letter XVII. To Maximus," in *A Select Library of the Nicene and Post-Nicene Fathers of the Christian Church* vol. 1, *The Confessions and Letters of St. Augustine, with a Sketch of his Life and Work*, ed. Philip Schaff, Christian Classics Ethereal Library, 2005, https://www.ccel.org/ccel/schaff/npnf101.vii.1 .XVII.html.

[134] Tertullian, "To Scapula," trans. S. Thelwall, Early Christian Writings, 2017, http://www.earlychristianwritings.com/text/tertullian05.html.

[135] Andrew Rutherfurd, *The Passion of the Scillitan Martyrs*, trans. J. A. Robinson, Early Christian Writings, 2017, http://www.earlychristianwritings.com/text /scillitan.html.

[136] Speratus received most of the questions, while the others only spoke once. This gives the impression that he was likely the teacher (using the books at hand). The enthusiasm in the others was apparent in their witness. This was typical among youthful African martyrs in the early church.

[137] Wikipedia Contributors, s.v. "Pope_Victor_I," *Wikipedia, The Free Encyclopedia,* February 24, 2019, https://en.wikipedia.org/wiki/Pope_Victor_I.

[138] Perpetua demonstrates that neither mothering instinct, nor the grip of wealth and status was powerful enough to compromise her faith in the Lord Jesus Christ. For Felicitas, her status as a servant was no reason to doubt her value and status in eyes of the same Lord.

[139] Tertullian, *The Passion of Perpetua and Felicitas*, trans. Peter Kirby, Early Christian Writings, 2017, http://www.earlychristianwritings.com /text/tertullian24.html.

[140] Maureen A. Tilley, *The Bible in Christian North Africa: The Donatist World* (Minneapolis: Augsburg Fortress, 1997), 41.

Chapter 7: African Church Fathers (pre-Nicene)
(Late 2nd through Mid-3rd Century A.D.)

These Early Church Fathers of North Africa (and unnamed others) interpreted, understood, and defended Christian beliefs and way of life using their Old African books (Gospels, Apostle Paul's letters, and the Septuagint). They continued Jesus' call for intimacy with God and making disciples, which had been brought to their land by the Libyan and Egyptian missionaries in the upper room at Pentecost.

An emphasis on divine intimacy may have also been due to the fact that Christian doctrine, as we know it today, was yet to be firmly established from a critical review of Scripture. The development of such a review process would come through the scholars mentioned in this chapter.

A Penchant for Divine Intimacy

Their expression of faith resonated with biblical themes such as, Jesus' counsel to the rich young ruler that "If you want to be perfect, go, sell your possessions and give to the poor …" (Matthew 19:21); Apostle Paul's "put off" and "put on" themes (Ephesians 4:22-24; Colossians 2:11-15); and Jesus' promised inheritance (Matthew 5:10-12; Mark 10:29-30). Concurrent with the formation of Christian scholarship, a desire for deeper intimacy with God also arose in Egypt in the form of hermitage. Seekers embraced ascetic values that led to setting themselves apart from much of their previous living routines and material possessions. The objective of such separation was to avoid being distracted from running the race for Christ. So, in varying degrees early African Christians also practiced

> Restraint: To become spiritually grounded in faith one mustn't be deceived by the seeking or keeping of material things.
>
> Chasity: By denying oneself a family life, all attention could be devoted to the service of Christ and His church.
>
> Obedience: Submission to God's will at the expense of one's own, in terms of lifestyle, beliefs and in the service of the church.

Up to the early fourth century, a vast number of the Christians did not live according to a systematic theology, but rather, practiced their faith through intimacy.[141] This practice grew more so in the cities, then later spread to the countryside. The value they placed upon divine intimacy, while based on Scripture, had not been thoroughly tempered with a systematic understanding of Scripture. After all, during this time, with the exception of the Gospels and Paul's epistles, the New Testament canon was still fluid. Yet, their faithfulness to Christ was no less genuine.

Notable Pre-Nicene African Church Fathers

They had been emboldened by the ongoing persecution of their Christian brothers and sisters, particularly in Africa, and the need to clarify what it meant to live a Christian life. While explaining to others what Christians believed, they hammered out principles for interpreting and understanding right Scriptural teaching, in order to contrast it with false teachings in the surrounding culture.

PROFILE OF AN AFRICAN EARLY CHRISTIAN LEADER

Clement of Alexandria[142]

Lifespan	150-215 A.D.
Ancestry or Hometown	Not much is available about his birth place or his death. Most historians identify Athens, Greece as his birth place, but there is also a traditional belief in an Alexandrian birth.
Family Life	Pagan Greek
Conversion Experience	He had searched for knowledge and truth in many lands before finally finding fulfillment in Christianity in Alexandria, Egypt.
Contribution(s)	Early Church Father and theologian. His writings include • *Can the Rich Be Saved?* • *Protrepticus* (or *Exhortation*) • *Paedagogus* (or *The Tutor*) • *Stromateis* (or *The Miscellanies*)
Type of Death	Unknown
Social, Political, or Religious Setting	Christianity was regularly under attack by the Greco-Roman culture, Hellenistic movement, and worshippers of diverse pagan gods. Still young, the Catechetical School in Alexandria taught Christian leaders how to defend their faith in an orderly and intellectual manner. From there, the first body of theological knowledge and dogma was established.[143]

Clement studied philosophy and theology under many unknown teachers whom he referred to in his written work *Stromata*. In *Who Is the Rich Man That Shall Be Saved?* Clement advised his readers not to allow life's material goods to get in the way of more virtuous concerns. He argued that property itself does not bring a man closer to God.[144]

In *Stromata* he refutes Carpocrates' gnostic doctrinal heresy. One gnostic belief was that, since the body is inherently evil and the soul is pure, it doesn't matter what a person did with his or her body (random sex and drug abuse were okay). In his writings, Clement confirmed the immorality of the Carpocratians, claiming that orgies occurred at their Agape gathering.

A few fragments of Clement's secret works remain. Their contents suggest a familiarity with pre-Christian Jewish esotericism and Gnosticism. He argued that Greek philosophy originated among non-Greeks and that both Plato and Pythagoras were taught by Egyptian scholars. Origen and Alexander of Jerusalem were among his pupils.[145]

Clement was appointed head of the Catechetical School in Alexandria by his predecessor Pantaenus in 192 A.D. His lectures were attended by large numbers of pagans. Therefore, he began teaching them with truths that could be demonstrated from philosophy and nature, for the purpose of leading his hearers by degrees to embrace the Christian faith. He not only lectured, but also wrote numerous works for individuals unable to attend his lectures. He fled to Palestine in 202 A.D. because of persecution by Emperor Septimius Severus but returned four years later.[146]

PROFILE OF AN AFRICAN EARLY CHRISTIAN LEADER

Tertullian

Lifespan	160?-240? A.D.
Ancestry or Hometown	Berber; Carthage
Family Life	Well educated in a wealthy family of non-Christian parents. Wife was a Christian while he was a convert.[147]
Conversion Experience	Unknown
Contribution(s)	Early Church Father, theologian and writer. His writings would later help to maintain doctrinal integrity regarding the Trinity for Western Christianity. Whereas, Christianity in the east remained divided over the divine and human nature of Jesus.[148] His writings may be categorized as • Apologetic • Doctrinal • Contentious (or controversial) • Moral • Practical
Type of Death	Unknown
Social, Political, or Religious Setting	A contemporary when Christian churches in Carthage first came to the attention of the Roman proconsul Vigellius Saturninus in 180 A.D. and the proconsul put to death twelve Christians with the sword.

Tertullian was the first of the church writers to make Latin the language of Christianity, as he wrote Greek and Latin fluently.[149] Arguably, he is considered the father of Latin Christianity, which was founded and flourished first in Northern Africa—not in Italy. He used Latin even before Novatian (the first Roman theologian to use Latin).[150] Through written and spoken works Tertullian contentiously combated

1. The practice of persecution: His writing *The Apology* in 197 A.D. was addressed to the magistrates of the Roman Empire, particularly the proconsul of Carthage about the persecution of Christians.[151] Here are a few excerpts:

We don't worship an ass-headed god—we leave that to you, and your Anubis cult.[152] We don't worship the cross, a bit of wood. Worshipping bits of wood—idols—is your trick. In fact the trophies of victory you adore all hang off cross-shaped bits of wood, so that's you, not us, once again.

Instead we worship the one God, the creator. He gave us books to allow us to know him, unknowable as the infinite is of itself, and sent men to tell us about him. Antiquity is almost a superstition among you—consider the antiquity of these books of the Jews! And among them was Christ born, as they knew he must sometime be.

2. Gnostic heresy: Those who believed in salvation through knowledge, not through faith.

3. Marcionite Gnosticism: In *Prescription Against Heresies*, Tertullian reveals that Marcion attempted to reconcile himself to the church before his death.

4. Confusion about the nature of Christ: He wrote *Treatise Against Praxeas* to help reconcile the divinity of Christ with the unity of God.

In *On the Pallium*, Tertullian's opening reveals a consciousness about his heritage. He writes, "Men of Carthage, ever princes of Africa, ennobled by ancient memories, blessed with modern facilities ..."[153]

The phrases "The blood of martyrs is the seed of the church" and "It is certain because it is impossible" are attributed to Tertullian.

Today, Tertullian's teachings have shaped the Roman Catholic, Lutheran, Episcopalian, Presbyterian, and Methodist orthodoxy regarding the Trinity and the doctrine of Christ.[154]

PROFILE OF AN AFRICAN EARLY CHRISTIAN LEADER

Origen of Alexandria

Lifespan	185-255 A.D.
Ancestry or Hometown	Egyptian; Alexandria, Egypt
Family Life	Christian family
Conversion Experience	From his earliest years he was conversant with the Gospels, Apostle Paul's letters, and the Septuagint Scriptures. His father, Leonides, was martyred in his presence in 202 A.D., and the family fortunes were confiscated by the Roman Empire. Only the intervention of his mother (by hiding his clothes) prevented Origen from presenting himself to share his father's fate.[155]
Contribution(s)	Early Church Father, theologian and writer
	Origen was a man ahead of his time, particularly in terms of biblical scholarship and criticism. At only eighteen years old he was appointed Bishop of Alexandria. He not only reopened the disbanded African Catechetical School in Alexandria, but headed it. The teachers and students of this school were influential in many of the early theological controversies within Christendom. His view of the Scriptures as a sacrament (it was believed that a divine encounter could be experienced through the "Living Word") was a key contribution to the foundation of *Lectio Divina* (still used today by western monastic communities).[156]
	In Origen's day, Scripture was read aloud or recited during worship as a sacrament (this was long before the general availability of the text). Listening to Scripture was the practice of the spiritual disciplines of silence and contemplation, not for the purpose of exegetical analysis, contextual criticism, or proof-texting.
Type of Death	When Christian clergy were arrested for not sacrificing to Roman gods, Origen too suffered refined and continuous torture in prison where he died.
Social, Political, or Religious Setting	He was a contemporary during Rome's Edict of 202 A.D. when Christian conversions were illegal, which resulted in his father's martyrdom in his presence.
	Origen and others battled opposition to Christianity in an orderly and intellectual manner through the Catechetical school in Alexandria.[157]

Origen was a brilliant student who received the best education and the best Christian upbringing available. He was a student of Clement of Alexandria. In 202 A.D. when Origen was eighteen years old, he was appointed by Demetrius, Bishop of Alexandria, not only to reopen the disbanded Catechetical School in Alexandria, but to head it (the school had been left vacant after persecution under Emperor Septimius Severus compelled Clement to flee to Palestine). The school was the older of the two major centers of biblical exegesis and theological study during the third century A.D., the other being the School of Antioch.[158]

Origen is credited as being the father of theology and was active in the fields of commentary and comparative biblical studies.[159] His life's work also included

- In 214 A.D. traveling to Rome and from there visiting Arabia at the pagan governor's request.

- In 218 A.D. beginning his written works for Ambrosius, a wealthy friend who provided him with a staff of stenographers, copy writers and copiers. It has been said that Origen penned about 6,000 books.

- In 229 A.D. he received an invitation to Athens to help the church there deal with a Gnostic heretic.[160]

PROFILE OF AN AFRICAN EARLY CHRISTIAN LEADER

Cyprian of Carthage

Lifespan	200-258 A.D.
Ancestry or Hometown	Berber; Carthage (modern Tunisia)
Family Life	A wealthy aristocratic, pagan Berber family
Conversion Experience	Through a priest named Caecilius
	He was baptized when he was thirty-five years old. Afterwards, he gave away a portion of his wealth to the poor of Carthage. He described his own Christian conversion and baptism in *Epistola ad Donatum de gratia Dei* (detailed following this profile).
Contribution(s)	He defined five possible types of lapses in faith during persecution under Roman Emperor Decius. For each type he designated the appropriate amends. His resolution for addressing the lapse brought forgiveness and unity to the Christian churches throughout the provinces.[161]
	Early Church Father, theologian, and writer
	Some of his pastoral writings are • *Epistola ad Donatum de gratia Dei*[162] • *Testimoniorum Libri III* • *Testimonia ad Quirinum* • *De Ecclesiae Catholicae Unitate* (*On the Unity of the Catholic Church*) • *De Lapsis* (*On the Fallen*)
Type of Death	He was beheaded with a sword as his followers watched. He was the first African bishop to suffer a martyr's death for his faith.
Social, Political, or Religious Setting	Persecution by Roman emperors Decius and Valerian

Conversion Experience

Thascious Caecilius Cyprianus took the additional name Caecilius in memory of the priest to whom he owed his conversion. Before his conversion, Cyprian was a leading member of a legal fraternity in Carthage, an orator, a pleader (lawyer) in the courts, and a teacher of rhetoric. He described his own Christian conversion and baptism in the following words:

> When I was still lying in darkness and gloomy night, I used to regard it as extremely difficult and demanding to do what God's mercy was suggesting to me ... I myself was held in bonds by the innumerable errors of my previous life, from which I did not believe I could possibly be delivered, so I was disposed to acquiesce in my clinging vices and to indulge my sins ... But after that, by the help of the

water of new birth, the stain of my former life was washed away, and a light from above, serene and pure, was infused into my reconciled heart ... a second birth restored me to a new man. Then, in a wondrous manner every doubt began to fade ... I clearly understood that what had first lived within me, enslaved by the vices of the flesh, was earthly and that what, instead, the Holy Spirit had wrought within me was divine and heavenly.[163]

Persecution and Martyrdom

In 248 A.D. shortly after the death of the incumbent, Donatus of Carthage, Cyprian was quickly appointed to the priestly office of bishop. Unfortunately, before Cyprian had time to prove himself, persecution by Emperor Decius (249-251 A.D.) had fallen upon the church. This persecution was directed against Christian leaders. The bishops of Rome, Antioch, and Jerusalem were all executed. Cyprian of Carthage and Dionysius of Alexandria only escaped by going into hiding.

At the end of 256 A.D., persecution of Christians broke out again under Emperor Valerian. In Africa, through his written exposition entitled *De Exhortatione Martyrii*, Cyprian prepared Christians for the expected edict of persecution. Shortly thereafter, he was brought before the Roman proconsul Aspasius Paternus (August 30, 257 A.D.) where he refused to sacrifice to the pagan gods, but instead, steadfastly professed Christ. The proconsul banished him and his clergy to Curubis (modern-day Korba). Within one year he was recalled and kept a prisoner in his own home.

A new edict was given which demanded the execution of all Christian clergy.[164] On September 13, 258 A.D., Cyprian was imprisoned on the orders of the new proconsul, Galerius Maximus. His imprisonment was believed to be due to a claim that he was responsible for the pandemic that ravaged Rome from 250-270 A.D. (historians also refer to it as the Plague of Cyprian). He witnessed and described the plague himself.[165] Five thousand people were said to die per day, in Rome.

On the day following his imprisonment, Cyprian was examined for the last time and sentenced to die by the sword. His only reply was "Thanks be to God!" The execution was carried out at once near the city. He removed his garments without assistance, knelt down, and prayed. After he blindfolded himself, he was beheaded by the sword as his followers watched.[166]

In Pontius the Deacon's *The Life and Passion of Cyprian, Bishop and Martyr*, the third century A.D. author wrote,

> His passion being thus accomplished, it resulted that Cyprian, who had been an example to all good men, was also the first who in Africa imbued his priestly crown with blood of martyrdom, because he was the first who began to be such after the apostles. For from the time at which the episcopal order is enumerated at Carthage, not one is ever recorded, even of good men and priests, to have come to suffering.[167]

PROFILE OF AN AFRICAN EARLY CHRISTIAN LEADER

Arnobius of Sicca

Lifespan	?–330 A.D.
Ancestry or Hometown	Berber; region of Numidia
Family Life	Pagan
Conversion Experience	Arnobius attributed his 300 A.D conversion to Christianity in to a premonition from a dream, and thereafter defended Christianity by demonstrating to the pagans their own inconsistencies.
Contribution(s)	Early Church Father and writer
	Because of his former paganism, many clergy were suspicious of him; notably, the local bishop. As a pledge of his conviction, he composed the seven books *Adversus Nationes* (*Against the Pagans*).[168]
Type of Death	Unknown

Arnobius was born a pagan of Berber origin. According to Jerome's chronicle, before his conversion, Arnobius was a distinguished Numidian rhetorician at Sicca Veneria (El Kef, Tunisia), a major Christian center in Proconsular Africa. It was an important town, lying on the Numidian border to the southwest of Carthage. The translators of Arnobius' *Ad Gentes* describe the town as "the seat of that vile worship of the goddess of lust, which was dear to the Phoenician races."[169]

In Sicca Veneria, Arnobius taught rhetoric during the reign of Roman Emperor Diocletian. His writings were penned in the abrasive and solemn style that was called "African," through which he vigorously defended the Christian faith. He was more earnest in his defense of Christianity than he was perfectly established in its tenets. His books were composed in response to Diocletian's persecution of Christians and were a rebuttal to pagan arguments as to why the persecution was justifiable.[170]

In *Jerome and Gennadius: Lives of Illustrious Men*, Arnobius is credited for being the teacher of Lactantius (the Berber African Christian who would become the future advisor to Rome's first "Christian" emperor, Constantine).[171]

Research Assignment 7.1

Look at the date table in the "Chronological Perspective" section and the results of some of your other searches. Notice how early these theologically powerful men wrote in defense of their faith.

Also, use your preferred internet search tool to find information about the book Against the Pagans.

Chapter 7 Notes

[141] *A Survey of Church History*, "Pioneering Theologian: Origen."

[142] Though not African by descent, it was the spiritual and intellectual richness in early African Christianity that seized Clement's heart and compelled him to make Africa his home.

[143] Oliver, W.H.

[144] Clement of Alexandria, *Who Is the Rich Man That Shall Be Saved?* trans. Peter Kirby, Early Christian Writings, 2017, http://www.earlychristianwritings.com/text/clement-richman.html.

[145] Gerald A. Press, *Development of the Idea of History in Antiquity* (Montreal: McGill-Queen's Press, 2003), 83.

[146] Wikipedia Contributors, s.v. "Catechetical School of Alexandria," *Wikipedia, The Free Encyclopedia*, July 23, 2018, https://en.wikipedia.org/wiki/Catechetical_School_of_Alexandria.

[147] Rashidi, 35.

[148] Gonzalez, 252, 164.

[149] Rashidi.

[150] Teissier; Chevalier; Wikipedia Contributors, s.v. "Novatian," *Wikipedia, The Free Encyclopedia*, June 24, 2017, https://en.wikipedia.org/wiki /Novatian.

[151] To write against Christian persecution at the hands of the Roman ruling authorities in the midst of that persecution required a strong resolve. This suggests that Tertullian was very confident about whatever God did to confirm the truth of the gospel to him.

[152] This is a reference to the cult of Osiris in Rome who worshipped the Egyptian ass-headed god. A senior countryman of Tertullian, Apuleius of Madauros (124-170 A.D.), Numidian (and half-Gaetulian), was a priest of Isis and Osiris. Apuleius was also author of the ancient Roman novel *The Golden Ass*, and was a famous lawyer, poet, Christian critic, and historian who travelled extensively to Rome, Athens, Asia-Minor and Egypt.

[153] Tertullian, "On the Pallium," ed. Roger Pearse, trans. S. Thelwall, The Tertullian Project, 1998, http://www.tertullian.org/anf/anf04/anf04-03.htm#P128_5972.

[154] Noel Q. King, *Christian and Muslim in Africa*, (New York: Harper & Row Publishers, 1971), 6.

[155] The simple act of a mother hiding her son's clothing to save him resulted in a treasure of spiritual insight for leadership in the early Christian church.

[156] Wikipedia Contributors, s.v. "Lectio Divina," *Wikipedia, The Free Encyclopedia*, accessed April 6, 2017, https://en.wikipedia.org/wiki/Lectio_Divina; Raymond Studzinski, *Reading to Live: The Evolving Practice of Lectio Divina* (Trappist, KY: Liturgical Press, 2009), 28-29.

[157] Tour Egypt.

[158] Wikipedia Contributors, "Catechetical School of Alexandria," *Wikipedia, The Free Encyclopedia*, July 23, 2018, https://en.wikipedia.org/wiki/Catechetical_School_of_Alexandria.

[159] Ibid.

[160] G. A. Oshitelu, "Origen of Alexandria," in *Dictionary of African Christian Biography*, 2002, http://www.dacb.org/stories/egypt/origen.

[161] Justin Eimers, "Cyprian on Apostasy and Unity," Academia, December 8, 2012, http://www.academia.edu/8209280/Cyprian_on_Apostasy_and_Unity, 11-12.

[162] He testified to feeling shamed and convicted about the innumerable errors and sins from his past. He concluded that he had no choice except to acquiesce to his own vices and continue in sin. But after experiencing reconciliation of the heart, he received and trusted his second birth that the Holy Spirit worked in him.

[163] Cyprian, "The Epistles of Cyprian: Epistle I. To Donatus," trans. Ernest Wallis, in *Ante-Nicene Fathers*, vol. 5, *Hippolytus, Cyprian, Caius, Novatian, Appendix*, ed. Alexander Roberts and James Donaldson, Christian Classics Ethereal Library, 2005, http://www.ccel.org/ccel/schaff/anf05.iv.iv.i.html.

[164] Wikipedia Contributors, s.v. "Cyprian," *Wikipedia, The Free Encyclopedia*, June 3, 2017, https://en.wikipedia.org/wiki/Cyprian.

[165] Pontius the Deacon, "The Life and Passion of Cyprian, Bishop and Martyr," in *Ante-Nicene Fathers*, vol. 5, *Hippolytus, Cyprian, Caius, Novatian, Appendix*. ed. Alexander Roberts and James Donaldson, Christian Classics Ethereal Library, 2005, http://www.ccel.org/ccel/schaff /anf05.iv.iii.html.

[166] Oshitelu, "Cyprian."

[167] Pontius the Deacon.

[168] Arnobius demonstrated that when people doubt the genuineness of your Christian conversion, the best thing is to simply continue in the purpose in which God is leading you.

[169] Alexander Roberts and James Donaldson, eds., *Ante-Nicene Christian Library: Translations of the Writings of the Fathers,* vol. 19, trans. Hamilton Bryce and Hugh Campbell (Edinburgh: T&T Clark, 1871), xiii.

[170] Wikipedia Contributors, s.v. "Arnobius," *Wikipedia, The Free Encyclopedia*, May 24, 2017, https://en.wikipedia.org/wiki/Arnobius.

[171] Ernest Cushing Richardson, trans., "Jerome and Gennadius, Lives of Illustrious Men," in *A Select Library of the Nicene and Post-Nicene Fathers of the Christian Church*, second series, vol. 3, *Theodoret, Jerome, Gennadius, and Rufinus: Historical Writings*, Christian Classics Ethereal Library, 2005, http://www.ccel.org/ccel/schaff/npnf203.v.iii .lxxxii.html.

Chapter 8: Persecuted for Not Sacrificing to Roman Gods, Part 1
(Mid-3rd through End of the 3rd Century A.D.)

SOCIAL/POLITICAL FACTORS

Roman Emperor Decius' Edict of 250 A.D.

Where	Throughout the Roman Empire
When	250 A.D.
Source	Emperor Decius
What	His edict mandated that every citizen carry at all times a certificate, issued by the local authorities, testifying that he or she had offered sacrifices to the gods.

Events and Effects

End of Favor from Rome

Prior to Emperor Decius' reign, Christians had momentarily enjoyed favor in the highest government positions and were among the most capable literary men. That favor was not based on law, but on the good nature of local governors. Decius (249-252 A.D.) came to the throne as a reformer at a time when everything Roman seemed to be going wrong everywhere throughout the empire.

The government's practice of syncretism was being threatened by the spread of Christianity and Judaism.[172] For centuries Rome's "one country, two systems" policies had allowed all people (Greek, Syrian, Egyptian, Hebrew, etc.) to maintain their traditions, religious freedom, political freedom, and freedom of thought, though under a general [and strict] Roman perspective. This meant one could be a Christian, as long as it didn't offend Caesar. However, syncretism was also a source of tension for Hebrews and Christians. Their teachings emphasized God's word, Christlikeness, and God's role in human history as the standard for determining right, wrong, and moral living. Above all of these was their "one God and Him only" monotheistic belief.

The more Rome's population converted to Christianity or Judaism, the more aware citizens were of the huge contrast between God's way and Rome's way. Seekers of truth and knowledge in and around North Africa began to experience the contradictions and conflicts between the two ways. This compelled them to be more ardent about revering Yahweh (for the Hebrews) and Jesus (for Christians) over Rome's way. Consequently, by the third century A.D., massive numbers of Christians chose death over compromise. Some estimate the number well over one million. Africa had become a breeding ground of persecution and martyrdom.[173]

In his zeal for the restoration of the historic national Roman gods, Emperor Decius organized an attempt to wipe out Christianity. Citizens not certified as Roman god worshippers were tortured with unprecedented ferocity. Some were beheaded, thrown to the lions, or burned alive. All were subjected to innovative torture techniques, regardless of age or sex.

In June of 250 A.D., Decius ordered a general sacrifice. Governors throughout the empire were commanded to search out everyone who rejected the national worship and to enforce the highest penalties.[174] This reached all classes, and no one was spared. The bishops were attacked first, with Fabian, Bishop of Rome, being an early victim. The bishops of Antioch and Jerusalem died in prison. The great church scholar Origen, in spite of his old age and advanced learning, was not spared but suffered refined and continuous torture. He died in prison as a result of his suffering. Other bishops such as Cyprian of Carthage fled for safety and governed their flocks from a distance.[175]

The Catechetical School of Alexandria was closed by order of Roman authorities, but its members continued to meet in other secret places.

PROFILE OF AN AFRICAN EARLY CHRISITAN MARTYR

Africanus and 40 Companions

Ancestry or Hometown	Punic (Carthaginians traced their origins to the Berbers and Phoenicians)
Function/Status	Unknown
Stand	Would not renounce their faith and allegiance to Christ
Persecution Location	Carthage
Persecution Date	Sometime between 249 and 251 A.D.
Circumstances	Fortunianus, the Roman governor of Africa, attempted to force Africanus and three of the others to renounce Christ. It is recorded that neither threats nor torture could influence these believers to change. Their torture included • Being burned with red-hot iron • Having vinegar poured on their wounds • Having salt sprinkled on their wounds • Having their skin raked with iron claws
	Africanus and three others were shown the bodies of the other thirty-six Christians who had already been slaughtered. Still refusing to renounce Christ, they were thrown into a prison cell.
Type of Death	They were beheaded.

Africanus and three others continued their refusal to renounce Christ.[176] The governor put heavy chains on them and gave orders to starve them to death. It was reported that at night, an angel of the Lord removed their chains and fed them. In the morning the guards found the four men cheerful and strong.

Fortunianus ordered sorcerers and conjurers to carry snakes and other poisonous creatures into the prison. When the guards looked into the cell through an opening in the ceiling, they saw the martyrs unharmed, praying, and with the snakes crawling at their feet. When the sorcerers opened the door of the prison cell, the snakes bit them. Furious, Fortunianus gave orders to behead the men.[177]

PROFILE OF AN AFRICAN EARLY CHRISITAN MARTYR

Isidore of Chios

Ancestry or Hometown	Egyptians; Alexandria, Egypt
Function/Status	Officer in the Roman Navy
Stand	Refused to worship the Roman gods
Persecution Location	Island of Chios
Persecution Date	251 A.D.
Circumstances	Confessed to the commander of the fleet that he was a Christian while on the island of Chios
Type of Death	Tortured, beheaded, and body tossed into a cistern[178]

Church Life under Emperor Decius

According to Maureen Tilley, by this time, Christians were not caught off guard by the existence of persecution. They didn't need to make sense of what was happening, because they perceived persecutors to be agents of the devil. Martyr stories during the time revealed internal quarrels precipitated by the devil, about how to deal with believers—in particular, how to handle clergy who had a lapse in the faith—and the increasing authority of confessors (Christians who had been punished or tortured and survived without renouncing Christ). Their martyr stories focused heavily on the value of enduring to the end.[179]

Peculiar Nature of Persecution in Africa

From 253 to 260 A.D., Emperor Publius Licinius Valerianus vigorously renewed his predecessor, Decius' persecution of Christians. He executed African Church Father Cyprian of Carthage, in addition to thousands of others. John Foxe makes a brief statement about persecution in Africa under Emperor Valerian in *Foxe's Book of Martyrs*: "In Africa the persecution raged with peculiar violence; many thousands received the crown of martyrdom."[180] One example was the martyrdom of James, Marian, and their friends.

PROFILE OF AN AFRICAN EARLY CHRISITAN MARTYR

James, Marian, and Friends

Ancestry or Hometown	Numidia
Function/Status	James was a deacon who had already suffered as a confessor. Marian was a reader in the church.[181]
Stand	Refused to worship the Roman gods
Persecution Location	Near Cirta
Persecution Date	259 A.D.
Circumstances	Centurions surrounded the house and made several arrests. Marian and James both openly confessed their faith and acknowledged their holy orders.[182]
Type of Death	After being tortured on the rack and imprisoned, they were taken to a river valley along with other unnamed friends. The martyrs were placed in rows, blindfolded, and then beheaded. Their bodies were thrown into the Rummel River.

SOCIAL/POLITICAL FACTORS

Ancient Library of Alexandria in Ruins

Where	Alexandria, Egypt
When	273 A.D.
Source	Roman Emperor Aurelian (270-275 A.D.)
What	The royal quarter of the city of Alexandria containing the great Library of Alexandria was burned to the ground as a result of Emperor Aurelian's colonial jostling for control over Egypt with Queen Zenobia of Syria's Palmyrene Empire.[183]
	Alexandria had always been a volatile city, especially during the Roman period. In 48 B.C., fires authorized by Roman Emperor Julius Caesar destroyed parts of the great Library. As a result, historians are uncertain of the extent of the Library's contents and structure before the fire under Emperor Aurelian.[184]

Research Assignment 8.1

Use your preferred internet search tool to find information about the following:

a. Decius' Edict of 250 A.D.
b. Africanus and 40 Companions
c. Isidore of Chios
d. The Library of Alexandria
e. Roman Emperor Aurelian

But meanwhile, in the desert region of Egypt ...

PROFILE OF AN AFRICAN EARLY CHRISTIAN LEADER

Anthony the Great

Lifespan	250-356 A.D.
Ancestry or Hometown	Egyptian; desert of Egypt
Family Life	The barely literate son of a prosperous Egyptian village merchant
Conversion Experience	He had been left an orphan at a young age. Then at twenty years old, he was struck by the admonition, "If thou wilt be perfect, go and sell all that thou hast." Anthony began his new life by moving into an ancient Egyptian tomb not far from his village, where he lived as a hermit for several years, gardening, praying intensely, and fasting.
	In addition to seeing visions of angels, it was reported that he was attacked by and wrestled with powerful demons that left him for dead.
Contribution(s)	The life of Anthony the Great would later serve as a spiritual guide to such Christian contributors as Athanasius, Jerome, Basil, and Augustine of Hippo (indirectly).
	Father of monks; credited as the founder of solitary living
Type of Death	Upon sensing his end approaching, Anthony requested that his disciples give his staff to Macarius, one sheepskin cloak to Athanasius, and the other sheepskin cloak to Serapion, his disciple. He asked that his body be buried in an unmarked, secret grave.

In about 294 A.D., after having made sure things were running well in the "monastery" that he had established, Anthony headed east towards the Red Sea to a desolate place near a spring of fresh water, where he established a new hermitage.

Around 342 A.D., Anthony was told in a dream about the existence of an older Egyptian desert hermit (Paul of Thebes) and went to find him. Jerome wrote that Anthony the Great and Paul met when the latter was 113 years old. They conversed with each other for one day and one night.[185]

In the Egyptian desert, Anthony and Pachomius the Great (also Egyptian), were the first champions of Christian monasticism.[186] Note that Western monasticism would not be founded for another 250 years by Benedict of Nursia. The African theologian Athanasius' biography of Anthony the Great helped to spread the concept of monasticism, particularly in Western Europe through Latin translations. Anthony was the first known ascetic to go into the wilderness.[187]

Research Assignment 8.2

Use your preferred internet search tool to find information about the following:

a. The father of monasticism
b. The life of Anthony the Great
c. Paul of Thebes
d. Pachomius the Great
e. Benedict of Nursia

SOCIAL/POLITICAL FACTORS

The Crisis within the Roman Empire

Where	Roman Empire (east and west)
When	235-268 A.D.
Source	Caused by a confluence of crises in national security, soldier salaries, political unrest, coin devaluation, financial instability, de-urbanization, and economics.
What	An Imperial Crisis (also known as the Military Anarchy) nearly caused the Roman Empire to collapse.

Events and Effects

The crisis began with the assassination of Emperor Severus Alexander by his own troops in 235 A.D. Subsequently and throughout the century, the following adverse events ensued:[188]

- National security was threatened by invasions from the Germanic people, Persian Empire, Carpians, Goths, Vandals, and the Alamanni.

- Increases in military expenditures (particularly in soldiers' salaries).

- Civil unrest broke out as twenty-six rivals with ambitions to assume imperial power over all or part of the empire vied for the title of Emperor.

- Years of coinage devaluation caused economic depression.

- Financial instability and invasions resulted in lasting disruptions of Rome's extensive internal trade network. The empire's economy had depended in large part on trade between Mediterranean ports and across the extensive road systems to the Empire's interior.
- Slowly, smaller walled cities became common and began to replace the large, open cities of the classical Rome of antiquity. Large landowners who had become more self-sufficient became less mindful of Rome's central authority and grew hostile towards its tax collectors.
- The common people of the empire (Rome and its colonies) lost economic and political status to the land-holding nobility. Middle class business owners faded away, especially upon experiencing disruptions in trade ports and roads.

By 268 A.D., the Roman Empire had split into three competing states: the Gallic Empire (which included their province of Gaul), Britannia, and Hispania. Two decades later, tension and unrest from the common people of Gaul had increased so much that additional military reinforcement was needed.

Research Assignment 8.3

Use your preferred internet search tool to find information about the following:

a. The Imperial Crisis
b. Third century A.D. invaders of Rome

Chapter 8 Notes

[172] Nova Roma, "Syncretism," 2009, http://www.novaroma.org/nr/Syncretism.

[173] JesusCentral.com, "First Century Context of Palestine (Israel)," accessed October 9, 2018, http://www.jesuscentral.com/ji/historical-jesus/jesus-firstcenturycontext.php?show=Editor.

[174] G.A. Oshitelu, "Cyprian."

[175] Ibid.

[176] If these African Christians had a faith that was imposed upon them or was a scam for personal gain, they would not have kept it through torture and death. It would have been more rational to abandon a faith that had not absorbed the core of their being.

[177] John Matusiak, "Martyr Africanus and 40 Others, Beheaded at Carthage," Orthodox Church in America, 2017, https://oca.org/saints/lives/2017/04/10/101043-martyr-africanus-and-40-others-beheaded-at-carthage.

[178] OrthodoxWiki Contributors, s.v. "Isidore of Chios," *OrthodoxWiki*, https://orthodoxwiki.org/Isidore_of_Chios.

[179] Tilley, 46-47.

[180] Foxe.

[181] Tilley, 45.

[182] David Farmer, "Marian and James," in *The Oxford Dictionary of Saints*, 2011. http://www.oxfordreference.com/view/10.1093/oi/authority. 20110803100134500.

[183] "The Roman Theban Legion," Bible Probe for Christians and Messianic Jews, 2014, accessed June 6, 2017, http://bibleprobe.com/theban.html.

[184] Brian Haughton, "What Happened to the Great Library at Alexandria?" in *Ancient History Encyclopedia*, 2011, https://www.ancient.eu/article/207/what-happened-to-the-great-library-at-alexandria/.

[185] Jerome, "The Principal Works of St. Jerome," trans W. H. Fremantle, G. Lewis, and W. G. Martley, in *A Select Library of the Nicene and Post-Nicene Fathers of the Christian Church*, second series, vol. 6, *Jerome: Letters and Select Works*, Christian Classics Ethereal Library, 2005, http://www.ccel.org/ccel/schaff/npnf206 .ii.html.

[186] Illiterate and without the support of family, Anthony listened to and obeyed what he had—God. What made him famous was his use of what others might view as his misfortune: being limited to what he heard or saw (couldn't read), loneliness (no family) and waiting (no plans). By embracing these, he established the virtue and pattern for monasteries around the world for centuries to come.

[187] ReligionFacts: Just the Facts on Religion, "St. Anthony of Egypt," 2016, http://www.religionfacts.com/anthony-egypt.

[188] Wikipedia Contributors, s.v. "Crisis of the Third Century," *Wikipedia, The Free Encyclopedia*, https://en.wikipedia.org/wiki/Crisis_of_the_Third_Century.

Chapter 9: Persecuted for Not Sacrificing to Roman Gods, Part 2
(Late 3rd through Early 4th Century A.D.)

SOCIAL/POLITICAL FACTORS

Roman Emperor Diocletian's Persecutions and Tetrarchy

Where	Mauretania, Numidia, Proconsularis, Libya, Egypt
When	284-305 A.D.
Source	Emperor Diocletian
What	Diocletian's reforms and reconfiguration of Rome's government into a tetrarchy (a form of government where power is divided among four individuals) resulted in mass executions throughout Africa. It was so savage against Coptic (Egyptian) Christians that during his reign, they designated the day of his military election as emperor as the beginning of the Era of the Coptic Martyrs. That date marked the start of the Coptic calendar known to the Western world as *Anno Martyrum* (A.M.), or the Year of the Martyrs.

Events and Effects

The tetrarchy was formed by dividing the Roman Empire in half (west and east), with an Augustus Emperor and a subordinate Caesar Emperor in each half. Then each Augustus Emperor would delegate ruling authority over a significant portion of his half to his Caesar.

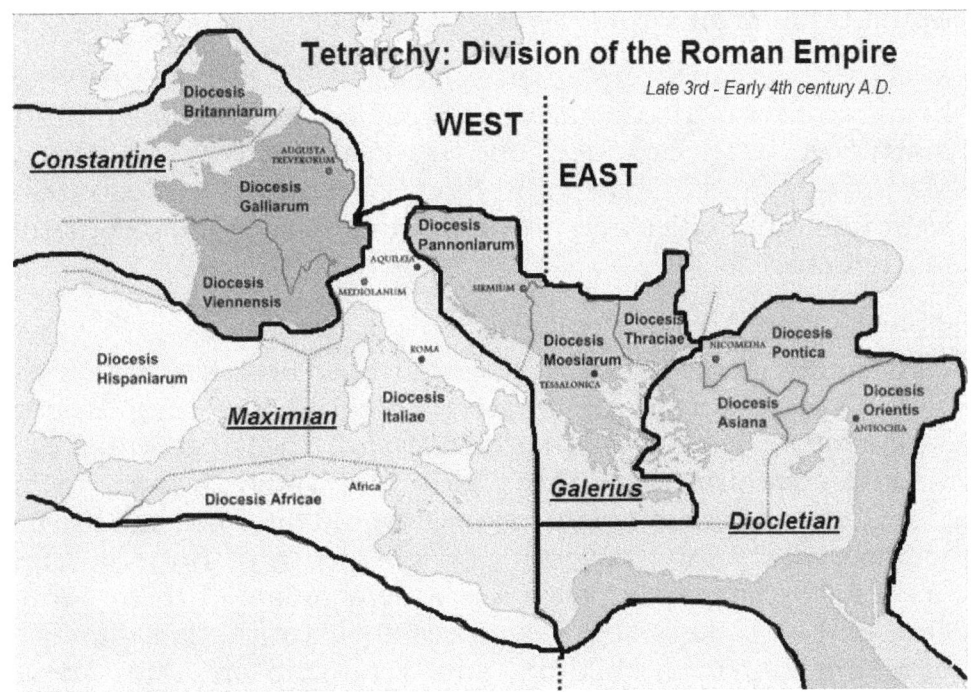

The four ruling emperors of Diocletian's tetrarchy were himself as Augustus in the eastern half of the empire with Galerius as his Caesar, and Maximian as Augustus in the western half of the empire with Constantine as his Caesar (see map above). Such decentralization of authority ensured greater precision when implementing reforms for stabilizing the weakening empire and enabled timely and regionally appropriate responses to situations that threatened the Roman way.

Africa Gave the Tetrarchy Most of Its Martyrs

In Stephen Williams' book, *Diocletian and the Roman Recovery* he states that "It was Africa that gave the West most of its martyrdoms."[189] Yet today, the names of African martyrs under Diocletian are scarcely honored. Their martyrdom stories are at risk of being eradicated along with recognition for their contributions.

Martyrs as Seeds

Remember, the Early Church Father Tertullian (a Berber) referred to the blood of second and early third century persecuted Christians as seeds of the church. In *The Apology* he stated, "Nor does your cruelty, however exquisite, avail you; it is rather a temptation to us. The oftener we are mown down by you, the more in number we grow; the blood of Christians is seed."[190]

It stands that, if the blood of earlier church martyrs was seeds, then Egypt in the eastern half of the tetrarchy was a storehouse for seeds during this time period.

- The Coptic Church has credited Tertullian with declaring in the third century that, "If the martyrs of the whole world were put on one arm of the balance and the martyrs of Egypt on the other, the balance would tilt in favor of the Egyptians."[191]

- In *The Church History of Eusebius*, the fourth century church historian wrote, "How could anyone, again, number the multitude of martyrs in every province, and especially of those in Africa, and Mauretania, and Thebais, and Egypt? From this last country many went into other cities and provinces and became illustrious through martyrdom."[192]

Unique Sacrifices of Young Women

As Diocletian's peculiar form of persecution raged across North Africa from Numidia to Egypt, it was met with the unique faith of several African girls and young women. They made sacrifices with the same valor as other martyrs. The commitment of these girls and young women to remain virgins for Christ set the template for what would later become the lifestyle and the vows of chastity, poverty, and obedience of nuns in monastic communities. In their tender years—pre-teens, some of them—and often in defiance of their parents, they sacrificed their youth, their families, and the prospect of marriage, children, and wealth, in order to take a bold stand for Christ. Without any formal orders or titles, these Africans were willing to live and die for their faith.[193]

These young women were the forerunners of what we know today as nuns. While researching information about the origin of nuns, it was discovered that the concept did not originate within Western Catholicism, but their roots are firmly planted in African soil. These young women will be identified throughout this survey by a ❀ image in their profile.[194]

Rome's Unique Attitude Towards the African Church

Steuart Erskine describes the Roman attitude towards Christians of Africa like this:

> "... the conciliatory attitude of the Romans towards the natives, whose gods they welcomed into their sanctuaries. This spirit [within the Romans] was absent in all dealings with the pernicious sect of the [African] Christians, who were always persecuted and suppressed."[195]

Persecution, Martyrs, Events, and Church Leaders During the Tetrarchy

From this point forward within the chapter, the general persecution narratives, martyrdom stories, events, and profiles are chronicled by their geographic region and then their date. Described from west to east, mainly in North Africa, these regions are Mauretania, Gaul, Numidia, Africa Proconsularis, Libya, and Egypt.

Persecution in or Around Mauretania (under Maximian)

The native inhabitants of Mauretania were of Berber ancestry and known to the Romans as the Mauri (or Moors) and the Masaesyli. In 293 A.D., Diocletian's reform further divided Mauretania into three provinces: Sitifensis, Caesariensis, and Tingitana, with Maximian as emperor.

Christians there, particularly those in the military, chose execution rather than renouncing their faith in Jesus Christ. A few accounts of Africa's Mauretanian martyrs follow.

PROFILE OF AN AFRICAN EARLY CHRISITAN MARTYR

Marcellus the Centurion

Ancestry or Hometown	Berber
Function/Status	A Roman Centurion stationed at Tingis (a Berber town, now modern-day Tangiers, Morocco).
Stand	He refused to participate in the birthday celebrations of Roman Emperor Maximian, which included sacrifice to the Roman gods.
Persecution Location	Tingis
Persecution Date	298 A.D.
Circumstances	He threw off his military belt, weapons, and vine branch (the insignia of his rank), then declared aloud that he was a soldier of Jesus Christ, the eternal King.[196]
Type of Death	By the sword

Marcellus was immediately brought before a prefect named Anastasius Fortunatus. The prefect turned his case over to Maximian and Constantius, thinking the latter, who was friendly to Christians, would show mercy. However, Marcellus was taken to the deputy Praetorian prefect Aurelius Agricolan instead. Marcellus pleaded guilty to renouncing his allegiance to the earthly Roman leader. There he was executed with a sword by the deputy Praetorian prefect.[197]

PROFILE OF AN AFRICAN EARLY CHRISITAN MARTYR

Cassian the Stenographer

Ancestry or Hometown	Tingis (a Berber town, now modern-day Tangiers, Morocco)
Function/Status	Court stenographer at Marcellus the Centurion's hearing.
Stand	Refusal to record the court proceedings of Marcellus the Centurion being put to death because of his faith
Persecution Location	Tingis
Persecution Date	298 A.D.
Circumstances	He was angry about the death sentence given to Marcellus.
Type of Death	By the sword

It was said that Cassian, the official court shorthand writer, was so outraged by Marcellus the Centurion's death sentence that he refused to record the court proceedings and was executed as well.[198]

PROFILE OF AN AFRICAN EARLY CHRISITAN MARTYR

Arcadius of Mauretania

Ancestry or Hometown	Caesarea, the capital of Mauretania (present-day Cherchell)
Function/Status	Unknown
Stand	Refused to sacrifice to Roman gods
Persecution Location	Caesarea
Persecution Date	302 A.D.
Circumstances	The governor lured him out of hiding by arresting one of his relatives, then offered to release him if he would sacrifice to the Roman gods. Arcadius quoted from a letter of Apostle Paul, "For me, to live is Christ, and to die is gain" (Philippians 1:21).
	The governor ordered that Arcadius' limbs be chopped off joint-by-joint, beginning with his toes.
Type of Death	Chopped up and bled to death[199]

Tradition holds that Arcadius was a citizen of Caesarea, the capital of Mauretania. In the distant past, Mauretania had been a part of the famous Berber kingdom. But in 302 A.D., a furious persecution raged, during which the Christians were cruelly dragged before idols and forced to make sacrifices. Arcadius, however, withdrew to a solitary place in the countryside to avoid being forced to worship the Roman gods.

Some sources have reported that after being lured out of hiding and chopped up, Arcadius' body had been reduced to a mere torso. It was reported that Arcadius gazed at his limbs and praised them, saying, "You are dearer to me than ever. I now know that I belong to Jesus Christ, as I have always desired." Then looking at the idolaters present, he urged them to "Adore the true God, who consoles me in these tortures; and abandon the worship of your false gods."[200] After Arcadius finished speaking, he died.[201]

PROFILE OF AN AFRICAN EARLY CHRISITAN MARTYR

Victor the Moor

Ancestry or Hometown	Berber native of Mauretania
Function/Status	Soldier in the Roman Praetorian Guard
Stand	He destroyed pagan altars
Persecution Location	Milan, Italy
Persecution Date	303 A.D.
Circumstances	Caught destroying pagan altars and arrested
Type of Death	Tortured and killed

Victor the Moor was born into a Christian Berber family that was native to Mauretania. According to tradition, he became a soldier who advanced through the ranks to become a member of the Roman Praetorian Guard.

His zeal for Christ became known to Emperor Maximian after Victor was caught destroying a pagan altar to a Roman god.[202] Victor confessed his lifelong love of Jesus Christ before the angry emperor. After refusing to renounce Christ, Victor was thrown into prison and tortured. As he continued to reject the emperor's calls to sacrifice to the pagan gods, Maximian finally ordered him beheaded in the emperor's garden.[203]

PROFILE OF AN AFRICAN EARLY CHRISITAN MARTYR

Salsa

Ancestry or Hometown	Tipasa, Mauretania
Function/Status	A virgin daughter of pagan parents who became a devout Christian at the age of fourteen. Most of the inhabitants there continued to be non-Christian until her martyrdom. Salsa was likely a nickname, though she born with a Carthaginian or an African name. [204]
Stand	She had a particular aversion to a brazen dragon with a gilded head and jeweled eyes that was greatly revered by the pagans. Salsa attended an annual pagan festival with her parents. While the people were fatigued from dancing, drunk, and had fallen asleep, she seized the head of the idol and hurled it into the sea.
Persecution Location	Tipasa
Persecution Date	Beginning of the 4th Century A.D.
Circumstances	Her deed went undiscovered until it was too late to track down the desecrator. She might have escaped had she not been obsessed with getting rid of the dragon's body as well. The noise from dragging it and toppling it into the sea alarmed the guardians who seized, beat and bruised her.
Type of Death	Stoned, then drowned when tossed into the sea.

PROFILE OF AN AFRICAN EARLY CHRISITAN MARTYR

Typasii the Veteran

Ancestry or Hometown	Mauretania
Function/Status	He had already served in the Roman army but was recalled. However, he became a Christian as a veteran.
Stand	He rejected being recalled into the army.
Persecution Location	Mauretania
Persecution Date	304 A.D.
Circumstances	He didn't reject the recall because it involved idolatry, but because he had finished with military combat and had graduated to spiritual warfare.
Type of Death	Beheaded[205]

Persecution in Gaul (under Maximian)

A spiritually heroic martyrdom story of African Christians in the Roman army took place in Gaul (encompassing present day France, Luxembourg, Belgium, most of Switzerland, northern Italy, parts of the Netherlands, and Germany). Though it took place within Emperor Maximian's region of the tetrarchy, the soldiers were from Emperor Diocletian's region.

PROFILE OF AN AFRICAN EARLY CHRISITAN MARTYR

Maurice the African, Roman General

Ancestry or Hometown	Coptic Egyptian; Thebes, Egypt
Function/Status	Roman General over the Theban Legion (6,600 soldiers)
Stand	Maurice and each individual of the Theban Legion refused to (a) sacrifice to the Roman gods, (b) take the oath of allegiance, or (c) swear to assist in the extermination of Christianity in Gaul.
Persecution Location	Aguanum (present day Switzerland)
Persecution Date	286 A.D.
Circumstances	Emperor Maximian called upon General Maurice to put down a revolt by a group of peasant insurgents in Gaul. When Maurice's Theban Legion arrived at Gaul, they discovered that those insurgents were Christians. His legion was composed of Theban Christians who had enjoyed a reputation for passionate and devout Christianity. Emperor Maximian was so greatly outraged that he ordered the legion to be decimated (death by tenths). When that didn't change the legion's resolve, the emperor commanded that the remaining legion be put to death.
Type of Death	By the sword

Maurice (250–287 A.D.) was an Egyptian who became a general in the Roman army. His legion was entirely composed of Christians who had been called from Thebes in Egypt. The people of Thebes had always enjoyed a reputation for passionate and devout Christianity. Theban Christians had celebrated many martyrs who refused to yield their faith during previous centuries of persecution, at the hands of Rome's regime.

General Maurice's Theban Legion passed through the Alpine mountain range into Gaul only to discover that the insurgents they were to suppress were Christian believers as well. Rome's pre-assault activities involved a general sacrifice, in which the whole army was to assist. Maximian commanded that the Theban Legion participate as well. Then they were to take the oath of allegiance and swear, before assisting in the extermination of Christianity in Gaul. The legion refused to sacrifice to Roman gods, take the oath, or slaughter fellow Christians.[206] The insurgents were not soldiers but common people of Gaul who resisted their way of life being massively submerged by the Roman culture. They felt there was little to lose.

Maximian ordered the Theban Legion to be punished by the process of decimation, whereby a tenth of the soldiers were randomly selected and executed. After several rounds of decimation, the legion still refused and were encouraged by Maurice's stance. Finally, in response to their refusal to use violence against fellow Christians, Maximian ordered the remaining members of the 6,600 strong legion to be executed.[207]

Persecution in and Around Numidia (under Maximian)

Under Diocletian's reorganization, Numidia was divided into two provinces. The northernmost region became Numidia Cirtensis, while the south, which included the often-raided mountainous terrain, became Numidia Militiana (or Military Numidia).[208]

For the Numidians, to hand over Scriptures was an act of terrible apostasy because Africa had long been home to the Church of the Martyrs. In Numidia, martyrs and confessors held more religious authority than the clergy. They were devout, uncompromising in matters of faith, valued martyrdom even over life, and believed the state of Rome to be a tool of Satan.

Many of the Christians murdered for their faith were from Numidian territories, as Africa gave the Christian west most of her martyrs.

PROFILE OF AN AFRICAN EARLY CHRISTIAN LEADER

Lucius Caecilius Firmianus Lactantius

Lifespan	250-325 A.D.
Ancestry or Hometown	Berber; Cirta, Numidia
Family Life	Non-Christian family
Conversion Experience	Unknown
Contribution(s)	Early Church Father, theologian, writer, and advisor to the first Christian Roman emperor
	Some of Lactantius' notable writings are • *De Opificio Dei* (*The Works of God*) • *Institutiones Divinae* (*The Divine Institutes*) • *An Epitome of the Divine institutes* • *De Ira Dei* (*On the Wrath of God or On the Anger of God*) • *De Mortibus Persecutorum* (*On the Deaths of the Persecutors*) • *Opera* (*Works*)
	Tutored Constantine's son
	Advisor of Rome's first Christian Roman emperor
Type of Death	Unknown
Social, Political, or Religious Setting	Effective as a rhetorician in his home town, Lactantius was requested by the new Emperor Diocletian to be an official professor of rhetoric in Nicomedia. While a professor he converted to Christianity just prior to Diocletian's first edict against the Christians.

Lactantius first met Constantine and Galerius while teaching in Nicomedia. However, he resigned the post as professor of rhetoric just before Diocletian's purging of Christians from his immediate staff and before the publication of Diocletian's first *Edict against the Christians* in 303 A.D.[209]

Now jobless as a result of his resignation and Diocletian's purge, Lactantius lived in poverty (some accounts state that he was homeless). The persecution had forced him to leave Nicomedia. Though he managed to eke out a living by writing, he continued to live in poverty.[210]

PROFILE OF AN AFRICAN EARLY CHRISITAN MARTYR

Maximilian of Tebessa

Ancestry or Hometown	Berber; Theveste, Numidia
Function/Status	A Christian, draft-eligible young man; son of Fabius Victor, also a Christian and soldier in the Roman army
Stand	Maximilian refused to swear allegiance to the emperor, which would have been required of him as a soldier.
Persecution Location	Theveste, Numidia (now Tébessa, Algeria)
Persecution Date	295 A.D.
Circumstances	Maximilian refused to enlist in the Roman army, stating that as a Christian he could not serve in the military.
Type of Death	Immediately Beheaded

The young man Maximilian of Tebessa (274-295 A.D.) was required to enlist at the age of 21.[211] But on March 12, 295 A.D., when he was brought before the proconsul of Africa Proconsularis, Cassius Dio, to swear allegiance to the emperor as a soldier, he refused ... stating that as a Christian, he could not serve in the military.[212] He was immediately beheaded by the sword. Maximilian is credited with being the earliest recorded conscientious objector. It is believed that other Christian young men at the time also refused military service and were executed.[213]

PROFILE OF AN AFRICAN EARLY CHRISITAN MARTYR

Crispina

Ancestry or Hometown	Thagara (modern-day Tunisia)
Function/Status	A wealthy, mature woman with children and member of a distinguished family
Stand	Brought before the proconsul Annius Anullinus and ordered to sacrifice to the Roman gods. Instead, she declared her honor to only one God.
Persecution Location	Theveste, Numidia
Persecution Date	304 A.D.
Circumstances	Her head was shaved, and she was exposed to public ridicule. Steadfast in her faith, unmoved even by the tears of her children, she thanked God and offered her head for execution with joy.[214]
Type of Death	Beheaded[215]

Nearly a century after her martyrdom, the post-Nicene Church Father (and African) Augustine praises Crispina in his commentary on Psalm 121. He wrote:

> The persecutors raged against Crispina, whose birthday we are today celebrating; they were raging against a rich and delicate woman: but she was strong, for the Lord was her defence upon the hand of her right hand. He was her Keeper. Is there any one in Africa, my brethren, who knoweth her not? For she was most illustrious, noble in birth, abounding in wealth: but all these things were in her left hand, beneath her head.[216]

Persecution in or Around Africa Proconsularis (under Maximian)

After Diocletian's reorganization of the Roman Empire, the Africa Proconsularis was divided into two territories. In the north was Africa Zeugitana which retained the name Africa Proconsularis. In the south was Africa Byzacena. Both were within Augustus Emperor Maximian's region of the tetrarch.

The proconsul of Africa appointed by Maximian was eager to assert his authority over the region. He went as far as to expand the emperor's persecution edict to include destroying Christian Scriptures and churches, and compelling Christians to sacrifice to the gods.[217]

PROFILE OF AN AFRICAN EARLY CHRISITAN MARTYR

Felix the Bishop of Thibiuca

Ancestry or Hometown	Thibiuca (credible sources place this town near Carthage).[218]
Function/Status	Bishop
Stand	He refused to turn over the sacred books. Given several days to think it over, Felix returned and stated, "It is better for me to be burned in the fire than the sacred scriptures, because it is better to obey God than any human authority" (Acts 5:29).
	After another sixteen days in the lower region of the prison, Felix still refused.[219]
Persecution Location	Thibiuca
Persecution Date	303 A.D.
Circumstances	Testimonies of Lactantius and Eusebius indicate that Diocletian's edict commanded that copies of the Scriptures were to be burned and church properties, both real and moveable, were to be confiscated.
Type of Death	Beheaded

PROFILE OF AN AFRICAN EARLY CHRISITAN MARTYR

Victoria of Albitina

Ancestry or Hometown	Albitina; North Africa
Function/Status	Devout virgin bride of distinguished North African nobility. After becoming a Christian in her tender years, she expressed a desire to lead a single life. Her pagan parents would not agree to it, because they had promised her in marriage to a rich, young nobleman.
Stand	On the day of her arranged wedding to an abusive bridegroom, she leaped from a window in her parents' house to worship Christ in Octavius Felix's home with Saturninus' family and others. Soldiers caught them illegally worshipping Christ.[220]
Persecution Location	Carthage
Persecution Date	304 A.D.
Circumstances	She proclaimed before the judge, "Certainly, I am a member of this assembly; I've celebrated the Lord's supper with my brothers and sisters because I am a Christian."
	Although the judge was willing to release her, she refused, stating, "I am a Christian. ... My mind is made up. ... I've never changed."
Type of Death	Tortured with the others and remanded to prison where she starved to death

PROFILE OF AN AFRICAN EARLY CHRISITAN MARTYR

Saturninus, His Children, and Companions

Ancestry or Hometown	Albitina; North Africa
Function/Status	A priest
Stand	Refused to renounce Christ
Persecution Location	Albitina
Persecution Date	304 A.D.
Circumstances	All were arrested while worshipping and celebrating the Lord's Supper in a home.
Type of Death	All were tortured and remanded to prison where they starved to death.

By this time, Diocletian's persecution had already raged an entire year in Africa. While some Christians had renounced Christ, many more defended the faith with their own blood. Albitina, a city of the proconsular province of Africa, was the location of their bloody triumph. It went down as follows:

> Saturninus, a priest of the city, worshiped on a Sunday in the house of Octavius Felix. They were taken into custody by the town's magistrates and soldiers stationed there. Forty-nine men, women, and children were all seized. Saturninus, the leader, was with his four children.
>
> When brought before the magistrate, they were quizzed and given a chance to renounce Christ. But when all of them resolutely confessed Jesus Christ, they were imprisoned and underwent the tortures of the rack, iron hooks, and clubbing. The women remained as steadfast as the men in their stand for Christ, including the young Victoria (mentioned previously). Confined and tortured, Saturninus, his children, and companions all died under the hardship of prison.[221]

PROFILE OF AN AFRICAN EARLY CHRISITAN MARTYR

Maxima, Donatilla, and Secunda of Tuburga

Ancestry or Hometown	Tuburga, six miles southwest of Carthage
Function/Status	Young girls who had taken personal vows of chastity
Stand	Refused to sacrifice to the Roman gods
Persecution Location	Tuburga
Persecution Date	304 A.D.
Circumstances	Emperor Diocletian issued an edict that all Christians must come and sacrifice. Any who refused to obey the edict would be punished and tortured.
Type of Death	Beheaded

Following Diocletian's persecution edict, many of the Christians who threw themselves to the ground to worship the Roman gods in fear for themselves, their children, and their spouses were ministers and deacons from all ranks of the clergy. Maxima and Donatilla were also brought to the Roman proconsul of the Africa Proconsularis for trial for failing to sacrifice to the gods of Rome. Fourteen-year-old Maxima told the proconsul, "It is better for me to receive a verdict from you than to defy the one and true God" (from Acts 5:29). Donatilla told the Roman proconsul, "Your tortures will be very useful to my soul." Then, they were led away to another location for sentencing.[222]

While on their way to the city for sentencing, twelve-year-old Secunda was looking from the balcony of her parents' home. Though her parents had arranged her to be married many times, she rejected them all because she loved the Lord. Suddenly, she leaped from the balcony to join the other two girls, leaving her parents' wealth behind. All of Maxima and Donatilla's attempts to discourage young Secunda from joining in on their fate failed.

Deprived of food, once again Maxima and Donatilla stood before the proconsul. Yet, neither of them wavered in their faith in Jesus Christ. The proconsul sentenced all three to be tortured and to fight wild beasts. When the hour came, the bear roared but did not harm the three girls. The proconsul then commanded that Maxima, Donatilla, and Secunda be executed by the sword.

PROFILE OF AN AFRICAN EARLY CHRISITAN MARTYR

Martyrs of Milevis

Ancestry or Hometown	Milevis, Numidia
Function/Status	Unknown
Stand	The historic record only contains Optatus, the Bishop of Milevis' reference to these martyrs in his six volume, untitled, anti-Donatists work sixty years after their deaths. In it he mentions an inscription in northern Numidia about an unspecified number of martyrs whom he stated, "suffered under the governor Florus in the city of Milevis in the days of incense burning."[223]
Persecution Location	Milevis
Persecution Date	304-305 A.D.
Circumstances	Unknown
Type of Death	Unknown

Alleged Betrayal by Bishop of Carthage and His Deacon

In 304 A.D. in Carthage, there was a riot outside the entrance to the prison. Christians coming in from the countryside to visit their imprisoned friends and relatives were pushed, shoved, whipped, and prevented from bringing comfort or showing support to the imprisoned confessors (believers who had refused to renounce their faith in Christ). These prisoners were being confined and tortured in dark cells until they renounced. The food and drinks, brought for those imprisoned in the dungeons, were knocked out of the visitor's hands onto the ground where the dogs would gulp it up. Fathers, mothers, friends, and neighbors of prisoners were also beaten into the gutters.[224]

Violent riots in Carthage were not much of a surprise. What is noteworthy about this instance was that these Christians were not beaten by Roman authorities, but by troops employed by their own Bishop of Carthage, Mensurius, and his deacon, Caecilian. In a letter to Secundus, Bishop of Tigisi (the senior bishop of Numidia), Mensurius declared that he had forbidden any to be honored as martyrs who had given themselves up voluntarily, or who had boasted about possessing copies of the Scriptures which they would not relinquish to Roman officials. He believed some of them were perpetrators, debtors or criminals of the state, who thought they might live off the state in prison, absolve themselves of misdeeds, and then enjoy the luxuries supplied by the kindness of Christian visitors.[225]

Mensurius did not want people visiting their families, friends, and neighbors who were in prison. This incident represents the first known recorded event wherein North African Christians conspired (allegedly) with the state of Rome against other African Christians.

Persecution in or Around Libya (under Diocletian)

What is now coastal Libya was known at the time as Tripolitania and Pentapolis (the territories between the Africa Proconsularis in the west and Cyrene in the east). In 296 A.D., Augustus Emperor Diocletian also separated the administration of Crete from Cyrene. Then he formed the new provinces of "Libya Superior" (with Cyrene as capital) and "Libya Inferior" (containing significant cities of Marmarica and Paraetonium). For the first time in history, the term *Libya* was used to describe a political state.[226]

Except for a few surviving fragments, many Libyan martyrdom stories were destroyed during Diocletian's persecution (or still buried under ruins). However, evidence of vast numbers of Christian monasteries in the Great Libyan Desert suggests that Christianity hadn't been exterminated. Rather, many Christians sought refuge in Libya's desert accessible to only the toughest monks or nomads.[227] But the Libyan martyrdom story below of Theodore of Cyrene and those that he had baptized did survive.[228]

PROFILE OF AN AFRICAN EARLY CHRISITAN MARTYR

Theodore of Cyrene

Ancestry or Hometown	Cyrene, Libya
Function/Status	Bishop of Cyrene. He had been a scribe or monk who quietly copied sacred Scriptures for public reading before being ordained as bishop.
Stand	He was ordered to hand over his copies of the sacred texts and to bring all who had publically read the testimony of the apostles with him before the court. He refused.
Persecution Location	Cyrene, Libya
Persecution Date	302-305 A.D., or as early as 292 by some accounts
Circumstances	He was beaten with leaden-tipped whips, and his tongue was cut out. Two other public readers named Serapion and Ammonious had their tongues cut out for reading Scriptures in common worship. The holy women of Libya, Cyprilla, Lucia, and Aroa were also executed.
Type of Death	Some accounts have Theodore surviving as a confessor without a tongue, while others report his death by unknown circumstances.

The readiness of Libyan Christians to die for their faith extended from the Cyrenaican Hebrews at Pentecost to the holy women Cyprilla, Lucia, and Aroa.

The Deacon Arius

Arius was a Libyan theologian of Berber descent who was a respected ascetic and leader in the Christian church in Alexandria, Egypt. He is believed to have been a student at the exegetical school in Antioch.[229] Having returned to Alexandria, Arius, according to a single source, sided with Meletius of Lycopolis in his dispute over the readmission into the church those who had renounced Christ under fear of Roman torture.

He was ordained as a deacon by Peter I of Alexandria in 306 A.D. Arius' teachings asserted that Jesus Christ is the Son of God, but who was created by God the Father at some point in time, and His nature is distinct from the Father's. Therefore, according to Arius, the Son is subordinate to the Father, yet the Son is still also God. Though such thinking has been labeled Arianism, it did not originate with Arius; he simply intensified it in North Africa.[230] Such thinking had been flourishing north of the Mediterranean Sea since the third century A.D.

In any event, disputes over Arius' teachings led the bishop to excommunicate him. Reconstructing his life and doctrine has proven to be a difficult task, as none of his original writings survived (more about him in Chapter 11).

Persecution in or Around Egypt (under Diocletian)

PROFILE OF AN AFRICAN EARLY CHRISITAN MARTYR

Timothy the Church Reader and His Wife Maura

Ancestry or Hometown	Egyptian; son of a priest named Pikolpossos
Function/Status	He was a reader among the church clergy and a keeper and copyist of the divine service books (liturgy and Scripture).
Stand	When the governor demanded that he hand over the sacred books, he refused.
Persecution Location	Egyptian Thebaid region
Persecution Date	286 A.D.
Circumstances	The emperor ordered the books to be confiscated and burned. Timothy refused and was subjected to horrible tortures, such as having red-hot iron rods shoved into his ears, which resulted in his loss of hearing and sight. His wife Maura boldly confessed herself a Christian. The governor commanded that the hair be torn from her head, and her fingers cut off her hands. Maura underwent the torment with joy and even thanked the governor for the torture, which she endured so that her sins might be forgiven. The people demanded an end to the abuse of this innocent woman, but Maura turned and said, "Let no one defend me. I have one Defender, God, in Whom I trust."[231]
Type of Death	Crucified over a period of ten days on crosses facing each other[232]

Alexandrian Christians Detest Diocletian

To fund his elaborate and expensive restructure of government, Diocletian also reorganized the tax system of the empire. His attempts to bring the Egyptian tax system in line with Roman standards stirred severe discontent in Egypt. A revolt swept the region. Diocletian moved upon Egypt to suppress rebels in the region of Thebes in the autumn of 297 A.D. By December of the same year, he had secured control of the Egyptian countryside. The city of Alexandria, however, held out until early 298 before being suppressed.

Early church historian Eusebius explains in his writing why Alexandrian Christians detested Diocletian. He states,

> "Such was the conflict of those Egyptians who contended nobly for religion in Tyre. But we must admire those also who suffered martyrdom in their native land; where thousands of men, women, and children, despising the present life for the sake of the teaching

of our Saviour, endured various deaths ... numberless other kinds of tortures, terrible even to hear of, were committed to the flames; some were drowned in the sea; some offered their heads bravely to those who cut them off; some died under their tortures, and others perished with hunger. And yet others were crucified; some according to the method commonly employed for malefactors; others yet more cruelly, being nailed to the cross with their heads downward, and being kept alive until they perished on the cross with hunger.

It would be impossible to describe the outrages and tortures which the martyrs in Thebais endured ... Others being bound to the branches and trunks of trees perished. For they drew the stoutest branches together with machines, and bound the limbs of the martyrs to them; and then, allowing the branches to assume their natural position, they tore asunder instantly the limbs of those for whom they contrived this.

All these things were done, not for a few days or a short time, but for a long series of years. Sometimes more than ten, at other times above twenty were put to death ... and yet again a hundred men with young children and women, were slain in one day, being condemned to various and diverse torments.

We, also being on the spot ourselves, have observed large crowds in one day; some suffering decapitation, others torture by fire; so that the murderous sword was blunted, and becoming weak, was broken, and the very executioners grew weary and relieved each other."[233]

From Alexandria, Diocletian traveled further into Egypt's southern frontier. There he encountered the inhabitants of Nubia—the Nobatae and Blemmyes tribes. Unable to subdue them, he entered into a peace treaty with them. The terms of the treaty resulted in his troops withdrawing its borders back northward near Aswan at the other side of the desert frontier and providing the two tribes with an annual gold stipend from Rome. Diocletian's withdrawal was inscribed within the temple of Kalabsha in northern Nubia.[234]

History may offer additional perspective about why Diocletian chose to withdraw. Over three centuries prior, in 21 B.C. the Roman General Petronius attempted but failed to subdue the Nubian forces (described in chapter 1). That may have been a consideration that prompted Diocletian in 298 A.D. to enter into a treaty with the Nubians, rather than continue his military's southern quest into Africa. This survey found no further Roman military activity into Africa past Aswan, Philae, and Elephantine.

PROFILE OF AN AFRICAN EARLY CHRISITAN MARTYR

Rais of Alexandria

Ancestry or Hometown	Egyptian; daughter of a Christian priest.
Function/Status	At age twelve she was sent to live in a women's monastery at Tamman.
Stand	Rais went to a well to draw water with other women of the monastery. On the way, they saw a ship with a group of women and men of the monastery, as well as other Christians in chains who were being abused by Loukianos. Rais berated the abusers and insisted that they kill her as well if they were killing Christians.[235]
Persecution Location	Egyptian Thebaid region
Persecution Date	303 A.D.
Circumstances	They imprisoned Rais as well. When Loukianos yelled, "I spit upon the Christian God," Rais objected, stepped up and spat in the tyrant's face. Loukianos ordered the girl to be tortured and beheaded. When the ship reached Antinopolis, Rais was one of the first to die.
Type of Death	Beheaded

PROFILE OF AN AFRICAN EARLY CHRISITAN MARTYR

Theodora (and Didymus)

Ancestry or Hometown	Egyptian
Function/Status	Young girl who had taken a personal vow of chastity
Stand	Would not renounce Christ because she had dedicated herself to God and had resolved to remain a virgin for the name of Christ.
Persecution Location	Alexandria, Egypt
Persecution Date	304 A.D.
Circumstances	Because of her religious beliefs, Theodora was on trial before the prefect Eustratius of Alexandria, where she boldly confessed being a Christian.
	With the help of Didymus she escaped but returned to be executed with him (he had gotten caught helping her to escape).
Type of Death	Beheaded, then burned at the stake

Theodora boldly confessed being a Christian while standing trial before the prefect Eustratius of Alexandria because of her religious beliefs.

> The prefect: Of what condition are you?
>
> Theodora: I am a Christian.
>
> The prefect: Are you a slave or a free woman?
>
> Theodora: I am a Christian, and made free by Christ; I am also born of what the world calls free parents.
>
> The prefect asked why she had not married.
>
> Theodora replied that she had dedicated herself to God and had resolved to remain a virgin for the name of Christ.

Eustratius gave her three days in prison to renounce Christ, or she would be forced to serve as a prostitute in the local brothel. After the three days, she remained as true to her faith as before in spite of the threat. She was taken to the brothel. There, two young men fought over who would have her first. Didymus, dressed in a soldier's uniform, chased the young men away and gave Theodora his uniform. She escaped unnoticed.

Arrested and interrogated, Didymus confessed to helping Theodora escape and was sentenced to death. To the surprise of all, Theodora ran to the place of his execution and insisted that she die with him.[236] Without hesitation, the prefect honored her request. Theodora was beheaded first, and Didymus' beheading followed. Their bodies were then burned at the stake.[237]

PROFILE OF AN AFRICAN EARLY CHRISITAN MARTYR

Catherine of Alexandria

Ancestry or Hometown	Egyptian; Alexandria, Egypt
Function/Status	Daughter of Constus, the governor of Alexandria, Egypt. She was a noted scholar and princess who became a Christian around the age of fourteen. She converted hundreds of people to Christianity.[238]
Stand	Catherine would not renounce Christ because she had dedicated herself to God and resolved to remain a virgin for the name of Christ.
Persecution Location	Alexandria, Egypt
Persecution Date	305 A.D.
Circumstances	The emperor called fifty of the best pagan philosophers and orators to debate her, hoping to refute her pro-Christian arguments, but the eighteen-year-old Catherine won the debate. She was then cursed and thrown into prison.
Type of Death	Beheaded[239]

Church Life under the Tetrarchy

Christians understood the nature of Christ, faith in Him, and the cost of being a disciple.[240] The Roman Empire had been crippled by an Imperial Crisis and the Plague of Rome. The tetrarchy's massive reconstruction of Rome's government required a massive army to enforce control, in order to keep things stable while reorganizing and rebuilding. Recruiting able-bodied men was essential to this success. Maintaining the favor of pagan gods (idolatry) and emperor worship were integral parts of a soldier's life. As a result, there were a high number of military related martyrdom accounts within the tetrarchy.[241]

Concurrently, there was also a slight rift developing within the African Church. It began at the Council of Cirta, held in Cirta (once the capital of the Berber kingdom of Numidia) from 303 to 305 A.D. A dozen bishops met to appoint a qualified successor to be consecrated and to replace a recently deceased bishop. The proposed criterion was whether a bishop had been faithful during persecution and had not handed over the sacred book to be burned by the Romans. One by one, each candidate was given an opportunity to refute charges against his conduct. A rift developed when a couple of incongruities in the selection process were pointed out:[242]

- For bishops, the church required martyrdom rather than have sacred books burned, however there were bishops in the selection/

process who had burned books themselves in order to avoid persecution..

- One candidate even admitted to murdering his nephews with cause. But the council didn't take issue with that. Instead, the issue that the council was concerned with was whether a crime was related to his candidacy based upon their criteria. The presiding bishop declared that God's judgment upon him regarding the murder would be enough.

Seemingly, avoiding a split within was more of a concern to the African bishops, at this time, than murder, or even handing over sacred books.

Research Assignment 9.1

a. Use your preferred internet search tool to find information about the following:
   1. Roman Gaul
   2. Maurice the African, Roman General
   3. Verroliez
   4. Order of Saint Maurice, and Sardinian Order of Saint Maurice
   5. Maurice en Valais
   6. Each profile of martyrs and leaders in this chapter

b. Answer the following questions:
   1. If these African Christians thought that Christianity was someone else's religion imposed upon them, do you believe they would have remained true to it when faced with death for doing so?
   2. Rome had Christians in its city and persecuted them there. Rome was far from being a Christian state. So how could the Roman Empire have imposed any brand of Christianity upon the African Christians?
   3. What empire at the time had the power and the Christian faith to impose its religious beliefs upon another empire, nation, or group? What do you think influenced the spirituality of these African Christians?

Dichotomies Rippling Through Time and Cultures

Diocletian's persecution failed to stop the rise of Christianity, particularly in Africa.[243] However, his tetrarch's east-west empire-wide divide not only distinguished Tripolitania from Cyrene, but for centuries to come, its effect also distinguished

- Church of the West/Church of the East
- Latin speaking/Greek speaking
- Capitalist/Communist
- Catholic/Orthodox
- Carthage/Alexandria
- Church as an independent entity/Church-state power complex[244]
- Intimate shared life with Christ/Syncretism with the state[245]

Biblical Anticipation of African Martyrs

There are indirect New Testament references to the martyrs of the early African Church. Apostle John received them in a vision while banished on the island of Patmos. Consider the observations recorded by Apostle John:

> When he opened the fifth seal, I saw under the altar the souls of those who had been slain because of the word of God and the testimony they had maintained. They called out in a loud voice, "How long, Sovereign Lord, holy and true, until you judge the inhabitants of the earth and avenge our blood?" Then each of them was given a white robe, and they were told to wait a little longer, until the full number of their fellow servants, their brothers and sisters, were killed just as they had been. (Revelation 6:9-11)

> I saw thrones on which were seated those who had been given authority to judge. And I saw the souls of those who had been beheaded because of their testimony about Jesus and because of the word of God. They had not worshiped the beast or its image and had not received its mark on their foreheads or their hands. They came to life and reigned with Christ a thousand years. (Revelation 20:4)

But there's a debate over the year that John wrote the Book of Revelation.[246] One faction places the writing during the reign of Nero, between 64 and 68 A.D. at the earliest. The other, suggests 95-96 A.D., during the reign of Emperor Domitian as the latest date. But it doesn't matter in terms of the point being made here, because both sides of the debate agree that John had been banished to Patmos sometime after Nero's first persecution began in 64 A.D.

We can believe that the references in Revelation are inclusive of the African Church because included under the altar were souls already persecuted by Nero who claimed allegiance to the word of God (Scriptures) and whose testimony was that they were Christians. They were given white robes and told to wait for others like themselves (the "full number of their fellow servants, their brothers and sisters"). This means that, as of the writing of the Book of Revelation, more persecution of Jesus' Church was yet to occur. There would be more souls to be killed (mostly beheaded) after either faction's suggested date of John's writing.

At the time of the Apostle John's writing, the "full number" had not been reached. So by necessity, the number needed to include the others. Specific to this survey, it needed to also include the martyred Christians of the African Church. The African Church's earliest documented martyrs, Speratus and his pupils, were recorded in Rome's official court transcripts about a century after John's writings in 180 A.D.

All of the Christian martyrs have a set apart and unique purpose in God's eschatological plan. According to Revelation 5 and 6, no one in heaven or on earth was worthy enough to break open any of the seals, except the Lamb (whom we know as Jesus). Jesus Himself is the unique proclaimer of the sacred content in the fifth seal—solely about the martyrs of the faith. African Christian martyrs were on the mind of God. Their devout contributions have been captured and sealed in His revelation. Their deaths were counted towards the attainment of the "full number," in accordance with God's end-time plan for humanity. According to Revelation 20, they too, will reign with Christ during the thousand years of peace.

Given the significance of the seals, the contents of the fifth seal, the prophetic nature of the references, and the souls destined to reign with Christ, it is safe to say that to dismiss the faithful stand and scholarship of the early African Church martyrs is to ignore something profoundly sacred to the Lamb.

> Research Assignment 9.2
>
> Use your preferred internet search tool to find information about the following:
>
> a. *Anno Martyrum*
> b. Roman Emperor Diocletian
> c. Tertullian's *The Apology*

Chapter 9 Notes

[189] Stephen Williams, *Diocletian and the Roman Recovery* (New York: Routledge, 1997), 179.

[190] Tertullian, "The Apology," ed. Allan Menzies, trans. S. Thelwall, in *Ante-Nicene Fathers*, vol. 3, *Latin Christianity: Its Founder, Tertullian.* Christian Classics Ethereal Library, 2005, http://www.ccel.org/ccel/schaff/anf03.iv.iii.i.html.

[191] St. Antonius Coptic Orthodox Church, "The Church of Martyrs," 2017, http://www.antonius.org/about/the-coptic-orthodox-church/.

[192] Eusebius Pamphilius, "Those in the Palace," in *A Select Library of the Nicene and Post-Nicene Fathers of the Christian Church*, second series, vol. 1, *Eusibius Pamphilius: The Church History of Eusebius,* trans. Arthur Cushman McGiggert, Christian Classics Ethereal Library, 2005, http://www.ccel.org/ccel/schaff/npnf201.iii.xiii .vii.html.

[193] Barbara Joyce Brooks (editor), in discussion with the author, May 31, 2019.

[194] Ibid.

[195] Erskine, *"Vanished Cities of Northern Africa,"* 109.

[196] When faith fills the soul, our power, successes, and accomplishments will seem trivial in comparison, and even appear to be an obstacle.

[197] Edward Gibbon, "Chapter XVI: Conduct Towards the Christians, From Nero to Constantine.—Part VI," in *History of the Decline and Fall of the Roman Empire*, Christian Classics Ethereal Library, 2005, http://www.ccel.org/ccel/gibbon/decline.iv.vi.html ?highlight=marcellus,the,centurion#highlight.

[198] Dan Graves "Cassian and Marcellus Beheaded for Their Bold Stand," Christianity.com, 2007, http://www.christianity.com/church /church-history/timeline/1-300/cassian-and-marcellus-beheaded-for-their-bold-stand-11629631.html; After seeing the Christ in Marcellus stand up, Cassian could not simply sit and do his job, so he stood as well.

[199] James Fitzhenry, "Saint Arcadius," Roman Catholic Saints, 2011, http://www.roman-catholic-saints.com/saint-arcadius.html.

[200] Through his suffering the truth of the gospel becomes more evident. A person does not suffer to the end like this for a fable or figurative story.

[201] Fitzhenry.

[202] Although he was a Roman Praetorian Guard with many other important things to do, apparently Victor couldn't ignore the status quo idolatry and let things be as they were.

[203] OrthodoxWiki Contributors, s.v. "Victor of Milan," *OrthodoxWiki*, https://orthodoxwiki.org/index.php?title=Victor_of_Milan&oldid=112248.

[204] Erskine, *"Vanished Cities of Northern Africa,"* 110-111.

[205] Augustine of Hippo and Optatus of Milevis, *Donatist Martyr Stories: The Church in Conflict in Roman North Africa*, trans. Maureen A. Tilley (Liverpool: Liverpool University Press, 1996), 49.

[206] After discovering the truth about the rebels, Maurice didn't simply continue as commanded. In spite of expectations and protocol, Maurice and his soldiers chose to stand with God, even at the threat of death. Apparently, these men didn't have a mere superficial understanding of Christ. They stood as a people who had personal relationships with Him.

[207] Tribunus, "Saint Maurice: Martyr, Black Saint, Knight Commander of the Theban Legion and Patron Saint of the Holy Roman Empire," *Roman Christendom* (blog),

September 26, http://romanchristendom.blogspot.com/2008/09/saint-maurice-martyr-black-saint-and.html.

[208] Wikipedia Contributors, s.v. "Numidia," *Wikipedia, The Free Encyclopedia*, October 2, 2018, https://en.wikipedia.org/wiki/Numidia; Wikipedia Contributors, s.v. "Diocletianic Persecution," *Wikipedia, The Free Encyclopedia*, October 8, 2018, https://en.wikipedia.org/wiki/Diocletianic_Persecution.

[209] Wikipedia Contributors, s.v. "Lactantius," *Wikipedia, The Free Encyclopedia*, May 25, 2017, https://en.wikipedia.org/wiki/Lactantius.

[210] Ibid.

[211] Philip Schaff and Henry Wace, eds., *The Canons of the 318 Holy Fathers Assembled in the City of Nice, in Bithynia*, in *A select Library of the Nicene and Post-Nicene Fathers of the Christian Church*, vol 14, *The Seven Ecumenical Councils*, Christian Classics Ethereal Library, 2005, https://www.ccel.org/ccel/schaff/npnf214.vii.vi.i.html; David Woods, "St. Maximilian of Tebessa (BHL 5813)," The Military Martyrs, 2003, https://www.ucc.ie/archive/milmart/Maximilian.html#B.

[212] In his era to not follow the career of one's father, refuse the military draft, or the emperor himself, would have required an influence far greater than a philosophy, carved statue, or "free spirit." This goes to the strength of Maximilian's faith in Christ.

[213] Wikipedia Contributors, s.v. "Maximilian (martyr)," *Wikipedia, The Free Encyclopedia*, March 13, 2017, https://en.wikipedia.org/wiki/ Maximilian_(martyr); Wikipedia Contributors, s.v. "Order of Maximilia," *Wikipedia, The Free Encyclopedia*, February 21, 2017, https://en.wikipedia.org/wiki/Order_of_Maximilian.

[214] As her children watched, Crispina seized the opportunity to instill a sense of the supremacy of Christ in their lives.

[215] Wikipedia Contributors, s.v. "Crispina," *Wikipedia, The Free Encyclopedia*, August 20, 2016, https://en.wikipedia.org/wiki/Crispina.

[216] Augustine of Hippo, "Psalm CXXI," in *A Select Library of the Nicene and Post-Nicene Fathers of the Christian Church*, ed. Philip Schaff, vol. 8, *St. Augustine: Expositions on the Book of Psalms*, ed. A. Cleveland Coxe, Christian Classics Ethereal Library, 2005, http://www.ccel.org/ccel/schaff/npnf108.ii.CXXI.html.

[217] Wikipedia Contributors, s.v. "Africa (Roman province)," *Wikipedia, The Free Encyclopedia*, October 9, 2018, https://en.wikipedia.org/wiki/Africa (Roman province); Wikipedia Contributors, s.v. "Diocletianic_Persecution," *Wikipedia, The Free Encyclopedia*, October 8, 2018, https://en.wikipedia.org/wiki/Diocletianic_Persecution.

[218] Augustine of Hippo and Optatus of Milevis, 7-8.

[219] Ibid., 9-11.

[220] Ibid., 25, 33, 41-42.

[221] Alban Butler, "SS. Saturninus, Dativus, and Others, Martyrs of Africa," in *The Lives of the Fathers, Martyrs, and Other Principal Saints*, vol. 2, February, *The Lives of the Saints*, Bartleby.com: Great Books Online, http://www.bartleby.com/210/2/111.html.

[222] Augustine of Hippo and Optatus of Milevis, 18-24.

[223] Graeme Clarke, "Third-Century Christianity," in *The Cambridge Ancient History: XII The Crisis of Empire, A.D. 193-337*, ed. Alan Bowman, Averil Cameron, and Peter Garnsey (Cambridge: Cambridge University Press, 2005), 652; Yvette Duval, "Loca Sanctorum Africae: le cult des martyrs en Afrique du IVe au VII siecle (Collection de l'Ecole Francaise de Rome 58; Rome, 1982), 245-7.

[224] Augustine of Hippo and Optatus of Milevis, 20.

[225] Catholic Online, *Catholic Encyclopedia*, s.v. "Donatists" Catholic.org, 2019, https://www.catholic.org/encyclopedia/view.php?id=3972.

[226] Wikipedia Contributors, s.v. "Roman Libya," *Wikipedia, The Free Encyclopedia*, September 11, 2018, https://en.wikipedia.org/wiki/ Roman_Libya.

[227] Oden, *Early Libyan Christianity*, 133-135.

[228] Ibid., 130.

[229] Originalpeople.org, "Arius: Libyan Christian Priest of Alexandria, Egypt and the Council of Nicaea," 2013, http://originalpeople.org/arius-libyan-christian-priest-alexandria-egypt-council-nicaea/.

[230] Ibid.

[231] John Matusiak, "Martyr Timothy the Reader and his wife in Egypt," Orthodox Church in America, 2017, https://oca.org/saints/lives/2011/05/03/101278-martyr-timothy-the-reader-and-his-wife-in-egypt.

[232] The faith of these early African Christians was simple trust. Since their experiences with God were real, there was no way they could betray it.

[233] Early Church History – CH101, "Persecution under Diocletian," https://churchhistory101.com/century4-p3.php.

[234] Wikipedia Contributors, s.v. "Roman–Nubian relations," *Wikipedia, The Free Encyclopedia*, September 16, 2018, https://en.wikipedia.org/wiki /Roman%E2%80%93 Nubian_relations; Wikipedia Contributors, s.v. "Diocletian," *Wikipedia, The Free Encyclopedia*, October 11, 2018, https://en.wikipedia.org/wiki/Diocletian; Gawdat Gabra and Hany Takla, eds, *Christianity and Monasticism in Aswan and Nubia* (New York: The American University of Cairo Press, 2016), 66.

[235] Wikipedia Contributors, s.v. "Saint Rais," *Wikipedia, The Free Encyclopedia*, June 28, 2018, https://en.wikipedia.org/wiki/Saint_Rais.

[236] Like Jesus' love, the power of their love compelled them both to risk and lose their lives for the other.

[237] Wikipedia Contributors, s.v. "Theodora and Didymus," *Wikipedia, The Free Encyclopedia*, May 30, 2016, https://en.wikipedia.org/wiki/Theodora_and_Didymus.

[238] Catherine was not a closet believer, nor did she hide behind the safety of family status. For the gospel's sake, she made herself vulnerable in order to win souls for Christ.

[239] Wikipedia Contributors, s.v. "Catherine of Alexandria," *Wikipedia, The Free Encyclopedia*, May 31, 2017, https://en.wikipedia.org/wiki/Catherine_of_Alexandria.

[240] Luke 14:25-35.

[241] Tilley, 46-47.

[242] Ibid., 51.

[243] Frank E. Smitha, "Order under Diocletian, to Constantine," MacroHistory: WorldHistory, http://www.fsmitha.com/h1/rome22.htm.

[244] Even today in many European countries, a church-state power complex still exists. Queen Elizabeth of England is the head of the Church of England. The Lutheran Church in Scandinavia and parts of Germany is supported by tax money. The Catholic Church in Rome and the Church in Spain are supported by tax money.

[245] Oden, *Early Libyan Christianity*, 243-246; Hippo and Milevis, xii.

[246] Wolfgang Schneider, "When Was the Book of Revelation Written?" BibelCenter, 2010, http://www.bibelcenter.de/bibel/studien/e-std310.php.

Chapter 10: Dissenting African Congregations
(Early 4th Century A.D.)

SOCIAL/POLITICAL FACTORS

Origin of Their Dissent[247]

Where	Numidia and Carthage
When	304-Beyond 533 A.D.
Source	Riot outside of a Carthaginian prison
What	It began with an incident while Diocletian's persecution against Christians was still in full effect. Confessors (those who refused to renounce Jesus Christ) from Abitinae, Numidia had been imprisoned in Carthage. Their friends and relatives came to visit, as commonly practiced. On one occasion, however, the visitors encountered resistance from a local mob. The visitors were harassed, beaten, and whipped. The food they had brought for imprisoned love ones was scattered on the ground.
	Ironically, the mob had been sent by the Christian Bishop of Carthage, Mensurius, and his deacon Caecilian to prevent visiting friends and families from providing support and comfort to confessors.

Events and Effects

The Dispute

In 311 A.D., seven years after the riot in the city of Carthage, dissension erupted! Mensurius, the Bishop of Carthage an alleged traitor, had died.[248] An uproar resulted after the heavily contested appointment of his successor Caecilian as the official representative of all regional churches, which included Numidia and Carthage.[249] He, too, was accused of being pro-Rome, a traitor, and having been improperly ordained by Felix the Bishop of Aptunga, in proconsular Africa.

The dissenting congregations refused to accept Caecilian's appointment based on

- Biblical grounds, that he was not above reproach (1 Timothy 3:2).[250]
- Legal grounds, that he hadn't been properly ordained in the first place; claiming that Felix himself had been accused and tried as a traitor during Diocletian's persecution.[251]

Caecilian's appointment was like a thorn in the foot for these Numidian congregations. Not only did they contest it on legitimate grounds, but they also did so because, as dissenters, they were a majority. Yet, their preferred candidate to replace the deceased bishop was not selected.

Dissenting Congregations Categorized as Donatists

The dissenters selected Donatus Magnus (of Berber descent) to represent their interests. Unfortunately, due to the destruction of his correspondences and written works, very little is known about Donatus' earlier life. He first appears in early church records in October 313 A.D., when he was consecrated as Bishop of Carthage (although he may have been designated bishop before arriving there, as early as 311 A.D.)[252]

Donatus struggled unsuccessfully against the Christian clergy in Rome to obtain church recognition as the Bishop of Carthage and the legitimate representative of all churches in Africa's western part of the Roman tetrarch. In 315 A.D. he appealed a number of times to Constantine, the new Roman emperor over the region, but without success.

From that point forward, these dissenters from the Numidian region became known as "Donatists," after their representative. Their distinct perspective and sentiment were rooted in the long-established Christian communities around the Africa Proconsularis region (see their range of influence in the map below.).

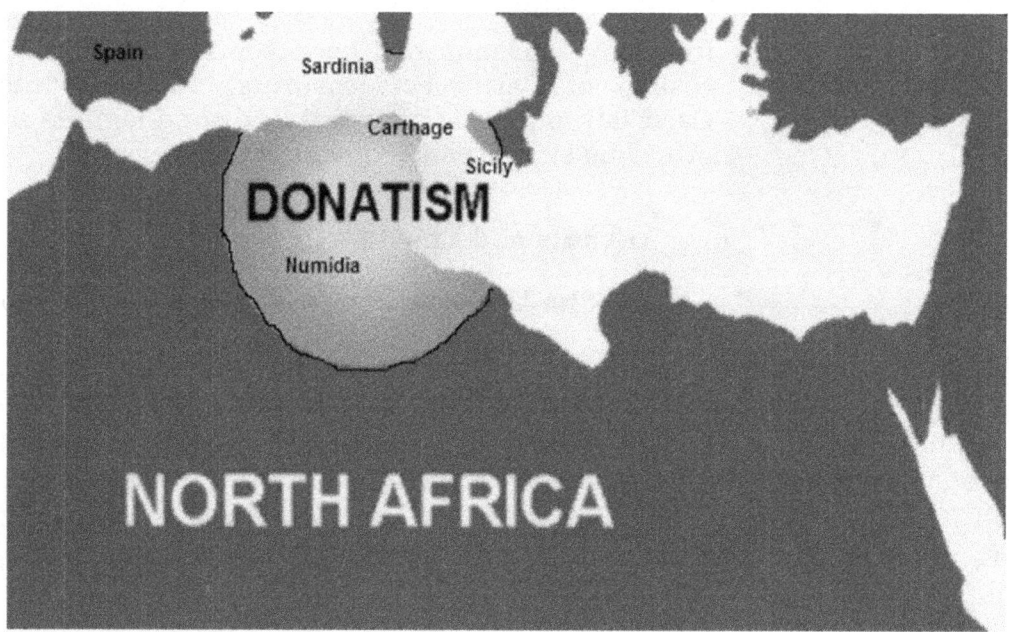

Donatist Christian communities continued through the fourth, fifth, and sixth centuries. They placed a high regard upon divine intimacy in the expression of their faith. They

- Honored their martyrs and rendered honors to their graves.
- Found it disheartening that their Carthage African clergy partners would support the Roman government's attempt to starve confessors until they renounced their faith in Jesus Christ.
- Forbade anyone to compromise, such as disclose the identities of Christians or hand over Scriptures to Roman authorities.

- Refused to accept church sacraments or prayers performed by any clergy or person who had renounced Christ during persecution, or to even recognize their authority. They believed the sacrament or prayer would be ineffective and invalid.

- Believed that the church must be a church of saints (redeemed), and not sinners (unredeemed).

Other influential Christian congregations without such an emphasis (yet also had experienced persecution) felt that a person could be absolved of such sins through years of penance. Donatists steadfastly believed that anyone who had renounced their faith after having been baptized should not be allowed to hold any kind of post or have authority within the church. The reasons for their beliefs were both practical and religious.

Remember the African Church Father Cyprian from Chapter 7? Well, back in 251 A.D. he had called a council of North African bishops from the African Proconsularis, Numidia, and Mauretania regions to address the issue of lapses of faith at the end of Decius' persecution. But for lapses during the time of the Donatists, the fear was that Cyprian's retrospective solution after Decius' persecution might be used prospectively by some to avoid Diocletian's persecution. The explanation below is key to understanding the Donatists' dissenting position:

> Before Emperor Decius' persecution, there was no prescribed method for the church to handle a lapse in one's faith. Cyprian saved the day by establishing a retrospective method for mercifully addressing the lapse. His solution had been socialized throughout the church for fifty years before Diocletian's persecution began. Donatists likely feared that a believer facing this new persecution would view intentionally lapsing in faith as a viable alternative to torture or death. After all, thanks to Cyprian, they believed amends could be made, and they would be restored by the church.

The Donatists, whose faith was more intimacy based, saw a prevailing tendency to lapse and then make amends. They viewed this tendency as the devaluing of the sacrifices of their martyrs and the cheapening of what it meant to be intimate with or devoted to Jesus Christ.

Research Assignment 10.1

Use your preferred internet search tool to find information about the following:

a. Mensurius, the Bishop of Carthage
b. Caecilian versus Donatists
c. Felix of Aptungi
d. Donatus Magnus' appeal to Constantine

Chapter 10 Notes

[247] The Donatist controversy is among the most serious and noteworthy splits in the history of Christianity. It was not even a doctrinal issue, but more about spiritual integrity than anything else. It resulted in the existence of two parallel churches in northern Africa, which endured for centuries. Mainstream and institutional history about the two Churches were written from the prevailing Church's perspective. Most of the Donatists' literature has been destroyed by rival Catholic congregations, particularly Rome's Church and State power complex.

[248] J.C. Robertson, "Chapter XXI: St. Augustine (A.D. 354-430) in *Sketches of Church History: From AD 33 to the Reformation*," Christian Classics Ethereal Library, June 1, 2005, https://www.ccel.org/ccel/robertson/history.iii.xxi.html; Wikipedia Contributors, s.v. "Felix of Aptunga," *Wikipedia, The Free Encyclopedia*, November 11, 2018, https://en.wikipedia.org/wiki/Felix_of_Aptunga; Wikipedia Contributors, s.v. "Secundus of Tigisis," *Wikipedia, The Free Encyclopedia*, May 10, 2018, https://en.wikipedia.org/wiki /Secundus_of_Tigisis#Meeting_of_305 AD.

[249] Tilley, 9-10; J.M. Fuller, "Caecilianus, Archdeacon and Bishop of Carthage," in *Dictionary of Christian Biography and Literature to the End of the Sixth Century A.D., with an Account of the Principal Sects and Heresies*, ed. Henry Wace and William Piercy, Christian Classics Ethereal Library, July 13, 2005, http://www.ccel.org/ccel/wace /biodict.html?term=Caecilianus, archdeacon and bishop of Carthage.

[250] Tilley, 9-10, 142.

[251] H.W. Phillot, "Felix (26) I., bp. of Aptunga," in *Dictionary of Early Christian Biography and Literature to the End of the Sixth Century A.D., with an Account of the Principal Sects and Heresies*, ed. Henry Wace and William Piercy. Christian Classics Ethereal Library, July 13, 2005, http://www.ccel.org/ccel/wace/biodict.html?term=Felix %20(26)%20I.,%20bp.%20of%20Aptunga; Wikipedia Contributors, s.v. "Felix of Aptunga," *Wikipedia, The Free Encyclopedia*, November 11, 2018, https://en.wikipedia.org/wiki/Felix _of_Aptunga.

[252] Wikipedia Contributors, s.v. "Donatus Magnus," *Wikipedia, The Free Encyclopedia*, August 1, 2017, https://en.wikipedia.org/wiki/Donatus_Magnus.

Chapter 11: Rome Ends Its Persecution of Christians
(Early to Mid-4th Century A.D.)

An Abrupt Loss of Roman Emperors Shakes Up the Tetrarchy

Unexpected illness, death and abdication strikes the eastern and western part of the Roman Empire.

- In 305 A.D. in the east, Diocletian retires due to illness.
- In 305 A.D. in the west, Maximian abdicated with Diocletian. His son Maxentius assumes power.
- In 306 A.D. in the west, Constantine restored Christians to full legal equality and returned property that had been confiscated during the persecution.
- In 306 A.D. in the west, Maxentius promised full religious toleration.
- In 307 A.D. in the west, Maximian recalled to the throne to help son defeat a rival.
- In 308 A.D. in the west, Maximian and son quarrel. Maximian seeks refuge.
- In 310 A.D. in the east, Galerius contracted a disease which he believed to be vengeance by the God of Christians.
    - On his death bed he issued what is called today the Edict of Toleration, ending the persecution of Christians throughout the entire empire. He then asked Christians to pray that he might live.

PROFILE OF AN AFRICAN EARLY CHRISTIAN LEADER

Pope Miltiades (a.k.a. Melchiades the African)

Lifespan	?-314 A.D.
Ancestry or Hometown	Berber; North Africa
Family Life	Unknown
Conversion Experience	Unknown
Contribution(s)	In 311 A.D., three months after the Edict of Toleration, Miltiades was elevated to pope. As the first pope of Constantine's reign as emperor of Rome, Miltiades' leadership coincided with the peace Constantine gave to the church.
	Constantine commissioned Miltiades and three Gallic bishops to call a council to resolve the Donatists' protest against Caecilian's appointment as their representative. Unwilling to jeopardize his relationship with the emperor, but also unwilling to preside over a council with an uncertain outcome, Miltiades changed the proceedings into a regular church synod and appointed an additional fifteen Italian bishops.
	The council followed the strict rules of evidence and argument for Roman civil proceedings. Frustrated by such proceedings, the Donatists left the council without presenting their case. This left Miltiades with no choice but to rule in favor of Caecilian.[253]
Type of Death	Unknown
Social, Political, or Religious Setting	A Donatist Bishop accused Miltiades and his associates of surrendering sacred texts and offering incense to Roman gods.

SOCIAL/POLITICAL FACTORS

The Edict of Milan in 313 A.D.

Where	Milan, Italy
When	313 A.D.
Source	Constantine was Rome's emperor of its western provinces of Gaul and Britannia, and Licinius, was emperor of its eastern provinces. Before Galerius died, he had abruptly appointed his friend Licinius to replace him as emperor.
What	This was the second edict of toleration. It granted religious freedom throughout the Roman Empire and ordered the restitution of property confiscated from Christians.

Emperor Constantine Reunites with Lactantinus

Constantine reunites with the former professor Lactantinus, now living in poverty, (see Chapter 9) and becomes his sponsor. Being twenty-two years older than Constantine, Lactantius became an advisor to Constantine, guiding his religious policy as it developed. He was also a tutor to Constantine's son.[254]

Lactantinus' *De Mortibus Persecutorum* describes a dream that Constantine had in 312 A.D., before the famous Battle of the Milvian Bridge. According to him, Constantine had a vision of a cross in the sky and heard a voice utter something to the effect of, "Go, and in this symbol, conquer."[255]

What the Edict of Milan Afforded Christians

The Edict of Milan, the second edict to address the toleration of Christians, went beyond the first of 311 A.D. The first edict was a shift from hostility towards neutrality towards Christains. The Edict of Milan provided a shift from neutrality to friendliness and protection by preparing the way for the legal recognition of Christianity.[256] However, as stated in the edict, the motive was so that any god (Christian God or Roman gods) would look favorably upon Rome's public welfare and security. Here's an excerpt:

> When I, Constantine Augustus, as well as I, Licinius Augustus, fortunately met near Mediolanurn (Milan), and were considering everything that pertained to the public welfare and security, we thought, among other things which we saw would be for the good of many, those regulations pertaining to the reverence of the Divinity ought certainly to be made first, so that we might grant to the Christians and others full authority to observe that religion which each preferred; whence any Divinity whatsoever in the seat of the heavens may be propitious and kindly disposed to us and all who are placed under our rule.[257]

The empire was fragmented due to the nature of a tetrarch. This edict served as a salve for healing several empire-wide ailments. Still, Rome hadn't made Christianity its state religion. That would not occur for another sixty-seven years.

Constantine's Aggression Against Donatists After the Edict of Milan

The romanized classes of the African Proconsularis saw the advent of Constantine and his benevolence to the church as a positive development. Seeing that they could now be both a good Roman as well as a good Christian, they flocked into the church. But Christians from the lower classes, and in Numidia and Mauretania tended to see the new developments as the progression of corruption into the church. From their perspective, the evil of Rome - that they had experienced and hated - was now becoming a part of the church. Soon, they feared, the powerful social-political Roman machinery would also control the church. Therefore, resisting the progression was deemed a necessity. They did not hesitate to remind the newly converted romanized classes that when they were still worshiping pagan gods, the supposedly ignorant Numidians, Mauretanians, and others knew the truth about Jesus.[258]

The Donatist's persistence in preserving their intimacy-based expression of Christianity resulted in their repression by Roman authorities. For support, the Donatists drew upon African sentiment, while their rival "pro-Caecilian" congregations had the support and force of Rome.[259] Caecilian was elected with the support of the romanized Christians of Carthage. His election was opposed by the lower classes in the African Proconsularis and by almost all the people and clergy of Numidia.[260] In 317 A.D., four years after the Edict of Milan (that ended persecution of Christians), Constantine issued a "death penalty" to all who "disturbed the peace of the kingdom."[261] The Donatists believed they were being targeted even though justified in their protest.

- Under this penalty they were not persecuted as Christians.
- They felt targeted for not supporting the appointment of Caecilian nor his appointees but rather, their own.
- Constantine persecuted the Donatists for civil disobedience by several measures:
    o He ordered the confiscation of Donatist churches and sent Donatist bishops into exile.
    o In one instance, an entire congregation was slaughtered inside a Carthaginian church.
    o Government troops disrupted Donatist assemblies and executed members of the congregation.
    o The government offered financial incentives to Donatist church leaders for submitting to the authority of the officially recognized bishops.

This aggression and injustice against Donatists continued through 321 A.D. It was for this reason that they did not recognize Emperor Constantine as the holy figure that he portrayed himself to be. Rome's continued military aggressive actions were unsuccessful in deterring the Donatists' resolve.

PROFILE OF AN AFRICAN EARLY CHRISTIAN LEADER

Alexander of Alexandria[262]

Lifespan	?-326 or 328 A.D.
Ancestry or Hometown	Egyptian; Alexandria, Egypt
Family Life	Little is known of Alexander's early years.
Conversion Experience	Unknown
	Alexander was the 19th Coptic Orthodox Pope of Alexandria, Egypt who succeeded from Mark the Evangelist.
Contribution(s)	Mentored the man who would be his successor, Athanasius of Alexandria, who became a leading Church Father.
	Alexander was designated to preside over the First Council of Nicaea, but instead delegated the responsibility to his deacon, Athanasius. Alexander led the opposition to Arianism at the council.
	Commissioned at the First Council of Nicaea to compute the date of Easter for use in place of the Hebrew's newly modified calculation. Egypt's computists deciphered the date using the nineteen-year Metonic cycle.[263] The circulation of their official results throughout Christendom began about 390 A.D. under the Egyptian Pope Theophilus of Alexandria.[264]
Type of Death	Unknown. However, as he was dying, he is said by some to have named Athanasius, his deacon, as his successor.[265]
Social, Political, or Religious Setting	During his time as a priest, he witnessed the bloody persecution of Christians by Emperors Diocletian and Galerius. At the First Council of Nicaea, he was praised for his service.

PROFILE OF AN AFRICAN EARLY CHRISTIAN LEADER

Athanasius

Lifespan	297?–373 A.D.
Ancestry or Hometown	Egyptian; Alexandria, Egypt
Family Life	Received a liberal education in secular learning, and was thoroughly instructed in the Scriptures
Conversion Experience	In 312 A.D., Bishop Alexander of Alexandria took him into his household as a companion, a secretary, and later as a deacon. He lived there as a son under the roof of this kindly and beloved bishop.
Contribution(s)	Early Church Father (post-Nicene), theologian. and writer
	Served as Bishop of Alexandria
	Chief spokesman during the First Council of Nicaea in 325 A.D. He provided clarification about the essence of Jesus' nature, and refuted false teachings and heretics.
	Athanasius identified the twenty-seven books of the New Testament to be used for the church 1,200 years before King James' commission of the Bible.
Type of Death	He died peacefully in his own bed, surrounded by his clergy and faithful supporters.
Social, Political, or Religious Setting	"Black Dwarf" was the tag given him by his enemies, and the short, dark-skinned Egyptian bishop had plenty of enemies. He was exiled five times by four Roman emperors, spending seventeen of the forty-five years he served as Bishop of Alexandria in exile.[266]

Though some of his teachers had been murdered during the persecution of 311 A.D., it hadn't deterred him. At the age of twenty-one, Athanasius published two apologetic works in support of Christianity and against paganism.

He was also delegated the responsibility of chief spokesman during Constantine's First Council of Nicaea in 325 A.D. One thousand eight hundred bishops from Christian churches within the Roman territories were invited (about 1,000 from the east and 800 from the west). However, in his letter "To the Bishops of Africa," Athanasius reported that only 318 bishops attended.[267] He is also credited for the Nicene Creed's emphasis on the Son being of one nature with, and the same substance as the Father.

The Nicene Creed is still recited in churches throughout the world today.[268]

- This creed was created to clarify divinely inspired scriptural teaching, and to distinguish right teaching from the heretics' "flavor-of-the-month" teachings (such as Gnosticism or Arianism).

- The creed is the most widely accepted statement of faith among Christian churches.

- The creed was established to identify conformity of beliefs among Christians as a means of recognizing heresy or deviations from established biblical doctrines, and as a public profession of faith.

When Bishop Alexander died around 328 A.D., Athanasius, barely thirty years old, was unanimously chosen to succeed the great leader. In his annual Festal Letter to the churches of Alexandria, Egypt in 367 A.D., Athanasius listed the books of the New Testament that are found in our Bible today as undisputable for the Church.[269]

It was Athanasius' writings that shaped the future of the Church.

SOCIAL/POLITICAL FACTORS

The First Council of Nicaea

Where Nicaea

When 325 A.D.

Source The revered Egyptian Alexander of Alexandria was chosen as spokesperson. But he delegated the responsibility to his deacon, Athanasius of Alexandria.

The primary purposes of this council were to (a) standardize the practices and behaviors of clergy, (b) differentiate Church teachings from of false teachings, (c) determine how to handle deviant teachers, and (d) honor the ancient Libyan and Egyptian Christian traditions.

Who From African churches in the empire's east[270]

- The Egyptian region
    - Alexander of Alexandria and his deacon Athanasius
    - Paphnutius – Bishop of Thebes (a Confessor who was a disciple of Anthony the Great)
    - Potamon – Bishop of Heraclea in Egypt (also a Confessor)
- The Libyan Pentapolis region
    - Secundus of Ptolemais
    - Theonus of Marmarica
    - Zephyrius and Dathes (excommunicated from the church along with Arius)

From the African Church in the empire's west

- The controversial Caecilian, Bishop of Carthage
    - The Donatists did not consider themselves represented by Caecilian, as they did not recognize him as bishop.

        As far as the Donatists were concerned, their interests were not represented at this council.

Some Outcomes from the First Council of Nicaea

The following clergy, traditions and locations, which are linked to Africa, were addressed by this council:

- The sixth canonical outcome (church rule) states, "The ancient customs of Egypt, Libya, and Pentapolis shall be maintained, according to which the bishop of Alexandria has authority over all these places..."[271]
    - Undoubtedly, this decision showed deference and honor to the missionary work of the Christ-believing Libyans and Egyptians in the Upper Room (Acts 2).
- The council crafted a letter specifically addressing the African bishops of the Church in Alexandria, Egypt and their brethren in Egypt, Libya, and Pentapolis. Amongst other things it included
    - The letter's purpose: "It seemed absolutely necessary that the holy synod should send you a letter so that you may know what was proposed and discussed, and what was decided and enacted."
    - A condemnation of Arius and his followers as heretics, calling his opinions evil and his terminology blasphemous. Arius was banished to Illyria. Constantine ordered all of his writings confiscated and burned.[272] Those works which survived this purge were later destroyed by his Trinitarian opponents.[273]
    - It mercifully stripped Meletius' authority to represent the church, to nominate or to ordain clergy (this also applied to the men he had ordained).
        - This was for creating a split in the church in Egypt; where Meletius had disapproved the ease with which traitors were welcomed back into the church.
    - The letter closes by giving honor to the great Egyptian Bishop Alexander, who was present at the council. It states, "Welcome our fellow minister, your bishop Alexander, with all the greater honor and love. He has made us happy by his presence, and despite his advanced age has undertaken such great labor in order that you too may enjoy peace."
- It was decided that all churches should follow a single rule for celebrating Easter, which should be computed independently of the Hebrew calendar (due to perceived errors that Hebrews had made in their revised calculations for the date of Passover).
    - Because Alexandria, Egypt had the advanced scholarly knowledge in this specialized field of study, it was decided to task them with computing an accurate date for Easter. Therefore, it became the duty of the great bishop and

patriarch Alexander to oversee this effort and to announce it to all other Christian churches.

- o The method for calculating the date for Easter by the African Church in Alexandria became authoritative.[274]

> Research Assignment 11.1
>
> Use your preferred internet search tool to find information about
> a. Emperors Constantine and Licinius
> b. The Edict of Milan
> c. Constantine's dream
> d. Lactantius (Constantine's advisor)
> e. The Battle of the Milvian Bridge
> f. The First Council of Nicaea
> g. Alexander of Alexandria and the date for Easter
> h. Athanasius' letter of 367 A.D.
> i. The sixth canon from the Council of Nicaea

Dueling Congregations

Donatist Theology and Growth

Heretics were exposed and excommunicated at the First Council of Nicaea. Yet nothing from this council impugned the Donatists' teachings, nor were Donatist clergy accused of any heresy. Their beliefs were the same as those of the other churches present at the council. Sadly, these two overlapping Christian churches were separated over practices of grace and integrity, not doctrine.

Though Bishop Caecilian represented territories occupied by Donatists at this council, their dissent remained strong and prevalent, and was not going away. It was their main distinction from the Nicaean Christian unity. Though they were unified in doctrine, they rejected the imported brand of Christianity perceived to be a government-sponsored institution. Instead, they embraced Christianity as a personally devout worship, and a way of living that was worth dying for.

As a non-Nicaean Christian dissident movement, Donatist congregations increased in number. They continued to redefine their identity and distinction from Nicaean congregations for decades. They also continued to establish themselves as far as Rome and Spain.[275]

Targets of Aggression Yet Again?

Thirty-three years after the Edict of Milan, in 346 A.D., the Nicaean Bishop of Carthage died. According to thirty-year-old protocol, a leader of the Donatist congregation in that city was in line to become the next bishop. When he was not recognized as such, the Donatists appealed to Emperor Constans (Constantine's son) for recognition as sole Bishop of Carthage.

In response, the emperor sent military officials with troops to investigate and make peace. However, the emperor's religious advisor seized the occasion to enforce an edict of unity—but under the leadership of the Nicaean group. This led to civil authorities offering financial incentives for Donatists to convert to Nicaeans. But when persuasion and bribery failed, the government resorted to force.

From 346-348 A.D., a renewal of strife between the Donatists and Nicaeans created new martyrs and new martyrdom stories. While both groups used the Bible as the authoritative source for their position, it remains unclear exactly how the Donatists' bible interpretations and/or applications differed from that of the Nicaeans.[276]

The Hunt for Heresy and Heretics

During the middle of the fourth century in Numidia, a bizarre northwest African phenomenon emerged. Bands of Berber extremists, who also regarded martyrdom as a virtue, wandered and would allegedly provoke others to kill them. They were labeled *Circumcellions*. Initially, they were concerned with remedying social inequalities. They condemned poverty and slavery. They advocated free love, canceling debt, and freeing slaves.

The term "Circumcellions" was attributed to them because "they roved about among the peasants, living on those they sought to indoctrinate." They disagreed with Bishop Donatus Magnus' primacy of chastity, sobriety, humility, and charity. Instead, they went to extreme measures to bring about their own martyrdom, typically, by provoking Roman soldiers, judges, or armed travelers to kill them in the name of their faith. Because of this practice the Circumcellions were deemed a heretical sect, and placed on the hit list.[277]

In the mid-370s A.D., about fifty years after the First Council of Nicaea, there was a resurgence of interest in heresy and heretics among Nicaean churches north of the Mediterranean and in the east. The concern was not so much to defend or cleanse Christian ideology internally, as much as it was to identify the various external adversaries to Nicaean Christianity.[278]

- A product of this resurgence of interest were extensive "hit lists" of heretics. The lists provided identity profiles by which Nicaean Christians could recognize any one of many adversaries they encountered.

Our research suggests that it is from the context of a Nicaean attempt to understand outsiders that the knowledge and writings about the Circumcellions emerged. Almost all known writings about the Circumcellions come from sources external to Africa (including Augustine's)[279] but not from Africans writing about African Christianity.[280] These external sources were also connected to the dominant eastern and northern Mediterranean church-state power struggles during the time.[281] In addition, that same Nicaean church-state power complex also placed the Donatists on the heretics list because of their perceived association with the Circumcellions (perhaps due to their common Numidian origins and reverence for martyrs). Even though many of the Circumcellion practices were very violent and displeasing to some, for reasons lost to oblivion, Donatists did not disassociate themselves from the Circumcellions.[282]

- In some respects, many Donatists blamed the Christian world in general for the crimes of these unknown Africans.[283] Undoubtedly, the Donatists perceived the heretics lists to be linked to the specific power aims of the Nicaean Church and its involvement with the Roman state.

- Donatists believed that the interest in heretics was part of a strategy to officially label them, by association with the Circumcellions, as dangerous heretics and thereby undermine their acceptance and influence.

Descriptions of the Circumcellions that have survived to this day were developed externally to Africa, based on writings from north of the Mediterranean. These descriptions have taken on a life of their own without any reference to writings, writers, or any reality that is internal to Africa.[284]

Read more in Chapter 13 about the struggle for identity and recognition of Donatist Christian congregations in Africa, particularly after Rome eventually adopted Christianity as its state religion.

PROFILE OF AN AFRICAN EARLY CHRISTIAN LEADER

Didymus the Blind

Lifespan	313-398 A.D.
Ancestry or Hometown	Egyptian; Alexandria, Egypt
Family Life	Despite becoming blind at the age of four, before he had learned to read, he successfully mastered all of the sciences known at that time.
Conversion Experience	He studied with a passion. His night studies were long and frequent, not for reading but for listening. He wanted to gain by hearing what others obtained by seeing. When a reader became tired and fell asleep, Didymus did not sleep himself, but reflected on what he had heard until he committed it to memory.
Contribution(s)	Theologian, writer, math scholar, and academic dean

Didymus' many works include

- Commentaries on all of the Psalms
- *The Gospel of Matthew*
- *The Gospel of John as Against the Arians*
- *On the Holy Spirit*
- Commentaries on Isaiah, Hosea, Zechariah, Job, and others

His writings show a remarkable knowledge of the Scriptures and are of great theological value.

Head of the Catechetical School of Alexandria |
| **Type of Death** | Unknown |
| **Social, Political, or Religious Setting** | He lived during a time when monasticism was one of the most significant manifestations of the Christian spirit, originating in Egypt and spreading to Palestine, Syria, and the whole Mediterranean world, producing literature and illuminating the life of the ancient church. Anthony the Great, Ammonas, Pachomius, and Evagrius Ponticus (who was the first monk to write in a habit of arranging his material in groups of a hundred aphorisms[285]) were Didymus' contemporaries. |

Didymus excelled academically because of his incredible memory. It was so powerful that he mastered dialectics and geometry without the benefit of sight. He found ways to help blind people to read through his experiments with letters carved into wood.[286] In 340 A.D., Athanasius the Great made him head of the influential Catechetical School of Alexandria, a position he held for fifty years.

Research Assignment 11.2

Use your preferred internet search tool to find information about the following:

a. Roman aggression towards Donatist congregations after the Edict of Milan
b. The Late fourth century A.D. heretic "hit list"
c. Didymus the Blind as head of the Catechetical School of Alexandria
d. Didymus the Blind and braille

Chapter 11 Notes

253 Wikipedia Contributors, s.v. "Pope Miltiades," *Wikipedia, The Free Encyclopedia*, March 14, 2019, https://en.wikipedia.org/wiki/Pope_Miltiades.

254 Wikipedia Contributors, s.v. "Lactantius," *Wikipedia, The Free Encyclopedia*, https://en.wikipedia.org/wiki/Lactantius; God raised up a Berber from a non-Christian family to eventually advise Rome's first "Christian" emperor nearly seventy years before Rome declared Christianity its state religion. This was also over seven-hundred years before the Roman Catholic faction, then a state religion, split off from the Christian Orthodox Church.

255 Richard Cavendish, "The Battle of the Milvian Bridge," History Today, October 10, 2012, http://www.historytoday.com/richard-cavendish/battle-milvian-bridge; Lactantius, "Of the Manner in Which the Persecutors Died," in *The Ante-Nicene Fathers: Translations of the Writings of the Fathers Down to A.D. 325*, vol. 7, *Fathers of the Third and Fourth Centuries*. trans. Alexander Roberts and James Donaldson, Christian Classics Ethereal Library, 2005, http://www.ccel.org/ccel/schaff/anf07.iii.v.xliv.html.

256 Philip Schaff, "The Edicts of Toleration. A.D. 311–313," in *History of the Christian Church*, vol. 2, *Ante-Nicene Christianity*, Christian Classics Ethereal Library, 2005, http://www.ccel.org/ccel/schaff/hcc2.v.iv.xiv.html.

257 Ibid.

258 Gonzalez, 155.

259 Wikipedia Contributors, s.v. "Donatism," *Wikipedia, The Free Encyclopedia*, July 28, 2017, https://en.wikipedia.org/wiki/Donatism.

260 Gonzalez.

261 Tilley, 57-70.

262 Thomas Campbell, "St. Alexander," in *The Catholic Encyclopedia*, vol. 1, 1907, http://www.newadvent.org/cathen/01296a.htm.

263 By this time, Egypt's advanced mathematical knowledge had been well known and respected for millenniums. In fact, by the sixth century B.C., when the famous Greek philosopher and mathematical and scientific discoverer Pythagoras was born, the science and mathematics used to build the Egyptian pyramids were already two thousand years old.

264 Wikipedia Contributors, s.v. "Computus," *Wikipedia, The Free Encyclopedia*, October 5, 2018, https://en.wikipedia.org/wiki/Computus.

265 Aziz S. Atiya, *The Coptic Encyclopedia* (New York: Macmillan Publishing Company, 1991).

266 G.A. Oshitelu, "Athanasius," in *Dictionary of African Christian Biography*, 2002, http://www.dacb.org/stories/egypt/athanasius.

267 Athanasius of Alexandria, "To the Bishops of Africa," in *A Select Library of the Nicene and Post-Nicene Fathers of the Christian Church*, second series, vol. 4, *Athanasius, Select Works and Letters*, Christian Classics Ethereal Library, 2005, http://www.ccel.org /ccel/schaff/npnf204.xxiv.ii.html.

268 JoHannah Reardon, "The Nicene and Apostles' Creeds," Christian Bible Studies, July 30, 2008, http://www.christianitytoday.com/biblestudies/articles /churchhomeleadership/nicene-apostles-creeds.html; Adrian Roberts, "The Nicene

Creed," Church on the Net, 2017, http://www.church-on-the-net.com/reference/creed.aspx.

[269] Archibald Robertson, *Select Writings and Letters of Athanasius, Bishop of Alexandria*, Northwestern Theological Seminary, 2010, http://www.ntslibrary.com/PDF%20Books/Athanasius%20Select%20Writtings%20and%20Letters.pdf.

[270] Papal Encyclicals Online, "First Council of Nicaea – 325 AD," February 20, 2017, http://www.papalencyclicals.net/Councils/ecum01.htm.

[271] Ibid.

[272] Wikipedia Contributors, s.v. "Augustine of Hippo," *Wikipedia, The Free Encyclopedia*, June 2017, https://en.wikipedia.org/wiki/First_Council_of_Nicaea.

[273] Wikipedia Contributors, s.v. "Arius," *Wikipedia, The Free Encyclopedia*, September 26, 2018, https://en.wikipedia.org/wiki/Arius; Originalpeople.

[274] Wikipedia Contributors, s.v. "Coptic Calendar," *Wikipedia, The Free Encyclopedia*, September 11, 2018, https://en.wikipedia.org/wiki/Coptic_calendar#Date_of_Easter; Wikipedia Contributors,s.v. "Computus," *Wikipedia, The Free Encyclopedia*, October 5, 2018, https://en.wikipedia.org/wiki/Computus#History.

[275] Tilley, 69.

[276] Ibid., 171-174.

[277] Wikipedia Contributors, s.v. "Circumcellions," *Wikipedia, The Free Encyclopedia*, July 9, 2017, https://en.wikipedia.org/wiki/Circumcellions.

[278] Brent D. Shaw, *Bad Boys: Circumcellions and Fictive Violence* - Version 2.1, February 3, 2006, https://www.princeton.edu/~pswpc/pdfs/shaw/020603.pdf.

[279] Shaw, 8.

[280] Shaw suggests that the African theologian and scholar Augustine did write about the Circumcellions, but in keeping with a style that imitates narratives from writings that originated to the north of the Mediterranean (Europe). Descriptions of Circumcellion violence that Augustine did write about did not include some of the other deranged claims about the Circumcellions. Shaw also suggests that writings about the Circumcellions attributed to the African theologian and ecclesiastical writer Tyconius were not his, but from writers to the north of the Mediterranean

[281] Shaw, 4.

[282] Ibid., 8-9.

[283] Ibid., 9.

[284] Ibid., 19.

[285] *Encyclopaedia Britannica*, s.v. "The Post-Nicene Period. Patristic Literature," 2018, https://www.britannica.com/topic/patristic-literature/The-post-Nicene-period#ref8045.

[286] Didymus didn't perceive his blindness as a weakness. Instead, he used his condition to understand how to help the blind. He developed a system similar to braille, whereby letters engraved into the surface of wood could be read by touch.

Chapter 12: Ethiopia
(Early 4th Century A.D.)

PROFILE OF EARLY CHRISTIANITY IN AN AFRICAN TERRITORY

Part of the Ancient Aksumite Empire

Key Location	Ethiopia
Modern-Day Name	Same
When	333 A.D.
How	Ethiopia had a thriving Christian community long before the events described here. But the formal adoption of Christianity as Ethiopia's state religion began during the reign of their Aksumite Emperor Ezana (320?–360 A.D.) As a young monarch, Ezana had been tutored by a former slave of the royal court named Frumentius, who converted him to Christianity.
Related Event(s)	The Ethiopian Orthodox Tewahedo Church maintains that Christianity was originally introduced to Ethiopia by the evangelist Philip, who <ul><li>Shared the gospel with the Ethiopian eunuch who was the treasurer to Candace, Queen of Ethiopia (Acts 8:26-40)</li><li>Was referred to as "the Evangelist" (Acts 21:8-9)</li><li>Had four daughters who prophesied (Acts 21:9)</li></ul>
Social, Political, or Religious Setting	Relations between Christian believers, and Axumite and Ethiopian authorities must have been cordial, because the believers openly sold goods and worked throughout Ethiopia.

Aksumite Emperor Ezana's Conversion

According to the historian Rufinus, around 313 A.D., Middle Eastern Christian Frumentius and his brother Edesius traveled with their uncle Metropius by ship from Tyre (modern-day Lebanon) to Ethiopia (territory under Axumite control at the time). While at harbor in the Red Sea region, the crew of their entire ship was slaughtered over a brawl that had erupted (another account says they were shipwrecked and lost their way).[287]

In any event, the two brothers, Frumentius and Edesius, managed to survive and were brought as slaves to the court of King Ousanas. The king favored the two, raising them to positions of trust. Before the king died, he liberated them from slavery. His widow, the acting regent Sofya, had the two (by then young adults) stay at the court and tutor her young son Ezana. Using their influence over the central administration of the kingdom, Frumentius managed to befriend Christian merchants living and working within the kingdom, along with converting Ethiopian Axumites to the Christian faith. His brother Edesius traveled back to their original home of Tyre to be ordained a priest. Frumentius, eager for the conversion of Ethiopia, accompanied his brother as far as Alexandria. There, he requested that Athanasius - Patriarch of Alexandria - send a bishop and some priests as missionaries to Ethiopia. However, by Athanasius' own account, he believed Frumentius to be the most suitable person for the job and consecrated him as bishop. Bishop Frumentius returned to Ethiopia to continue his missionary work, whereupon he baptized King Ezana.[288]

- Frumentius is honored in Ethiopian history as the Kesate Birhan (Revealer of Light) and Abba Salama (Father of Peace), and the first Abune, head of the Coptic Church of Ethiopia.

- He is also accredited with being the first to translate the New Testament into the Ethiopian writing system of Ge'ez.[289]

Earliest Illustrated Christian Bible

The world's earliest illustrated Christian Bible is from Ethiopia. The colored illustrations in the *Garima Gospels* are still vivid today. The monk Abba Garima wrote them on goat skin in the early Ethiopian language of Ge'ez. The two-book volume has been dated between the fifth and sixth centuries A.D. Also, as the fifth oldest book in the world today, experts believe it is the earliest example of book binding still attached to the original pages.[290]

Research Assignment 12.1

Use your preferred internet search tool to find information about the following:

a. The Aksumite Empire

b. Ezana's conversion to Christianity

c. Frumentius

d. Ethiopian Christians

e. Philip in Acts 8:26-40

Chapter 12 Notes

[287] A. K. Irvine, "Frumentius," in *Dictionary of African Christian Biography*, 1975, https://dacb.org/stories/ethiopia/frumentius/.

[288] Gonzalez, 262; Wikipedia Contributors, s.v. "Frumentius," *Wikipedia, The Free Encyclopedia*, March 10, 2019, https://en.wikipedia.org/wiki/Frumentius.

[289] Yohanes Jemaneh, "Ethiopia: Strengthening the Historical Tight Bond," *The Ethiopian Herald,* March 30, 2017, http://allafrica.com/stories/201703300590.html.

[290] France in Ethiopia: Embassy of France in Addis Ababa, "Inauguration Ceremony of Abba Garima Museum – Adwa," June 6, 2012, accessed April 28, 2019, https://et.ambafrance .org/Inauguration-ceremony-of-Abba; Oldest.org, "8 Oldest Books That Ever Existed," July 1, 2018, accessed April 28, 2019, http://www.oldest.org/culture/books-ever-existed/.

Chapter 13: Rome Adopts Christianity as Its State Religion
(End of 4th Century A.D.)

SOCIAL/POLITICAL FACTORS

Rome Becomes a Nicene Christian State

Where	Rome, Italy
When	380 A.D.
Source	Roman Emperor Flavius Theodosius Augustus I
What	The Edict of Thessalonica in 380 A.D. was issued by the three reigning Roman emperors (Theodosius I, Gratian, and Valentinian II). It made Nicaean Christianity the state religion of the Roman Empire.[291]
	Without consulting the church, Emperor Theodosius I decreed that only persons who believed in the Nicene Creed's consubstantiality of God the Father, Son, and Holy Spirit were to be considered "Catholic." Hence, the emperor reserved that term.[292]
	The edict stated that their subjects should profess the faith of the bishops of Rome and Alexandria, who were all Nicaean. Therefore, throughout the empire, the notion of being Catholic became synonymous with being Nicaean, and thereby in support of its Christian church-state complex.

Events and Effects

There had been an increase in brutal fights between competing Christian sects in the city of Rome. The fights were for religious supremacy, as paganism was a dying part of the dominant culture. Pagan temples that had been previously re-established by Emperor Julian were overrun by fanatic Christian mobs. Paganism in Rome continued on the path to virtual extinction. The final death blow to paganism came under the rule of Emperor Flavius Theodosius Augustus I (379-395 A.D.), an ardent Christian who recognized the amazing growth of the still relatively young religious sect. What ended the competing Christian sects was his adoption of Christianity, as described in the Nicene Creed, as the official religion of the Roman Empire.

Emperor Theodosius I devoted so much effort to promoting Nicaean Christianity that he seemed to have neglected other duties as emperor. So, it should be no surprise that he would also be the last emperor to rule both the eastern and western portions of the Roman Empire.

Donatists' Apprehension Confirmed

Since the era of the Nicene Council of 325 A.D., increased melding between the church and the state of Rome had finally solidified through

Theodosius' Edict of Thessalonica. A hawkish church-state political complex had emerged, whose decisions and actions resulted in a heavy-handed relationship with particular congregations of the African Church, to say the least. To the apprehension of Donatist congregations, all of the painful pieces seemed to have fallen into place.

- The Nicaean Christians becoming pro-Rome

- The traitor Caecilian's selection to represent them at the Council of Nicaea

- Exclusion of Donatists from Emperor Constantine's list of officially recognized Christian congregations (eligible for rebuilding funds and protection)[293]

- The renewed interest in heretics and heresy by churches north of the Mediterranean

- The inclusion of Donatists with Circumcellions on the late fourth-century list of heretics[294]

- Rome's lack of protection for Donatist congregations

Though the state of Rome was then Nicaean—or Catholic—it urged Donatists and Catholics to find a way to live together. No longer were the Donatists a major religious concern in the western region of the Roman Empire. By then, Rome's concerns were its traditionally pagan religions and the Arians, both of whom were persecuted by Emperor Theodosius I.

Gildo's Coup in Rome's African Territories

Emperor Theodosius I's insistence that Catholics and Donatists "find a way to live together" was reflected by his choice of officials to control Rome's African territories. They were men of high ranking who were not inclined to persecute Donatists.[295] However, one such official was a Roman army general. He seized the opportunity to take advantage of the emperor's relaxed policy with a bold, pro-African military maneuver.

Early in the 390s A.D., Emperor Theodosius I was in full control of the empire, and his borders were secure. In Africa, he felt assured about the confidence he had in his appointees. One rising officer in the Roman military was Gildo, the son of the Moorish Berber King Nubel. Even though Gildo's brother had revolted against Emperor Theodosius I fifteen years prior, Gildo remained loyal to Rome. He was eventually promoted to both Roman General and Magistrate of Africa, where he continued to serve the interests of the emperor.[296] General Gildo provided oversight of Rome's western region of North Africa.[297]

However, at the death of Emperor Theodosius I in 395 A.D., his two sons Honorius and Arcadius, neither of whom General Gildo respected or feared, assumed power over Rome.[298] When enemies entered the empire in the east and from the north and the two young emperors bickered over jurisdiction, General Gildo seized the opportunity to take control of Africa for himself. He declared the independence of the recaptured African territories and sought to restore North Africa to its former glory.

Catholic-Imperialist Repression of Donatists

The famous Berber Augustine had been ordained as a Catholic in 391 A.D. and began his active campaign against the Donatists. He took advantage of Donatist disunity and exploited the Donatists' reputation as associates of the usurper General Gildo and the violent Circumcellions. Augustine's goal was to cast a light on the Donatists as being heretics, and not merely a separate brand of Christians.

- In 393 A.D. Catholics sent representatives to imperial courts to advocate new legislation and renew old laws against Donatists.[299]

- In the first year of the new legislation, the Donatists were subjected to fines and threatened with deportation for disrupting the Catholic [Nicaean] Church.

- For the next two years, the state of Rome attacked the Donatists' institutional life. They were forbidden to ordain new bishops, then forbidden to assemble, ordain clergy, or teach.

- The following year, Donatists were forbidden to gather for any rituals.

- In 395 A.D. after Gildo declared independence from the Roman Empire, the emperors reasserted their authority by declaring anyone receiving help from Gildo as heretics. They would be treated as revolutionaries against Rome. In addition, the properties of Gildo's supporters and of Donatist bishops were confiscated.

- In 401 A.D. Gildo was overthrown by Rome. His failure to retain control of the African territories led to a severe imbalance of political and religious power between North Africa and the state of Rome. From that point forward[300]
    - Only Christians loyal to the two Roman emperor brothers and to Catholic Christianity were appointed to positions of power in North Africa.
    - Never again were African military leaders allowed to hold a command of Roman Troops in North Africa.
    - Never again would a North African or Donatist sympathizer be sent as a Roman representative to Africa.
    - Catholic fears heightened and they accelerated repressive legislation against the Donatists.
    - Catholics kept pressure on the imperial courts for more anti-Donatist legislation, as well as financial and civic penalties.

- In 410 A.D. the Roman emperor sent a new general and magistrate to Africa. He went with instructions to get Catholics and Donatists in a conference together. The objective was to put an end, once and for all, to the religious and political unrest in Roman territories of North Africa.

- After the Conference of Carthage in 411 A.D., Rome continued to propagate legislation against the Donatists.

Fortunately, neither the Donatists nor Catholics wanted a repeat of the era of martyrs and took precautions against it. However, the Donatists continued to be harassed, while the Catholics enjoyed their new status and imperial favor with Rome. Sporadic violence and pamphlet wars from both sides ensued. This conflict continued until the invasion of the Vandals in 439 A.D.

It would be reasonable to suggest that the Donatists realized that something was inappropriate about the union between the Catholics and the state of Rome one thousand years before Martin Luther posted his "Ninety-five Theses" in Wittenberg (credited as the beginning of the Reformation). Donatists wanted no part of it!

Differentiating Between Donatists and Catholics

Unfortunately, very little helped to resolve the divide between the Donatists and Catholics. Therefore, with the passage of time, both Donatists and Catholics became increasingly uncompromising. Attempts to reconcile them, by a number of popes and respected figures such as Augustine all failed. No Donatist clergy had been accused of a heresy. Their beliefs were the same as those of the other churches present at the first Nicaean Council. Yet, in varying degrees, both Christian congregations were separated, seemingly, over practices of *grace* versus *spiritual integrity* regarding the handling members with a lapse in faith.

Most of the time Donatists outnumbered the Catholics. But Catholics had the weight of Roman imperialism on their side. For the sake of perspective, following are a few differences between the two expressions of the Christian faith:

- Worship Style - The nature of their religious services began to drift apart. Donatist worship services became increasingly charismatic in nature. They developed a reputation for having energetic and unstructured services.

- Confession - Among the Catholics, the sacrament of confession became an individual one—private between priest and repenting member. But among the Donatists, confessions were public. The repenting member confessed sins before the entire congregation.

- Politics - Although the source of their differences was not theological, Donatism began to take the shape of nationalism, particularly in Numidia, Africa.[301] Catholics were in a church-state union with the Roman government.

- Spiritual Formation - Donatists contrasted their indigenous form of African Christianity (being more intimacy based) from the Catholics of Africa. Citing that the latter had embraced an "imported" and controlling brand of Christianity from the continent north of the Mediterranean.[302]

- Temperament - Catholics, who were heavily influenced by the church-state union with Rome, were sometimes put off by the fierceness of African Christianity of the Donatists.[303]
- Affiliations – Donatists, in keeping with their religious experiences, seemed resistant to being united with the state, at least to the extent that Catholics were.

These differences continued through the Vandal invasion of North Africa.

Research Assignment 13.1

Use your preferred internet search tool to find information about the following:

a. Roman Emperor Flavius Theodosius Augustus I
b. Roman General Gildo's coup
c. Repressive legislation against Donatists
d. The Edict of Unity

Chapter 13 Notes

[291] Wikipedia Contributors, s.v. "Christianity in the 4th Century," *Wikipedia, The Free Encyclopedia*, August 2, 2018, https://en.wikipedia.org/wiki/Christianity_in_the_4th_century.

[292] Adolf Lippold, "Theodosius I: Roman Emperor," in *Encyclopaedia Britannica*, 2018, https://www.britannica.com/biography/Theodosius-I.

[293] Tilley, 56

[294] Shaw, 6-9.

[295] Ibid, 130.

[296] Wikipedia Contributors, s.v. "Gildo," *Wikipedia, The Free Encyclopedia*, October 10, 2018, https://en.wikipedia.org/wiki/Gildo; Tilley, 132-133.

[297] Wikipedia Contributors, s.v. "Firmus (4th Century Usurper)," *Wikipedia, The Free Encyclopedia*, July 3, 2018, https://en.wikipedia.org/wiki/Firmus_(4th-century_usurper).

[298] Tilley, 132.

[299] Ibid, 135-137.

[300] Ibid, 132.

[301] *Encyclopedia.com*, s.v. "Christianity: Christianity in North Africa," October 9, 2018, https://www.encyclopedia.com/environment/encyclopedias-almanacs-transcripts-and-maps/christianity-christianity-north-africa.

[302] Joseph T. Kelley, *Saint Augustine of Hippo: Selections from Confessions and Other Essential Writings* (Woodstock, VT: SkyLight Paths Publishing, 2010), xxiv, Kindle.

[303] Ibid.

Chapter 14: Africa's Hardening of Christian Philosophy
(Mid-4th through Early 5th Century A.D.)

PROFILE OF AN AFRICAN EARLY CHRISTIAN LEADER

Aurelius of Carthage

Lifespan	?-429? A.D.
Ancestry or Hometown	Carthage
Family Life	Very little is known about his early life.
Conversion Experience	Unknown
Contribution(s)	His friend Augustine of Hippo reveals some of Aurelius' intangible contributions as a deacon at Carthage. In Augustine's *Of the Work of Monks*, *On Original Sin*, and *The City of God*, he informs us of Aurelius' charity and his opposition to the pagan rituals that Christians celebrated at the tombs of the martyrs.
	As archbishop of Carthage, he was a theologian and overseer of overseers. He denounced the Donatists as heretics and was the first to expose and condemn Pelagianism as heresy.
Type of Death	Unknown
Social, Political, or Religious Setting	The Roman Empire was being raided and collapsing. It was
	• Preoccupied with putting down invaders (the Visigoths, Vandals, Suevi, and Alans).
	• Closing its colosseum and officially ending gladiatorial combat.
	• Withdrawing its last legion in Britain and abandoning the province.
	• Experiencing its first external capture in 800 years.
	• Putting down revolts by Gildo, Heraclius, and Boniface in Africa.
	• Losing Mauretania to the Vandals under Genseric.

An Overseer of Overseers

In 388 A.D., while Africa provided intellectual leadership for the church worldwide, Aurelius was elevated to archbishop of Carthage.[304] In the footsteps of Cyprian of Carthage, Aurelius confirmed the church nominations in all the councils of the Church of Africa which were often held yearly. He continued to maintain a close relationship with Augustine of Hippo.[305]

Deemed Donatists Heretics Due to Their Practices

Donatist congregations within Bishop Aurelius' jurisdiction of Carthage required Christian clergy to be faultless, in order for their ministries to be effective and for their prayers and sacraments to be valid. Aurelius deemed such a practice to be flawed, and declared that "Bishop" Donatus Magnus and his followers were heretics.

Deemed Pelagians Heretics Due to Their Doctrine

In addition, a British monk named Pelagius rejected the African theologian Augustine's concept of grace. Instead, he taught that through human free will moral perfection was attainable, in this life, without the assistance of divine grace. It was Aurelius who met this crisis with decisiveness and wisdom. Aurelius was among the first to unmask and denounce Pelagianism as heresy.[306]

PROFILE OF AN AFRICAN EARLY CHRISTIAN LEADER

Augustine of Hippo

Lifespan	354-430 A.D.
Ancestry or Hometown	Berber; Numidian city of Thagaste (now Souk Ahras, Algeria)
Family Life	His mother, Monica (born in Numidia), was a devout Christian; his father, Patricius, was a Roman official who converted to Christianity on his deathbed.
	Augustine couldn't find truth in Christianity because he saw it as a religion for the simple-minded. After his primary education, at the age of seventeen, Augustine left home to further his education in Carthage. During his years as a student there (371–374 A.D.) he began living with a girlfriend who ultimately became his faithful companion for about thirteen years. While still a student, they had a son together named Adeodatus, who died at a young age.[307]
Conversion Experience	After nine years of holding to Manichaeism, Augustine became disillusioned by the failure of Faustus (the leading Manichaean teacher) to answer his questions.[308] He gradually drifted into Neoplatonism.[309] He partly owed his Christian conversion to reading Athanasius' biography on the great Egyptian hermit Anthony.[310]
	In 386 A.D., after having been moved by the story of Ponticianus and his friends and the life of Anthony of the Desert, Augustine converted to Christianity.[311] He reportedly heard a childlike voice telling him to "take up and read," which he took as a divine command to open the holy books and read the first thing he saw. Augustine read from Paul's letter to the Romans—the portion that includes chapters 12 through 15 of the epistle in our Bible today.[312]
Contribution(s)	Early Church Father (post-Nicene), theologian, writer, philosopher, and scholar.
	At thirty-seven he opened the first urban Christian monastery.[313]
	Augustine's large contribution of writings covered fields including theology, creation, ecclesiology, eschatology, Mariology, hermeneutics, original sin, predestination, sacramental theology, philosophy, and sociology. Following is a short list: • Psychological analogy of the Trinity • Philosophical and theological reasoning • Reasoning as a uniquely human cognitive capacity that comprehends deductive truths and logical necessity

	- Theory of time: Time is nothing in reality but exists only in the human mind's apprehension of reality
- Interpretation of the ultimate meaning
- Explanation of how small children learn and express language
- Faith seeking understanding: "Believe in order that you may understand."
- Refutation of skepticism
- Proof of the existence of God from eternal truths
- Response to the problem of evil: Evil is real it is not a substance, but evil is the absence of goodness
- Divine illumination: Human knowledge is directly dependent upon God
- Creation ex nihilo: God created the world "out of nothing" or "from nothing."
- The examined self: He was one of the first to write in depth about the self, particularly in relation to God[314]
Type of Death	Died of an illness during the Vandals' siege of Rome's North African provinces
Social, Political, or Religious Setting	Augustine waged the greatest theological debate of his life against the Pelagians during his last twenty years. It was also during this time that he and his friend and countryman Aurelius experienced the effects of a raided and collapsing Roman Empire. Rome was - Preoccupied with putting down invaders (the Visigoths, Vandals, Suevi, and Alans).
- Closing its colosseum and officially ending gladiatorial combat.
- Withdrawing its last legion in Britain and abandoning the province.
- Experiencing its first external capture in 800 years.
- Putting down revolts by Gildo, Heraclius, and Boniface in Africa.
- Losing Mauretania to the Vandals under Genseric.

Augustine was the Bishop of Hippo Regius (in modern-day Annaba, Algeria), located in Numidia (now Algeria and a part of Tunisia and Libya). His writings influenced the development of Western Christianity and Western philosophy. He is viewed as one of the most important Church

Fathers in Western Christianity for his writings during the Patristic Era.[315] Among his most influential works are *The City of God* and *Confessions*.[316]

Described as the greatest Catholic theologian and a millennium later the greatest Protestant theologian[317] and the first modern man.[318]

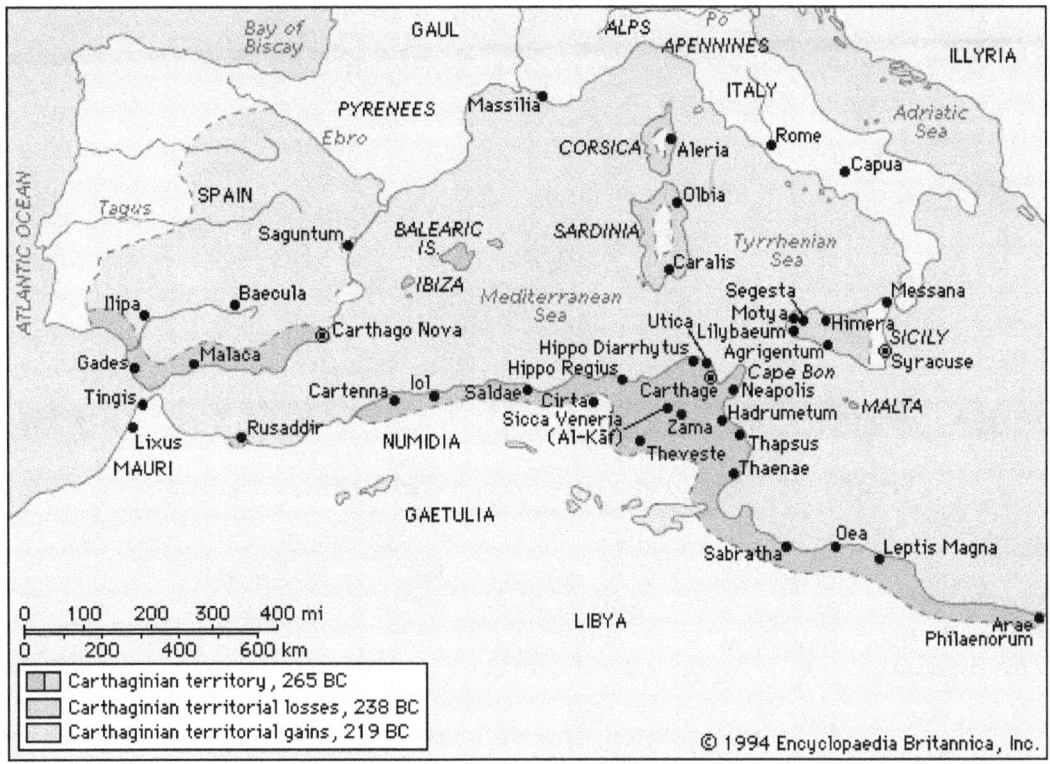

Evidence of Augustine's African Consciousness

As a powerful Christian theologian and philosopher, Augustine's writings also reveal his African consciousness and sense of heritage. In several of his writings he frequently calls out his countrymen using references such as "African bishops," "African council," "African Church," "African synod" and the "Old African version." Other examples are:

In *Answer to the Letters of Petilian*, twice he refers to his African heritage. He states, "It is evident that in Christ not only Africans or Africa, but all the nations through which the catholic Church is spread abroad, should receive the blessing which was promised so long before."[319]

In *Letter to Marcellinus* and in reference to Apuleius he writes, "Of whom I choose rather to speak, because, as our own countryman, he is better known to us Africans."[320]

In *Confessions* he writes, "Ponticianus, our countryman so far as being an African …"[321]

In *Contra Faustum Manichaean* he identifies Faustus the Manichaean by race, saying "Faustus was an African by race …"[322]

Finally, a noteworthy fact: The oldest city in America, St. Augustine, Florida, was named after Augustine of Hippo.[323]

> Research Assignment 14.1
>
> Use your preferred internet search tool to find for information about the following:
>
> a. Aurelius of Carthage
> b. Friendship between Aurelius and Augustine of Hippo
> c. Augustine's
>   1. Early Manichean beliefs
>   2. *Confessions*
>   3. *The City of God*
>   4. Interpretation of ultimate meaning
>   5. Influence upon Western philosophy
>   6. Mother Monica

PROFILE OF AN AFRICAN EARLY CHRISTIAN LEADER

Desert Fathers: Founders of Monastic Living

When	4th Century
Ancestry or Hometown	Desert regions of Thebes in Egypt
Who & What	An organized group of hermits who established the first monastic communities. They fled the cities for simple, disciplined and solitary living in the deserts of Egypt. Some settled religious communities there.
Walk with God	As hermits they sought to live simple, solitary lives, listening to and communing with God
Contribution(s)	Set the pattern for monasticism, convent communities, and monks throughout Christendom
	Provided spiritual insight and perspective to returning disciples seeking counsel

Providers of Spiritual Guidance and Counsel

These early hermits drew a sizeable following of individuals who were in search of salvation and unity with God.[324] Notable desert fathers were

- Paul of Thebes (227-342 A.D.) The first hermit recorded to have set the tradition of monastic abstinence and contemplation for unity with God.

- Pachomius of Thebaid (292-346 A.D.)

    Considered to be the founder of the early convent or monastic community.

- Anthony the Great of Egypt (see Chapter 8.) The revered father of monks. Two hundred fifty years prior to the founding of Western monasticism, he oversaw colonies of hermits in Egypt's middle region. He soon became the model of solitary living and a religious hero for the Western church (thanks to the enormous praise given in Athanasius' biography of him, *Vita S. Antoni*).[325]

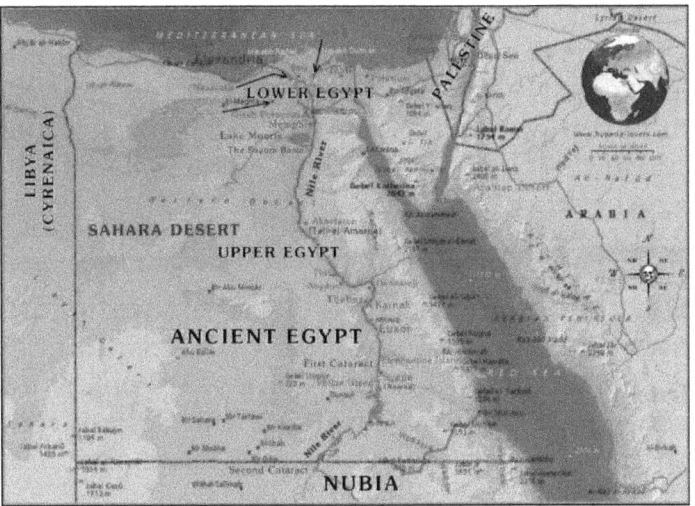

Western monasticism was patterned after these primitive hermits and religious communities.[326]

PROFILE OF AN AFRICAN EARLY CHRISTIAN LEADER

Moses the Black

Lifespan	330-407? A.D.
Ancestry or Hometown	Egyptian; Alexandria, Egypt
Family Life	Born into slavery to an Egyptian official's family, he was charged with theft and suspicion of murder. He escaped and became the leader of a gang of bandits.[327]
Walk with God	Hiding from local authorities, he took shelter with some monks in a monastic colony in Skete in the western desert near Alexandria. The dedication of the monks' lives and their peace and contentment seemed to have influenced Moses deeply. Eventually, he gave up his old way of life and became a monk himself.
Contribution(s)	He became a • symbol of monastic influence. • model of monastic conviction and commitment. • priest and spiritual leader of a colony of hermits.
Type of Death	In order to allow other monks to flee safely, Moses nonviolently engaged attacking bandits. He was martyred during the engagement.

<u>An Empathetic Judge</u>

When one brother of the colony committed a fault, a council met, and Moses was invited, but refused to attend. Someone went to him to let him know the others were waiting. Moses entered the meeting carrying a leaking jug filled with water on his shoulder (another version has him carrying a basket of sand with a hole in it). The others met him asking, "What is this?" With remarkable similarity to what Apostle Paul told young Timothy (1 Timothy 5:24) over three centuries prior, Moses replied, "My sins run out behind me and I do not see them, but today I am coming to judge the errors of another." Hearing that, they said no more to the erring brother, but forgave him.[328]

A Peacemaker

Having become a priest (uncommon for desert monks), Moses was the spiritual leader of the colony of hermits in the desert near Skete. In 407 A.D. when he was seventy-five years old, word came that a group of Berber renegades planned to attack the colony. The brothers wished to defend themselves, but Moses forbade such action. He told them to retreat rather than take up the sword. He and seven others stayed on to greet the invaders with open arms, but all were martyred by the bandits.[329]

Research Assignment 14.2

Use your preferred internet search tool to find information about the following:

a. Desert Fathers and the history of desert spirituality
b. Monasticism

Chapter 14 Notes

[304] Oden, *How Africa Shaped*, 29-31, 95; Aurelius was the person we all need in life—someone to keep us centered, a person who stands for what's right and is not afraid to tell us or correct us when we deviate.

[305] OrthodoxWiki Contributors, s.v. "Aurelius of Carthage," *Orthodox Wiki*, https://orthodoxwiki.org/index.php?title=Aurelius_of_Carthage&oldid=112392.

[306] Ibid.

[307] Kelley, loc. 185.

[308] Manichaeism was founded by a Persian prophet named Mani. He taught that the universe was comprised of dualistic forces. In it was a struggle between a good, spiritual world of light, and an evil, material world of darkness. Throughout human history, light is gradually removed from the world of matter and returned to the world of light, from which it came.

[309] Neoplatonists were heavily influenced by Plato and the Platonic tradition. They are a diverse group. Although they shared some basic assumptions about the nature of reality, there are considerable differences in their views and approaches. However, each Neoplatonist believes that the first principle of reality is an utterly simple, inexpressible, unknowable existence which is both the creative source and the intended end of all existing things. There is no name appropriate for the first principle. The most adequate names are "the One" or "the Good." It cannot even be said to exist or to be a being. Rather, the creative principle of all things is beyond being.

[310] Gonzalez, 147; Augustine of Hippo, *A Select Library of the Nicene and Post-Nicene Fathers of the Christian Church*, vol. 1, *The Confessions and Letters of St. Augustine, with a Sketch of his Life and Work*, ed. Philip Schaff, Christian Classics Ethereal Library, 2005, https://www.ccel.org/ccel/schaff/npnf101.i.html.

[311] Augustine was not a "fake it until you make it" Christian. If he didn't believe it, he did not pretend to live it. And when he believed in something, he was not casual about it, but defended it firmly.

[312] Augustine of Hippo, "Chapter XXII," in *The Confessions of St. Augustine*, Book XII, trans. Edward B. Pusey, Christian Classics Ethereal Library, 2005, https://www.ccel.org/ccel/augustine/confess.xiii.xxii.html.

[313] Kelley, loc. 243.

[314] Toni Shuma, "What are the Main Contributions of St. Augustine?" (blog), January 5, 2013, https://www.quora.com/What-are-the-main-contributions-of-St-Augustine; Augnet, "Life of Augustine," 2013, http://augnet.org/en/life-of-augustine/; Augnet, "Writings of Augustine," 2013, http://augnet.org/en/works-of-augustine/writings-of-augustine/.

[315] Gonzalez, 191.

[316] Steven Kreis, "The Church Fathers: St. Jerome and St. Augustine," The History Guide: Lectures on Ancient and Medieval European History, February 28, 2006, http://www.historyguide.org/ancient/lecture16b.html; Wikipedia Contributors, s.v. "Augustine of Hippo," *Wikipedia, The Free Encyclopedia*, June 4, 2017, https://en.wikipedia.org/wiki/Augustine_of_Hippo.

[317] Kelley, loc. 557.

[318] *A Survey of Church History: Part 1*, "Augustine."

[319] Augustine of Hippo, Chapter 50, in *The Three Books of Augustin, Bishop of Hippo, in Answer to the Letters of Petilian, the Donatist*, trans. J.R. King, in *A Select Library of the Nicene and Post-Nicene Fathers of the Christian Church*, vol. IV, *St. Augustin: The Writings Against the Manichæans and Against the Donatists*, ed. Philip

Schaff, Christian Classics Ethereal Library, 2005, http://www.ccel.org/ccel/schaff/npnf104.v.v.v.l.html.

[320] Augustine of Hippo, "Letter CXXXVIII, To Marcellinus," in *A Select Library of the Nicene and Post-Nicene Fathers of the Christian Church*, vol. 1, *The Confessions and Letters of St. Augustine, with a Sketch of his Life and Work*, ed. Philip Schaff, Christian Classics Ethereal Library, 2005, http://www.ccel.org/ccel/schaff/npnf101.vii.1.CXXXVIII.html.

[321] Augustine of Hippo, "Chapter VI, Pontitianus' Account of Antony, the Founder of Monachism, and of Some Who Imitated Him," in *A Select Library of the Nicene and Post-Nicene Fathers of the Christian Church*, vol 1, *The Confessions and Letters of St. Augustine, with a Sketch of his Life and Work*, ed. Philip Schaff, Christian Classics Ethereal Library, 2005, http://www.ccel.org/ccel/schaff/npnf101.vi.VIII.VI.html#vi.VIII.VI-Page_122.

[322] Augustine of Hippo, "St. Augustine: Reply to Faustus the Manichaen," in *A Select Library of the Nicene and Post-Nicene Fathers of the Christian Church*, vol. 4, *St. Augustin: The Writings Against the Manichaens and Against the Donatists*, ed. Philip Schaff, trans. J. R. King, Christian Classics Ethereal Library, 2005. http://www.ccel.org/ccel schaff /npnf104.iv.ix.iii.html.

[323] Wikipedia Contributors, s.v. "St. Augustine, Florida," *Wikipedia, The Free Encyclopedia*, October 3, 2018, https://en.wikipedia.org /wiki/St._Augustine,_Florida.

[324] In the tradition of their predecessor and countryman Anthony the Great, the Desert Fathers advanced the practice of listening to God in Scripture and remote community. They were the forerunners of religious communes and convents.

[325] Athanasius of Alexandria, *Vita S. Antoni* [*Vita S. Antoni*], Internet Ancient History Sourcebook, 1998, http://sourcebooks.fordham.edu /halsall/basis/vita-antony.asp.

[326] Emily K. C. Strand, "Desert Fathers," Solitary Life, Solitaries of De Koven, 1995, http://www.solitariesofdekoven.org/articles.html.

[327] Moses is proof that the power of God can radically change a person's deeds, temperament and preferences when he or she trusts Him completely.

[328] Tom DeWane, "History of St. Moses the Black Priory," St. Moses the Black Priory, 2009, http://www.stmosestheblackpriory.org/about_history.html.

[329] Ibid.

Chapter 15: Africa's Hardening of Christian Ecclesiology
(Early 5th Century A.D.)

SOCIAL/POLITICAL FACTORS

Code of Canons from Africa-Specific Church Councils

Where	Carthage and Hippo
When	African bishops met at least once a year, except during persecution, for what was called councils or synods. Six or seven of them were held while Cyprian was bishop (249-258 A.D.) There were more than fifteen while Aurelius was bishop (391-429 A.D.)[330]
Source	Cyprian's letters and Synod at Carthage
What	Twenty-one Africa-specific Church councils had been held since the first reported one in 251 A.D. (i.e. ten African councils held before the first Nicaean Council). African bishops continued to convene after Rome adopted Christianity. These councils addressed matters within the African Church (with some impacting all of Christendom). They set the pattern for ecumenical consensus used in Nicaea and today.

Events and Effects

In his book *Early Libyan Christianity: Uncovering a North African Tradition*, Thomas Oden makes the following statements:[331]

- "Many third-century questions were settled first in Africa through consensus by African Church councils. The first Synod of Rome was called by an African pope from Libya."

- "Africa set the pace for the maturing of ecumenical Christianity."

- "The consensual answers were often debated and formed first in Africa. These decisions ultimately became widely accepted by believers in the north and east in Europe and Asia."

According to Augustine, Carthage was formerly the head of the whole of Africa. As expected, a great number of councils we held there, convening church leaders from all the provinces of Africa.[332] The collection of African canons confirmed at the council in 419 A.D. was deemed *The Code of Canons of the African Church.*

On Doctrine, Jurisdiction, Religious Pride, and Closed Canon

Below are the Africa-specific church councils that convened around Africa-specific matters:[333]

- In 397 A.D., the African Council of Carthage was held to agree on the set of books that Christians were to regard as authoritative Scripture.

- In 411 A.D., a conference was held in Carthage to end the Donatist rift. It led to the violent suppression of the Donatists.[334]

The following two Africa-specific councils suggest that not only the Donatists in Africa, but now even the Catholics of Africa pushed back against the Catholic-Rome church-state power complex.

- In 418 A.D., the Council of Africa was called by Augustine of Hippo. He and Aurelius Bishop of Carthage took action concerning errors regarding redeeming grace, denounced the Pelagian doctrines, approved the views of Augustine and reinstated a deposed African priest. This council enacted a decree that whoever appeals to a court on the other side of the sea (meaning Rome) may not again be received into communion by anyone in Africa.[335]

- In 419 A.D., this council called by Augustine of Hippo and Aurelius Bishop of Carthage to
    - Condemn the pope in southern Italy for interfering with the African Church's jurisdiction by falsifying the text of Canon 5 of the First Council of Nicaea (325 A.D.)
    - Warn the pope and a predecessor not to "introduce the empty pride of the world into the Church of Christ" and to "keep their Roman noses out of African affairs."
    - Rule that no bishop may call himself "Prince of Bishops" or "Supreme Bishop" or any other title which suggested supremacy.
    - Rule that if any African clergy dared to appeal to Rome, "that very act itself casts them out of the clergy."[336]
    - Re-review all of the canons adopted at previous councils, with the greater part of them reconfirmed.

At or after the council in 419 A.D., the African Augustine declared the biblical canon closed (set selection of books for the Bible).[337]

African Canons as the Gold Standard Throughout Christendom

Initially, the canons from these Africa-specific Church councils were not adopted in Greek, but in Latin (the language of northwest Africa's Roman colonizer territory). Also, they were confirmed in Latin. Throughout the written narratives in the canons are references to African provinces, churches, bishops, councils, and synods. Both the Eastern and Western churches inserted these African canons into their ancient codes.[338]

Throughout history, and by diverse sources, these canons have been referred to by other names.[339]

- Dionysius named them *The Statutes of an African Council* (*Statuta Concilii Africani*).

- Hefele describes them as "the collection of those African Canons put together in 419 by Dionysius Exiguus."
- In *Migne Patrologia Latina's Codex Canonum Ecclesiasticorum*, no such title occurs, but an appropriate description does: "A Synod at Carthage in Africa, which adopted one hundred and thirty-eight canons."

Primacy and Influence

In 394 or 395 A.D. as Jerome (north of the Mediterranean) was translating the Septuagint Scriptures into Latin (producing the Vulgate Bible), Augustine, Bishop of Hippo, provided the following guidance and caution in a letter to him:

> We therefore, and with us all that are devoted to study in the African churches, beseech you not to refuse to devote care and labor to the translation of the books of those who have written in the Greek language most able commentaries on our Scriptures. You may thus put us also in possession of these men, and especially of that one whose name you seem to have singular pleasure in sounding forth in your writings [Origen]. But I beseech you not to devote your labor to the work of translating into Latin the sacred canonical books, unless you follow the method in which you have translated Job, viz. with the addition of notes, to let it be seen plainly what differences there are between this version of yours and that of the LXX., whose authority is worthy of highest esteem.[340]

In 401 A.D. Augustine wrote,

> As to the people of Vigesile, who are to us as well as to you beloved in the bowels of Christ, if they have refused to accept a bishop who has been deposed by a plenary Council in Africa, they act wisely, and cannot be compelled to yield, nor ought to be.[341]

In 418 A.D. Augustine wrote,

> After the conviction and condemnation of the Pelagian heresy with its authors by the bishops of the Church of Rome, – first Innocent, and then Zosimus, – with the co-operation of letters of African councils, I wrote two books against them: one On the Grace of Christ, and the other On Original Sin.[342]

<u>A Concern for Africa</u>

In the writings of the Early Church Fathers about the African Church, on a subtopic level, there are distinct discourses that make references to Africa, Africans, or the African Church, just as they do to the churches in Rome, Antioch, Jerusalem, and other regions. One recurring discourse in Augustine's rhetorical arguments seems intended to argue against a popular and radical notion that the church, gospel, or even God Himself was for Africa only. In these discourses there is a consensus amongst the Early Church Fathers that Jesus called for His gospel to be spread throughout the entire world. In Augustine's sermon based on Matthew 20:30 he states, "That good Sower, the Son of Man, hath scattered the good seed not in Africa only, but everywhere."[343]

> Research Assignment 15.1
>
> a. Use your preferred internet search tool to find the definition of the word *canon*. Write the definition that fits this chapter below.
>
> b. Search to find the following:
>   1. Ecumenical consensus
>   2. The location of the Mediterranean Sea
>   3. Closed biblical canon

Chapter 15 Notes

330 Wikipedia Contributors, s.v. "Hippo Regius," *Wikipedia, The Free Encyclopedia*, October 6, 2018, https://en.wikipedia.org/wiki/Hippo_Regius.

331 Oden, *Early Libyan Christianity*, 44.

332 Philip Schaff and Henry Wace, eds., "Introductory Note," in *The Canons of the CCXVII Blessed Fathers Who Assembled at Carthage. Commonly Called the Code of Canons of the African Church*, in *A Select Library of the Nicene and Post Nicene Fathers of the Christian Church*, vol. 14, *The Seven Ecumenical Councils*, Christian Classics Ethereal Library, 2005, https://www.ccel.org/ccel/schaff/npnf214.i.html.

333 Fourth Century Christianity, "Early Christian Councils," April 17, 2012, https://www.fourthcentury.com/councils-and-creeds/.

334 Wikipedia Contributors, s.v. "Councils of Carthage," *Wikipedia, The Free Encyclopedia*, September 7, 2018, https://en.wikipedia.org/wiki/Councils_of_Carthage

335 Wikisource Contributors, s.v. "1911 Encyclopaedia Britannica/Carthage, Synods of," January 17, 2016, https://en.wikisource.org/wiki/1911_Encyclop%C3%A6dia_Britannica/Carthage,_Synods_of.

336 Wikipedia Contributors, s.v. "Councils of Carthage," *Wikipedia, The Free Encyclopedia*, https://en.wikipedia.org/wiki/Councils_of_Carthage.

337 Wikipedia Contributors, s.v. "Development of the Christian Biblical Canon," *Wikipedia, The Free Encyclopedia*, October 5, 2018, https://en.wikipedia.org/wiki/Development_of_the_Christian_biblical_canon; Everett Ferguson, "*Factors leading to the Selection and Closure of the New Testament Canon,*" in *The Canon Debate,* eds. L. M. McDonald & J. A. Sanders (Peabody, MA: Hendrickson, 2002), 320; F. F. Bruce, *The Canon of Scripture* (Downers Grove, IL: Intervarsity Press, 1988), 230; The Book of Revelation was added later in 419 A.D. at the subsequent synod of Carthage.

338 Schaff and Wace, eds., "Introductory Note."

339 Ibid.

340 Augustine of Hippo, "From Augustine to Jerome (A.D. 394 or 395)," ed. Kevin Knight, New Advent, 2009, http://www.newadvent.org/fathers/1102028.htm.

341 Augustine of Hippo, "Letter 64 (A.D. 401) ed. Kevin Knight, New Advent, 2009, http://www.newadvent.org/fathers/1102064.htm.

342 Augustine of Hippo, "Extract from Augustine's Retractations," in *A Select Library of the Nicene and Post-Nicene Fathers of the Christian Church*, ed. Philip Schaff, vol. 5, *St. Augustine: Anti-Pelagian Writings*, Christian Classics Ethereal Library, 2005, http://www.ccel.org/ccel/schaff/npnf105.xv.ii.html.

343 Augustine of Hippo, "Sermon XXXVIII," in *A Select Library of the Nicene and Post-Nicene Fathers of the Christian Church*, vol. 6, *St. Augustine: Sermon on the Mount; Harmony of the Gospels; Homilies on the Gospels*, ed. Philip Schaff, trans. R. G. MacMullen, Christian Classics Ethereal Library, 2005. http://www.ccel.org/ccel/schaff/npnf106.vii.xl.html.

Chapter 16: Arian Invaders Persecute Donatists and Catholics
(4th and 5th Centuries A.D.)

SOCIAL/POLITICAL FACTORS

Anti-Trinitarian Invaders

Where	Beginning in northwest Africa and continuing eastward
When	4th and 5th Centuries A.D.
Source	King Genseric (also known as Gaiseric or Geiseric) and his son the successor King Huneric
What	The Vandals (a Germanic tribe from Eastern Europe) invaded North Africa. As believers in Arianism they rejected teachings of the Trinity (Godhead of the Father, Son, and Holy Spirit).

Events and Effects

In 429 A.D., the Vandals invaded North Africa with the help of the Maurii (Moors, Berbers of Northwest Africa). They went on to control coastal Numidia, including Carthage. However, they could not make a significant settlement further inland, due to being harassed by local Berbers.[344] During the Vandal occupation, several Berber revolts occurred in the former Roman Africa. Some Berbers detached themselves and established self-rule near border territories.[345]

Also, because Donatists and Catholics were Trinitarians, both became the targets of Vandal persecution. In 434 A.D. when it became clear that Vandal presence and violence could not be stopped by force, Rome removed its military and political presence from northwest Africa. This was to allow the Vandals to settle in the provinces of Numidia and Mauretania. This young Vandal kingdom continued, by conquest, to expand further into North Africa and the Mediterranean. African Catholics could no longer count on Rome's protection against the Vandals.

On October 24, 439 A.D., the Suevi, the Vandals and their allies the Sarmatian Alans, under the Vandal King Genseric, caught the Romans off-guard while they were heavily preoccupied with conflicts in Gaul. In his article entitled "History of the Vandals," Brian Adam describes the invasion as follows:

> King Genseric landed North Africa with over 80,000 men including Alans, Roman-Spaniards, former slaves and several Germanic tribesmen with their families. They seized lands from the local Berbers and some Romans near Tingi (Tangier), from there they overran the country and spread all over Mauretania. There was no limit to their savage atrocities and cruelties. Everything within their reach was laid waste, with looting, murders, tortures of all kinds, brigandry, and countless other unspeakable crimes, without any mercy to men, women, children, priests and ministers of God. Also

they destroyed church buildings. As the Vandals were Arians, they made the war with the Catholic Romans especially bitter.[346]

King Genseric also captured the strategic port city of Carthage, along with the Roman navy vessels docked there.

King Genseric's son Huneric succeeded him. Like his father, he and his advisors were ardent Arians. King Huneric had difficulty with both Arian and North African-established Christian churches co-existing. *Note: at this time the western region of the Roman Empire had collapsed; and the empire's eastern region (later called New Rome or the Byzantine Empire) was yet to come into its own as a significant power.* The North African Catholic [Nicaean] churches were left to protect themselves against Huneric's dislike about their co-existence. Taking advantage of these vulnerable Trinitarian Christians, King Huneric banished the Catholic bishops from their African jurisdictions and began a violent persecution of established African Christians, many of whom were put to death. These were not persecutions from Rome, but persecution by the hand of a Germanic king with Arian beliefs (beliefs that had been deemed heresy a century earlier at the Nicene Council; see Chapter 11).[347]

Once again, violent persecution erupted in North Africa. This time it was an Arian king persecuting Trinitarian Christians. The fifth century African bishop and historian of the Province of Byzacena (a sub-province within the Africa Proconsularis) by the name of Victor Vita (a.k.a. Victor of Vitensis) captured these atrocities in his three-volume book, *A History of the African Province Persecution, in the Times of Genseric and Huneric, the Kings of the Vandals*. The majority of his historic accounts were contemporary narratives about the cruelties perpetrated against the Catholic Christians of North Africa by the Arian Vandals. His accounts did not include reports of physical persecution against Donatist Christians. His first book provides an account of the reign of Genseric, from the Vandal invasion of Africa in 429 A.D. until the king's death in 477 A.D. The second and third books are his eyewitness record of events during Huneric's reign (477-484 A.D.)

Victor's works provide a coherent narrative of Vandal persecution where none had previously existed.[348] He sheds much light on the social and religious conditions in Carthage and on the African liturgy of his day. His historical account portrays the Vandals as being strongly and violently opposed to African Catholic Christianity.[349] Several documents that are inaccessible elsewhere are contained within his books.[350]

In his 2006 book, *Victor of Vita: History of the Vandal Persecution*, John Moorhead elucidates upon Victor's work, particularly about the status of the African Church at the time. He suggests the events that had occurred during the Vandal domination of Africa must be understood in light of what had already occurred between African Catholics and Donatists. In particular, this would explain why African Catholics were more susceptible as targets than Donatists. The latter were primarily of Berber descent. He states that

> Even while the Roman Empire was still pagan, African Christianity had displayed distinctive characteristics. It was immensely productive of martyrs ... and both literary and archaeological evidence indicate the popularity ... Africa was also productive of movements resistant to ecclesiastical authority.[351]

We know that the Vandals had not won the favor of Donatists. An editorial revision of an original Donatist literary work in Vandal Africa demonstrates that the same letters in the name "Gensericus" have the numerical value of 666.[352]

Huneric's Deceptive Oath Given to African Bishops

According to Victor of Vita, after confiscating the homes and churches of African bishops (Donatists or Catholics), King Huneric corralled them outside their cities to suffer hunger and nakedness, while wallowing in their dung. They were then ordered to a place called the Temple of Memoria and given a proposition. It was to swear that after the death of the king their wish would be to have his son Hildirit become king. He insisted that they not write to their peers on the other side of the Mediterranean Sea (the territory much closer to the Vandals' homeland) about the conditions under which they swore this. The king promised that if they swore to this oath, he would restore them to their churches.

Some bishops decided to swear to the oath. They did not want it said later that those who did not swear the oath were to blame for their churches not being restored. Other bishops felt the proposition was a deceptive trap, so they were unwilling to take the oath. After their decisions, both groups were taken to clerks who wrote down what each bishop had said and the town from which they came. Then, to the surprise of some bishops, both groups were taken into custody, and the deception was revealed.

For those who had sworn the oath, the king ordered that they would never see their towns or churches again. They were banished to cultivate fields and never be allowed to sing, pray, teach, preach, baptize, or even hold a book to read. As for those who had not sworn to the oath, the king banished them to the island of Corsica to cut timber for the king's ships. But the king had already initiated simultaneous tortures, beatings, hangings, and burning at the stake throughout the towns and provinces of all the bishops before exiling them. Not a single home or place was free from weeping and mourning. They did not spare people of any age or gender, except those who renounced their "Christ and the Father, same substance" belief.

Enormous Devastation to the Early African Church

Steuart Erskine describes the devastation to the Early African Church, by the invading Vandal people, as follows:[353]

"The Africa of their invasion was the Africa of Augustine [Bishop of Hippo] and many saintly people."

"Their [Vandals] rapacity knew no bounds, their cruelty was abnormal and they laid waste and never rebuilt."

"They found Africa flourishing and left it desolate ..."

"... its people reduced to slavery"

"The Church of Africa – so important in those early days of Christianity – practically non-existent."

Victor also writes about the cruelty. One example is a persecution account that he describes as "contrary to the laws of nature." In a particular town, a noblewoman was tortured entirely naked and in full view of the public. Her name was Dionysia.[354]

PROFILE OF AN AFRICAN EARLY CHRISITAN MARTYR

Dionysia of Africa

Ancestry or Hometown	Africa Proconsularis
Function/Status	Widowed noblewoman and mother in an established church. According to Victor Vita's narrative from her contemporary, she was a lady of rare beauty in Africa, and more courageous than the other married women.[355]
Stand	She was the first in her town to be persecuted by Huneric for being a Trinitarian Christian. She preferred tortures, shameful indignities, and death to renouncing her belief that Christ was both God and man.
Persecution Location	Africa Proconsularis
Persecution Date	484 A.D.
Circumstances	Beaten with rods at the stake until covered with blood and stripped of her clothing, yet in a bold voice she said, "You servants of the devil, what you think you are doing to my shame is in fact to my praise." Then using Scripture, she strengthened others being martyred.

Seeing her young son Majoricus weep fiercely, she called out to him saying, "Let us not lose the garment of our salvation, in case the host, when he comes, does not find the wedding garment and says to his servants: Cast him into the outer darkness ..." The boy was strengthened by her words.[356]

Many townspeople were gained for Christ through Dionysia: her sister and her sister's boyfriend, the bishop's daughter, a doctor, a religious man, and Boniface of Sibida. |
| **Type of Death** | Dionysia, Dativa, Leontia, Tertius, Emilianus, Boniface, and Majoricus[357] were tortured to death.[358] |

PROFILE OF AN AFRICAN EARLY CHRISTIAN LEADER

Pope Gelasius I

Lifespan	?-496 A.D.
Ancestry or Hometown	Berber; Rome
Family Life	Born of African Berber parents
Conversion Experience	Unknown
Contribution(s)	In 492 A.D. he was elevated to pope. It was during the time of an existing theological split between the Eastern Roman Emperor and the patriarch of Constantinople. The latter held the view that Christ's nature was singular (a common view in the east). However, the emperor of the eastern region of the empire held the view of the dual nature of Christ (which had been the western view before its collapse). In his book *On the Dual Nature of Christ*, Pope Gelasius I outlined the elements of Christ's dual nature as the universal point of view for Christendom.
	Gelasius advocated for the primacy of Rome over the entire Church, East and West. He presented this position in terms that set the model for subsequent popes asserting the claims of papal supremacy.
	In 494 A.D., Gelasius wrote a very persuasive letter, known as "Duo sunt" ("there are two"), on the topic of church-state relations. The impact of this letter was felt for almost a millennium. It is regarded as "the most celebrated document of the ancient Church concerning the priestly spiritual authority and secular temporal authority." The Gelasian doctrine articulates a Christian theology about division of authority and power.[359]
Type of Death	Unknown

PROFILE OF AN AFRICAN EARLY CHRISTIAN LEADER

King Masuna

Lifespan	Unknown
Ancestry or Hometown	Berber; Mauretania Caesariensis (western Algeria)
Family Life	Unknown
Conversion Experience	Masuna is assumed to have been Christian like his citizens. He ruled over a Romano-Moorish kingdom of Christian Berbers.
Contribution(s)	His kingdom maintained its independence by resisting occupation by the Vandals during the sixth century. Also, it is believed that his kingdom's independence was key to Donatism surviving the Vandal invasion as well.
Type of Death	Unknown

King Masuna was a Romano-Moorish king in Mauretania Caesariensis (western Algeria) from 508-535 A.D. In an inscription from Altava, Masuna described himself as *rex gentium Maurorum et Romanorum* (king of the Moorish and Roman peoples). By some accounts, Masuna's kingdom stretched over a sizeable part of Mauretania Caesariensis.[360] It extended beyond the borders of the former Roman Empire, encompassing Berber territories that had never been under Roman control.[361] It was a Christian Berber kingdom that existed in Tamazgha until the conquest of the Maghreb. This may shed light on why the Donatist Christian faction (predominately in Berber North Africa) were less susceptible to Vandal attacks.

Masuna is the earliest recorded ruler of this kingdom, which is assumed to have been established by the local Berber chieftains and rulers following the collapse of the Western Roman Empire and loss of Roman control over Mauretania. His reign would see the arrival of the Byzantine Empire's (eastern end of the Roman Empire) military in North Africa. Joining forces, they fought the Vandal Kingdom in Africa. During this Vandalic War of 533 A.D., King Masuna and the Byzantine Emperor Justinian defeated the Vandals, as well as other invading Berber tribes under a confederation.[362]

Research Assignment 16.1

a. Use your preferred internet search tool to find information about the following:
   1. Arians
   2. King Huneric
   3. The Vandals
   4. Dionysia and son Majoricus

b. Answer the following questions:
   1. At this point in history, the Vandals were invaders with colonizing power in Carthage. They forcefully imposed a "brand" of Christianity upon African Christians that had been declared to be false. These African Christians still chose death over denying what they believed to be true.
      a. What does this suggest about the Africans' comprehension of the Scriptures and commitment to their faith?
      b. Do you think Dionysia was simply towing the line of religious talk?
      c. Do you think Dionysia foolishly dragged her son into her religious fanaticism?
   2. Did these Africans embrace Christianity as a way of living, or simply obey it out of tradition?

Chapter 16 Notes

[344] Wikipedia Contributors, s.v. "Algeria," *Wikipedia, The Free Encyclopedia*, June 5, 2017, https://en.wikipedia.org/wiki/Algeria.

[345] Wikipedia Contributors, s.v. "History of Roman-era Tunisia," *Wikipedia, The Free Encyclopedia*."

[346] Brian Adam, "History of the Vandals," Internet Archive WaybackMachine, June 23, 2017, https://web.archive.org/web/20170623155644/http://www.roman-empire.net/articles/article-016.html.

[347] Wikipedia Contributors, "Huneric," Wikipedia, The Free Encyclopedia, May 31, 2017, https://en.wikipedia.org/wiki/Huneric.

[348] Andrew Merrills and Richard Miles, *The Vandals* (Chichester, UK: Wiley-Blackwell Publishers, 2010), 184-185.

[349] Ibid.

[350] Wikipedia Contributors, "Victor Vitensis," Wikipedia, The Free Encyclopedia, April 17, 2018, https://en.wikipedia.org/wiki/Victor_Vitensis.

[351] John Moorhead, trans., *Victor of Vita: History of the Vandal Persecution*, vol. 10, *Translated Texts for Historians* (Liverpool: Liverpool University Press, 2006, https://epdf.tips /queue/victor-of-vita-history-of-the-vandal-persecution.html.

[352] Victor of Vita, *Victor of Vita: History of the Vandal Persecution*, trans. John Moorhead (Liverpool, UK: Liverpool University Press, 2006), xiii.

[353] Erskine, "Vanished Cities of Northern Africa," 274.

[354] Victor of Vita, 69-72.

[355] Victor of Vita, 72.

[356] Ibid., 72-73.

[357] Dionysia's death is an unfortunate example of the extreme to which doctrinal differences can lead.

[358] Melanie Rigney, "Wednesday's Woman: St. Dionysia," *Faith, Saints and Life* (blog), December 2, 2015, http://melanierigney.com/blog/ catholicism/4201/.

[359] Wikipedia Contributors, "Pope Gelasius I," Wikipedia, The Free Encyclopedia, February 21, 2019, https://en.wikipedia.org/wiki/Pope_Gelasius_I; Wikipedia Contributors, "Famuli vestrae pietatis," Wikipedia, The Free Encyclopedia, December 18, 2017, https://en.wikipedia.org/wiki/Famuli_vestrae_pietatis.

[360] Andrew Merrills, *Vandals, Romans and Berbers: New Perspectives on Late Antique North Africa* (New York: Routledge Publishing, 2017), 41; Wikipedia Contributors, "Masuna," Wikipedia, The Free Encyclopedia, February 12, 2017, https://en.wikipedia.org /wiki/Masuna.

[361] Merrills, 5-7.

[362] John R. Martindale, *The Prosopography of the Later Roman Empire*: Volume 2, AD 395-527 (New York: Cambridge University Press, 2006), 734.

Chapter 17: Nubia
(4th through 6th Century A.D.)

PROFILE OF EARLY CHRISTIANITY IN AN AFRICAN TERRITORY

Christianity in Ancient Nubia

Key Locations	Nobatia; Makuria; Alodia and its northern frontier
Modern-Day Name	Sudan; South Sudan
When	4th-6th Centuries
How	Christianity gradually arose in Nubia through its Christian neighbors: Egypt to the north and Ethiopia to the southeast.
Related Event(s)	The Theban mountains and desert terrain served as a fitting resort for many hermits and monks. For these Egyptian hermits, as it is today, the attraction of the desert was a place to center oneself on Christ, attain spiritual clarity, and to hone their discernment of God's voice.[363]
Social, Political, or Religious Setting	In 298 A.D. as the fourth century approached, Emperor Diocletian's forces travelled south along the Nile River where they encountered the Nobatae and Blemmyes tribes—inhabitants of Old Nubia territory. Rome was compelled to enter into a peace treaty with them. The terms of the treaty resulted in (a) Rome withdrawing its borders back northward near Aswan, Egypt, at the other side of the desert frontier and (b) both tribes receiving an annual gold stipend from Rome.
	Diocletian's withdrawal was inscribed within the temple of Kalabsha in northern Nubia.[364] The Nubian tribesmen established a territorial delimiter to Rome's military control in the region.

Events and Effects

A desert frontier was where interactions occurred between people of diverse cultural backgrounds, as they traversed to and fro. It was there that diverse values and beliefs collided, combined, or were abandoned (even if only temporarily). A frontier was the perfect venue to facilitate a gradual movement of Christian ideas southward from Egypt into Nubian territory. During the fourth through the sixth centuries A.D., Egyptian desert hermits, their Theban desert communities, and Christian monks facilitated the flow of Christian ideology into the frontier territories between Egypt and Nubia.

Inscriptions and archaeological evidence in the frontier from converted pagan temples and artifacts attest to the Christianization of Nubia. Nubian royal tombs from the fifth and sixth century A.D. contain such evidence.

Location of Nubia

Nubia was the territory that included today's Upper Egypt to the north, the Sudan to the west and south, and borders Ethiopia on the southeast. The map of ancient Nubia (Nobatia, Makuria, and Alodia) reveals its geographical proximity to Egypt, the desert frontier, and Ethiopia. At one time ancient Nubia was a Nile Valley and a Sudanic civilization. Its history extended beyond the founding of Dynastic Egypt and Napatan-Meroitic Kush. Long after ancient Egypt had been subdued by the Greeks and Rome, ancient Nubian civilizations continued to thrive in late antiquity as an independent kingdom for 1,000 years.[365]

Gradual Christianization of Nubia

Contrary to the beliefs of many Western historians, Christianity gradually arose in Nubia between the fourth and sixth centuries A.D., a century before the arrival of Byzantine missionaries in the 600s A.D.[366] From the first through the fifth centuries A.D., its Christian neighbors Egypt and Ethiopia had vastly influenced the culture, values, and Nubian people in that region. The communities and other habitations of early Christian hermits, monks, and the Desert Fathers in and around the desert and the city of Thebes added to a flood of Christian ideas and beliefs.[367]

Influential Historic Events

- As described in Chapter 1, the Nubian army, led by Queen Amanirenas, defeated the Roman forces at Aswan, Philae, and Elephantine.[368] This may have influenced Emperor Diocletian, centuries later, to take soldiers into Nubian territory or to enter into a treaty with them.

- Egypt's ancient pharaonic civilization's relationship with the desert millenniums prior created the appetite, lure and mechanics embraced later in Egypt's Christian desert spirituality. Eventually, this relationship with the desert morphed into the rudiments of hermitages.[369]

- The traditions of hermits in the Theban desert and mountainous terrain nurtured and preserved Christian spirituality and theology in the region. Their desert spirituality relied upon solitude and separation away from the cities, to center themselves on Christ. Communities were often formed in the desert around this experience. There, they routinely practiced devotion to serving others, feeding the poor, caring for travelers, and becoming self-sufficient and hardworking. Theban Christians celebrated many martyrs who had refused to renounce their faith during the many persecutions in the first three centuries of the early African Church.[370] These communities made Christianity a way of life, unlike the stale, "belief-ism," academic, and liturgical Christianity that we see today.[371] Over time, desert communities became a place for thinking, teaching, religious engagement, and ultimately holding and preserving the key tenets of the Christian faith.

- In Ethiopia from 330 to 356 A.D., shortly after it declared Christianity its state religion, King Ezana fought and subdued the Nubians. He inscribed his victory on a stone tablet in praise of the Christian God. This stone is known today as the Ezana Stone.[372] King Ezana's victory was significant, in that, by the late fourth century and the entire fifth century A.D., Nubia had the influence of Coptic Christian Egypt and desert communities to its north and Christian Ethiopia to its southeast. These neighbors had already saturated Nubian territories with rich Christian thought and values long before Byzantine Christian influences.

Inscription Evidence of Gradual Christianization

<u>Nubian King Silko's</u>

In 1819, archaeologists discovered the triumphant inscription of the Nubian King Silko in the temple of Kalabsha. Dated a century before the arrival of Byzantine missionaries, the inscription suggests that Silko led a campaign to drive out the Blemmyes nomads around 537 A.D. It reads, "God granted me victory," and "I am a lion in the lower region and a bear in the upper regions." Silko is credited with making the way for Christianity to sprout in Nubia.[373]

The significance of his inscription is not only that bears were foreign to both Nubia and Egypt, but that the Nubian King Silko used the language of Old Testament prophets (1 Samuel 17:34-37; Lamentations 3:10; Hosea 13:8; Amos 5:19). It should be no surprise that he could have heard or read Old Testament accounts. As described in Chapter 4, nearly 700 years prior in Egypt, the entire Old Testament had already been translated from Hebrew into Greek by seventy Hebrew scholars. Whether Silko was a Christian or not is not the point. The point here is that his inscription in this frontier is evidence of the progression of Christian influence into the region. In this frontier, desert spirituality had been gradually replaced with the language of Scripture. In no small way, the unique interactions formed in the desert proved to be as strong an influence as political alliances, in terms of religious change.[374]

Paul the Priest's

Also in Kalabsha there are two Coptic inscriptions, dated in the mid to second half of the sixth century, written on the left pylon in front of the temple. They read, "I, Paul, the priest, prayed here for the first time," and "I, Paul, the priest, set up the Cross here for the first time."[375] There, a Christian priest named Paul converted and rededicated a pagan temple as a church.

Nubian King Eirpanome's

Using the same Coptic format as Paul the priest to declare the conversion of the pagan temple, the Temple of Dendur was rededicated as a Christian church. The dedication reads, "By the will of God and the order of King Eirpanome and the eager student of the word of God, Joseph, the exarch of Talmis [Kalabsha], and as we receive the Cross from Theodore the bishop of Philae [near Aswan], I Abraham, the most humble priest, set up the Cross on the day on which the foundation of this church were laid." This was the first official Christian document from Nubia. It goes on to state that from that time on, Christianity was the state religion of Nobatia.[376]

In addition to temple conversions by the priests, evidence of other Christian gatherings existed in Nubian territories without the need to convert pagan temples. These sixth century A.D. inscriptions serve as examples of the gradual cultural and religious shifts without an influx of organized missionaries, forced religious conversions, or colonial conquests. The Christianization of Nubia was not event driven, but a gradual and complex progression.

Artifact Evidence of Gradual Christianization

General Artifact Evidence up to Mid-6th Century A.D.[377]

Nubians likely expressed their Christian beliefs on many other artifacts. The following evidence is limited to the variety of artifacts that the nineteenth-century European excavators, archeologists, and historians could validate as being Christian, based upon corroboration with their understanding of "organized" Christian artifacts (i.e. churches, ritual utensils, symbols, crosses, tombs, inscription stories, books, or schools). Undoubtedly, other indigenous, sixth-century A.D. artifacts that expressed Christian beliefs - unique to Nubian culture -, would have gone unidentified even when in plain sight. These kinds of early-adopted

Christian artifacts would likely have predated any European recognizable artifacts in Nubia.

The European recognizable Christian artifacts discovered were
- Ritual lamps
- Wall paintings
- Many ecclesiastical remains
- A mud church
- Inscriptions
- Objects of daily use

Artifact Evidence among Royalty

Between 1931 and 1934, excavators Walter Bryan Emery and Laurence P. Kirwan discovered archaeological evidence of Christian influence in 122 Nubian royal tombs of the fourth and fifth centuries A.D. in Ballana and Qustul.
- They were dated to the time after the collapse of the Meroitic state (from around 360 to 420 A.D.), but before the founding of Byzantine Christian Nubia.[378]
- Emery reported, "Christian symbols have been found on possessions of obvious native manufacture such as leather quivers ... [and] on pottery after baking." He went on to describe "a silver reliquary with figures of Christ and the Apostles in relief."[379]

Research Assignment 17.1

Use your preferred internet search tool to find information about the following:
   a. The location and dates of the first two Arab invasions into Africa
   b. The Introduction to Islam's into Africa

Chapter 17 Notes

³⁶³ Gabra and Takla, 55-60.

³⁶⁴ Gabra and Takla, 66; Wikipedia Contributors, s.v. "Roman–Nubian Relations," *Wikipedia, The Free Encyclopedia*, September 16, 2018, https://en.wikipedia.org/wiki /Roman%E2%80%93Nubian_relations; Wikipedia Contributors, s.v. "Diocletian," *Wikipedia, The Free Encyclopedia*, October 11, 2018, https://en.wikipedia.org/wiki /Diocletian.

³⁶⁵ Salim Faraji, *The Roots of Nubian Christianity Uncovered: The Triumph of the Last Pharaoh* (Trenton: Africa World Press, 2012), back cover.

³⁶⁶ Ibid., 63, 68.

³⁶⁷ Ibid., 70.

³⁶⁸ Wikipedia Contributors, s.v. "Amanirenas," *Wikipedia, The Free Encyclopedia*, September 28, 2018, https://en.wikipedia.org/wiki/Amanirenas; The Freeman Institute, "Ancient Nubia," 2018, http://www.freemaninstitute.com/Gallery/nubia.htm.

³⁶⁹ Gabra and Takla, 55-60.

³⁷⁰ Faraji, 239-244.

³⁷¹ Henry L. Gates, "Great Ancient African Civilizations," VHS, produced and directed by Henry L. Gates, Public Broadcasting Service, 2017.

³⁷² Wikipedia Contributors, s.v. "Ezana Stone," *Wikipedia, The Free Encyclopedia*, June 28, 2018, https://en.wikipedia.org/wiki/Ezana_Stone.

³⁷³ Faraji, 63, 86-91; Gabra and Takla, 66-67.

³⁷⁴ Gabra and Takla, 66-67.

³⁷⁵ Ibid, 67.

³⁷⁶ Ibid., 68; Jitse H.F. Dijkstra, *Philae and the End of Ancient Egyptian Religion: A Regional Study of Religious Transformation (298-642 CE)* (Louvain Belgium: Peeters Publishers, 2008), 299-302.

³⁷⁷ Gabra and Takla, 51.

³⁷⁸ Faraji, 129-130.

³⁷⁹ Ibid., 238-239.

Chapter 18: Decline of Christianity in Northwest Africa
(6th through 7th Century A.D.)

What Happened to Donatists and Nicaeans?

The indigenous Berbers already in Mauretania and Numidia survived the Vandal invasion and their 100-year occupation by reviving their old culture in some places. They were key to the survival of Donatist members. Berbers even survived the Arab conquest in the eighth century and persisted until modern times. After the Vandalic War of 533 A.D., Emperor Justinian intended to unify what was left of the Catholic [Nicaean] Church with what remained of the Roman Empire. He discouraged all divisive tendencies within the church, including Donatism.

Due to Numidia's geographic proximity to King Masuna's kingdom, the Donatists were able to survive the Byzantine reconquest of old Roman North African territories. Through subsequent African theologians such as Bishop Facundus of Hermiane and other challenges in the seventh century A.D., we know that the independent nature of African Christianity continued to be demonstrated, even after the Byzantine reconquest.[380] Although their wealth appeared to have dwindled, the Donatists maintained an independent presence in North Africa until the Arab conquest of northern Africa in the seventh and eighth centuries.

Reflections on the Decline of Christianity in Northwest Africa

The Donatist controversy was never actually resolved, and remained a divisive point with Catholics.[381] Dr. Noel Quinton King, one of the few scholars belonging to the old school of learning, who founded the University of California at Santa Cruz's department of the History of Religion reports that:

> "The main reason for the disappearance of Christianity in the northwest of the African continent may well have been the beauty of in-coming young Islam, compared with the tired Christianity left by the great struggle between Catholics and the others, eking out an existence in a society ruined by barbarian invasion and East Roman reconquest."[382]

Whereas Steuart Erskine reports:

> "The Muslim empire, without boundaries, without political divisions, swept over Northern Africa carrying the Berbers in its onrush, like a great tidal wave."[383]

> "The early Christian Church in Africa ... will be remembered, ruined by the seditions that rose up. The Africans were sincere believers, but independent, argumentative, intensely combative. They were only too ready to fight to the death with anyone who opposed their convictions; they sacrificed to their prejudices the whole future, not only to Christianity, but of civilisation."[384]

Africa's Eastern Coast Stronghold

In his review in the *Journal of African History*, Noel Q. King details African Christianity's perseverance along its eastern coastline. He states:

> There has been no break in the continuity of life of the Coptic and Ethiopian Churches, and their importance for the future of Christianity in Africa is not lightly to be passed over. ... Even the Church of Nubia whose pillars now lie in the dust made its contribution to African Christianity as a whole.[385]

However, during the seventh century A.D., whether by military force or peaceful socialization, Arabs conquered North Africa, bringing a new religion, language, and alien customs to the native Berber tribes. By 700 A.D., Carthage, Maghreb, and Mauretania fell to the Arabs, and most of the North Africans (except for the Egyptian Copts) converted to Islam.[386] According to Cheikh Anta Diop's research, there was never an Arab conquest of Mozambique or any other East African territory.[387]

While Islam entered Africa from the north and the west, Egypt's Coptic Christians, Nubian Christians, and Ethiopian Christians secured Africa's Christian heritage along its eastern shores.

Author's Reflection:

Scriptural Context
African Christian martyr stories reveal a community of individuals who valued an individual relationship with the Lord, not merely the belief-ism, creed based and national religion. To appreciate their Christian spiritual formation (shaped while under colonial oppression) we must first understand the broader source of oppression upon all humanity. Evidence suggests that they clearly understood it. For starters, we must interpret Psalm 116:15 as the Lord's response to a declaration from the dark realm of heaven, which asserts,

> Declaration: "Skin for skin!" Satan replied. "A man will give all he has for his own life. But now stretch out your hand and strike his flesh and bones, and he will surely curse you to your face." Job 2:4-5

> Response: Precious in the sight of the Lord is the death of his faithful servants. Psalm 116:15

In African Christianity, particularly in the north, it was more honorable to join the souls beneath the altar (Revelation 6:9-11) with one's faith intact, waiting to be avenged, even when faced with being swiped from the face of this earth. They believed this as an individual on trial for being a Christian, as well as, a whole faith community being forced to embrace the faith of the heavy handed spirituality of a Church-State unison. From the Lord's point view, their decline or disappearance is a win, not a loss.

<u>Earthly Context</u>

So much is unchronicled, lost, or yet revealed. But I thank the Lord Jesus Christ for allowing me to provide every Christian a glimpse into the spirit of early African Christians. Too often, their genuine and independent spirit - strong in conviction – had to be expressed through situations of persecution and oppressed. Their resistance to ecclesiastical authority may well have been to the particular brand imposed by the Church-State union, under which they often found themselves.

Rome's persecution of Christians and the Vandal's invasions were chiefly responsible for dimming the light of the Church, both in the north and most of the south of the Mediterranean Sea. This contributed to Europe's Dark Ages. Fortunately, through the Lord's providence, Augustine of Hippo's influence crossed a millennium to reach church reformers like Martin Luther and John Calvin who brightened His light for Europe. But church historians neglected to shine the light on Africa's contribution.

But what's done in the dark shall come into the light! I liken early African Church history to the resilience of the once fortified African Berber village of Thugga. This village had preserved some of its native characteristics despite having been darkened as a Carthaginian colony, obscurely-Romanized city, fallen to the Vandals, being a Byzantine citadel and inhabited by Arabs. Yet, in the early twentieth century Thugga was found back as an African village. Like Thugga, once again surviving, the history of the early African Church shines through this book.

Chapter 18 Notes

[380] Victor of Vita, xiii-xiv.

[381] David Benedict, History of the Donatists, The Reformed Reader, 1999, http://www.reformedreader.org/history/benedict/donatists/toc.htm; Early Christian History, "Controversies: Donatism," 2018, http://www.earlychristianhistory.net/donatus.html.

[382] King, *Christian and Muslim*, 8.

[383] Erskine, "Vanished Cities of Northern Africa," 162.

[384] Ibid., 131.

[385] Noel Q. King, review of *The Planting of Christianity in Africa*, by C.P. Groves, *The Journal of African History* 1, no. 1 (January 1960) 158.

[386] Eamonn Gearon, "Arab Invasions: The First Islamic Empire," *History Today*, June 2011, https://www.historytoday.com/archive/arab-invasions-first-islamic-empire; Kat Cendana, "North Africa Converts to Islam and Arab Slave Trade Begins in 700 AD," Amazing Bible Timeline with World History, November 15, 2016, https://amazingbible timeline.com/blog/north-africa-converts-to-islam-and-arab-slave-trade-begins-in-700-ad/.

[387] Cheikh Anta Diop, *Precolonial Black Africa* (Brooklyn, NY: Lawrence Hill Books, 1978), 102.

Africa's Prominence in Church History at a Glance

Throughout the history of the early African Church, we see the descendants of the sons of Ham weaving it into existence.[388] The descendants of Cush, Egypt, Put and Canaan each had a providential role in shaping the Christian mind more than a millennium before European Christian missionaries arrived in Africa and the King James Bible was compiled. Just as their progenitor Ham had helped his father Noah build the ark, his descendants helped establish the foundation of Western Christianity.[389]

> **Canaan** (Phoenicians): Introduced a variant of the Hebrew language across North Africa, and founded the city of Carthage from which Christian teachers, theologians and martyrs emerged.[390]
>
> **Egypt**: Helped raise the baby Jesus; established the great university in Alexandria where Christianity was first subjected to rigorous studies that created its theology and dogma, as well as the hermits who preserved that theology and dogma in desert communities.
>
> **Put** (Libyans): Assisted Jesus with carrying His cross. Were among the leaders who planted the church in Antioch where believers were first called Christians. It was from this church that God separated Saul (later used Paul) before his first missionary journey. [391].
>
> **Cush** (Ethiopians and Nubians): The Ethiopian eunuch who brought the gospel back home. Nubians who halted the Roman army under Emperor Diocletian from advancing further south into Africa, thereby affording an unabated natural, yet gradual flow of Christian beliefs and values into Nubia. They helped form a strong Christian presence along Africa's eastern coastline.[392]

The contributions of Africa and Africans that shaped Western Christianity were already in place by the fifth century A.D. That's approximately

- Decades before the birth of Muhammad, the prophet and founder of Islam
- 235 years before the first monastery in Europe
- 500 years before Roman Catholics became a separate church faction
- 550 years before the first Roman Catholic Crusade
- 900 years before Gutenberg invented the printing press for Rome
- 900 years before Europeans kidnapped African citizens to use as permanently owned property
- 950 years before Europeans sent Christian missionaries to Africa
- 1,150 years before King James' Bible compilation was completed
- 1,350 years before Europeans divided and exploited Africa's natural resources
- 1,350 years before European Christian colonies settled in Africa

What Others Have Declared

I now realize how true it is that God does not show favoritism but accepts from every nation the one who fears him and does what is right. You know the message God sent to the people of Israel, announcing the good news of peace through Jesus Christ, who is Lord of all. You know what has happened throughout the province of Judea, beginning in Galilee after the baptism that John preached— how God anointed Jesus of Nazareth with the Holy Spirit and power, and how he went around doing good and healing all who were under the power of the devil, because God was with him ...

- Apostle Peter, Acts 10:34-38

Nearly all the Latin Fathers are Africans: Tertullian of Carthage, the Numid Arnobius of Sicca and his pupil Lactantius, Saint Cyprian of Carthage, the African Marius Victorinus, the Berber Saint Augustin, in short, all this glorious vanguard of Latin patristic culture. What splendid gifts these were from Africa to the Church of Rome while the latter had only the works of Saint Ambrose and of Saint Jerome to put in the Balance![393]

- Etienne Gilson's *The Philosopher and Theology*

The whole of North Africa was a glory of Christendom with St. Augustine, himself a Berber, its chief ornament.[394]

- "Paulist Fathers," *Catholic World*

Precious in the sight of the Lord is the death of his faithful servants.

- Psalm 116:15

Author's Closing Remarks

Hopefully, this survey has provided enough details to compel its reader to dig, probe, expand, and research even further. Perhaps by doing so, a work of even greater visibility will emerge. My prayer is twofold: for people around the world to acknowledge and appreciate the African roots of Christianity, and to honor God's faithful Berber servants with whom I share DNA.

Africa's Prominence in Church History at a Glance Notes

[388] Genesis 10:6

[389] Gonzalez, 251.

[390] Wikipedia Contributors, s.v. "Canaan," Wikipedia, The Free Encyclopedia, June 16, 2017, https://en.wikipedia.org/wiki/Canaan.

[391] Acts 11:20-21, 26, 13:1-3

[392] Acts 8:27-39

[393] Etienne Gilson, *The Philosopher and Theology* (New York: Random House, 1962) 195-196.

[394] "Paulist Fathers," *Catholic World*, vols. 175-176, 1952.

Bibliography

Academic Dictionaries and Encyclopedias, s.v. "Afri." http://latin_german.deacademic.com/1644.

Adam, Brian. "History of the Vandals." Internet Archive WaybackMachine. Accessed November 29, 2018. https://web.archive.org/web/20170623155644/http://www.roman-empire.net/articles/article-016.html.

Albright, William F. *The Archaeology of Palestine*. London: Penguin Books. 1949.

Algeria Carthage and the Berbers. "Carthage and the Berbers." 1993. Accessed April 5, 2017. http://workmall.com/wfb2001/algeria/algeria_history_carthage_and_the_berbers.html.

Ancient Names Galleria. "Names of Libya (Africa)." November 20, 2009. Accessed April 26, 2019. http://www.peiraeuspubliclibrary.com/names/libya.html.

Athanasius of Alexandria. *On the Incarnation of the Word*. Christian Classics Ethereal Library. 2005. Accessed March 28, 2017. https://www.ccel.org/ccel/athanasius/incarnation.v.html.

———. "To the Bishops of Africa." In *A Select Library of the Nicene and Post-Nicene Fathers of the Christian Church*. Second Series. Vol. 4, *Athanasius, Select Works and Letters*. Christian Classics Ethereal Library. 2005. Accessed May 23, 2017. http://www.ccel.org/ccel/schaff/npnf204.xxiv.ii.html.

———. *Vita S. Antoni* [*Life of St. Antony*]. Internet Ancient History Sourcebook. 1998. Accessed April 6, 2017. http://sourcebooks.fordham.edu/halsall/basis/vita-antony.asp.

Atiya, Aziz S. *The Coptic Encyclopedia*. New York: Macmillan Publishing Company. 1991.

Augnet. "Life of Augustine." Accessed October 12, 2018. http://www.augnet.org/?ipageid=376.

———. "Writings of Augustine." Accessed October 12, 2018. http://augnet.org/en/works-of-augustine/writings-of-augustine/.

Augustine of Hippo. Chapter 50. In *The Three Books of Augustin, Bishop of Hippo, in Answer to the Letters of Petilian, the Donatist*. Translated by J.R. King. In *St. Augustin: The Writings Against the Manichaens and Against the Donatists*. Edited by Philip Schaff. Christian Classics Ethereal Library, 2005. http://www.ccel.org/ccel/schaff/npnf104.v.v.v.l.html.

———. "Chapter VI. Pontitianus' Account of Antony, the Founder of Monachism, and of Some Who Imitated Him." In *A Select Library of the Nicene and Post-Nicene Fathers of the Christian Church*. Vol. 1, *The Confessions and Letters of St. Augustine, with a Sketch of his Life and Work*. Edited by Philip Schaff. Christian Classics Ethereal Library. 2005. Accessed May 31, 2017. http://www.ccel.org/ccel/schaff/npnf101.vi.VIII.VI.html#vi.VIII.VI-Page_122.

———. "Chapter XXII." In *The Confessions of St. Augustine*. Book XII. Translated by Edward B. Pusey. Christian Classics Ethereal Library. 2005. Accessed May 27, 2017. https://www.ccel.org/ccel/augustine/confess.xiii.xxii.html.

———. "Extract from Augustine's Retractations." In *A Select Library of the Nicene and Post-Nicene Fathers of the Christian Church*. Edited by Philip Schaff. Vol. 5, *St. Augustine: Anti-Pelagian Writings*. Christian Classics Ethereal Library. 2005. Accessed May 31, 2017. http://www.ccel.org/ccel/schaff/npnf105.xv.ii.html.

———. "From Augustine to Jerome (A.D. 394 or 395)." Edited by Kevin Knight. New Advent. 2009. Accessed May 23, 2017. http://www.newadvent.org/fathers/1102028.htm.

———. "Letter [12] XVII. To Maximus." In *A Select Library of the Nicene and Post-Nicene Fathers of the Christian Church*. Vol. 1, *The Confessions and Letters of St. Augustine, with a Sketch of his Life and Work*. Edited by Philip Schaff. Christian Classics Ethereal Library. 2005. Accessed May 19, 2017. https://www.ccel.org/ccel/schaff/npnf101.vii.1.XVII.html.

———. "Letter 64 (A.D. 401)." Edited by Kevin Knight. New Advent. 2009. Accessed May 23, 2017. http://www.newadvent.org/fathers/1102064.htm.

———. "Letter [138] CXXXVIII. To Marcellinus." In *A Select Library of the Nicene and Post-Nicene Fathers of the Christian Church*. Vol. 1, *The Confessions and Letters of St. Augustine, with a Sketch of his Life and Work*. Edited by Philip Schaff. Christian Classics Ethereal Library, 2005. Accessed May 31, 2017. http://www.ccel.org/ccel/schaff/npnf101.vii.1.CXXXVIII.html.

———. "Psalm L." In *A Select Library of the Nicene and Post-Nicene Fathers of the Christian Church*. Edited by Philip Schaff. Vol. 8, *St. Augustine: Expositions on the Book of Psalms*. Edited by A. Cleveland Coxe. Christian Classics Ethereal Library. 2005. Accessed May 31, 2017. http://www.ccel.org/ccel/schaff/npnf108.ii.L.html.

———. "Psalm CXXI." Edited by Philip Schaff. In *A Select Library of the Nicene and Post-Nicene Fathers of the Christian Church*. Vol. 8, *St. Augustine: Expositions on the Book of Psalms*. Edited by A. Cleveland Coxe. Christian Classics Ethereal Library. 2005. Accessed May 31, 2017. http://www.ccel.org/ccel/schaff/npnf108.ii.CXXI.html.

———. *A Select Library of the Nicene and Post-Nicene Fathers of the Christian Church*. Vol. 1, *The Confessions and Letters of St. Augustine, with a Sketch of his Life and Work*. Edited by Philip Schaff. Christian Classics Ethereal Library. 2005. Accessed May 27, 2017. https://www.ccel.org/ccel/schaff/npnf101.i.html.

———. "Sermon XXXVIII." In *A Select Library of the Nicene and Post-Nicene Fathers of the Christian Church*. Vol. 6, *St. Augustine: Sermon on the Mount; Harmony of the Gospels; Homilies on the Gospels*. Edited by Philip Schaff. Translated by R. G. MacMullen. Christian Classics Ethereal Library. 2005. Accessed May 31, 2017. http://www.ccel.org/ccel/schaff/npnf106.vii.xl.html.

———. "St. Augustine: Reply to Faustus the Manichaen." In *A Select Library of the Nicene and Post-Nicene Fathers of the Christian Church*. Vol. 4, *The Writings Against the Manichaens and Against the Donatists*. Edited by Philip Schaff. Translated by J. R. King. Christian Classics Ethereal Library, 2005. Accessed May 31, 2017. http://www.ccel.org/ccel/schaff/npnf104.iv.ix.iii.html.

Augustine of Hippo, and Optatus of Milevis. *Donatist Martyr Stories: The Church in Conflict in Roman North Africa*. Translated by Maureen A. Tilley. Liverpool: Liverpool University Press, 1996.

Barth, Heinrich. *Travels and Discoveries in North and Central Africa*. Vol. 5. New York: Harper & Brothers, 1857.

Beale, Philip, and Sarah Taylor. *Sailing Close to the Wind: An Epic Voyage Recreating the First Circumnavigation of Africa by the Phoenicians in 600 BC*. Warwickshire, UK: The Lulworth Press, 2012.

Benedict, David. *History of the Donatists*. The Reformed Reader. 1999. Accessed October 12, 2018. http://www.reformedreader.org/history/benedict/donatists/toc.htm.

Bercot, David W. *A Dictionary of Early Christian Beliefs*. Peabody, MA: Hendrickson Publishers, 1998.

Bible Probe for Christians and Messianic Jews. "The Roman Theban Legion." 2014. Accessed April 4, 2017. http://bibleprobe.com/theban.html.

Bolman, Elizabeth, ed. *Monastic Visions: Wall Paintings in the Monastery of St. Antony at the Red Sea.* Cairo: American Research Center in Egypt, 2002.

Bruce, F. F. *The Canon of Scripture.* Downers Grove, IL: Intervarsity Press. 1988.

Butler, Alban. "SS. Saturninus, Dativus, and Others, Martyrs of Africa." In *The Lives of the Fathers, Martyrs, and Other Principal Saints.* Vol. 2, February. *The Lives of the Saints.* Bartleby.com: Great Books Online. 2012. Accessed May 22, 2017. http://www.bartleby.com/210/2/111.html.

Campbell, Christopher L., Pier F. Palamara, Maya Dubrovsky, Laura R. Botigué, Marc Fellous, Gil Atzmon, Carole Oddoux, et. al. "North African Jewish and non-Jewish populations form distinctive, orthogonal clusters." PNAS: Proceedings of the National Academy of Sciences. August 21, 2012. Accessed February 9, 2019. https://www.pnas.org /content/109/34/13865.

Campbell, Thomas. "St. Alexander." *The Catholic Encyclopedia.* Vol. 1. New York: Robert Appleton Company, 1907. Accessed November 28, 2018. http://www.newadvent .org/cathen/01296a.htm.

Carrington, Philip. *The Early Christian Church: Volume 2, The Second Christian Century.* Cambridge, UK: University Press, 1957.

Carroll, James Milton. *The Trail of Blood.* Emmaus, PA: Challenge Press, 1931.

Cartwright, Mark. "Dido." In *Ancient History Encyclopedia.* 2016. https://www.ancient.eu /Dido/.

Catholic Online. *Catholic Encyclopedia*, s.v. "Donatists." Accessed March 17, 2019. https://www.catholic.org /encyclopedia/view.php?id=3972.

———. [Second] "2 Maccabees – Chapter 2," May 24, 2018, https://www.catholic.org/bible /book.php?id=21&bible_chapter=2.

CatholicBridge.com. Accessed December 7, 2018. http://catholicbridge.com/.

Cavendish, Richard. "The Battle of the Milvian Bridge." History Today. 2012. Accessed May 6, 2017. http://www.historytoday.com/richard-cavendish/battle-milvian-bridge.

Cendana, Kat. "North Africa Converts to Islam and Arab Slave Trade Begins in 700 AD." *Amazing Bible Timeline with World History.* November 15, 2016. Accessed April 17. 2019. https://amazingbibletimeline.com/blog/north-africa-converts-to-islam-and-arab-slave-trade-begins-in-700-ad/.

CenturyOne Bookstore. "Main Events in the History of Jerusalem." Jerusalem: The Endless Crusade. 2003. Accessed April 6, 2017. http://www.centuryone.com /hstjrslm.html.

Chevalier, Louis. *Le Problème Démographique Nord-Africain.* France: Presses Universitaires de France, 1947.

Clarke, Graeme. "Third-Century Christianity." In *The Cambridge Ancient History: XII The Crisis of Empire, A.D. 193-337.* Edited by Alan Bowman, Averil Cameron, and Peter Garnsey. New York: Cambridge University Press, 2005.

Clement of Alexandria. *The Stromata, or Miscellanies, Book IV.* Edited by Peter Kirby. Early Christian Writings. Accessed April 28, 2017. http://www.earlychristianwritings .com/text/clement-stromata-book4.html.

———. *Who Is the Rich Man That Shall Be Saved?* Translated by Peter Kirby. Early Christian Writings. Accessed April 28, 2017. http://www.earlychristianwritings .com/text /clement-richman.html.

CNA: Chaine Nord Africaine. "History of the Church in North Africa: North Africa Returning to Its Roots?" 2013. Accessed May 9, 2017. http://www.cna-sat.org/O1/index.php /history-of-the-church-in-north-africa.

Cruciani, Fulvio, Roberta La Fratta, Piero Santolamazza, Danielle Sellitto, Roberto Pascone, Elizabeth Watson, Valentina Guida, et. al. "Phylogeographic Analysis of Haplogroup E3b (E-M215) Y Chromosomes Reveals Multiple Migratory Events Within and Out of Africa." *American Journal of Human Genetics* 74, no. 5, 2004. Accessed April 4, 2017. http://www.sciencedirect.com /science/article/pii /S0002929707643651.

Cyprian, "The Epistles of Cyprian: Epistle I. To Donatus." Translated by Ernest Wallis. In *Ante-Nicene Fathers.* Vol. 5, *Hippolytus, Cyprian, Caius, Novatian, Appendix.* Edited by Alexander Roberts and James Donaldson. Christian Classics Ethereal Library, 2005. Accessed May 20, 2017. http://www.ccel.org/ccel/schaff/anf05.iv.iv.i.html.

Dalrymple, William. *From the Holy Mountain: A Journey among the Christians of the Middle East.* New York: Henry Holt & Company, 1997.

Desfayes, Michel. "The Names of Countries: Including Some Familiar Names of Provinces or Peoples." http://michel-desfayes.org/namesofcountries.html.

DeWane, Tom. "History of St. Moses the Black Priory." St. Moses the Black Priory. 2009. Accessed April 17, 2017. http://www.stmosestheblackpriory.org/about_history.html.

Diakonoff, Igor M. *Semito-Hamitic languages: An Essay in Classification.* Moscow: Nauka Publishing House, 1965.

Dijkstra, Jitse H.F. *Philae and the End of Ancient Egyptian Religion: A Regional Study of Religious Transformation (298-642 CE).* Louvain, Belgium: Peeters Publishers, 2008.

Dines, Jennifer. *The Septuagint.* London: T&T Clark, 2004.

Diop, Cheikh Anta. *Precolonial Black Africa.* Brooklyn, NY: Lawrence Hill Books, 1978.

Dunn, Marilyn. *The Emergence of Monasticism: From the Desert Fathers to the Early Middle Ages.* Malden, MA: Blackwell Publishers, 2000.

Duval, Yvette. *Loca Sanctorum Africae: le cult des martyrs en Afrique du IVe au VII siècle.* Collection de l'Ecole Francaise de Rome (Book 58). l'Ecole Francaise de Rome, 1982.

Early Christian History. "Controversies: Donatism." Accessed October 12, 2018. http://www.earlychristianhistory.net/donatus.html.

Early Church History – CH101. "Persecution under Diocletian." Accessed October 9, 2018. https://churchhistory101.com/century4-p3.php.

Eimers, Justin. "Cyprian on Apostasy and Unity." Academia. 2012. Accessed October 9, 2018. http://www.academia.edu/8209280/Cyprian_on_Apostasy_and_Unity.

Elowsky, Joel. "Why a Center for Early African Christianity (CEAC)?" *Center for Early African Christianity* (blog), February 6, 2012. Accessed April 5, 2017. http://earlyafricanchristianity.com/blog/post.php.

Encyclopaedia Britannica, s.v. "Hieroglyphic Writing." Accessed March 21, 2019. https://www.britannica.com/topic/hieroglyphic-writing/Christianity-and-the-Greek-alphabet.

———, s.v. "Numidia: Ancient Region, Africa." Accessed October 9, 2018. https://www.britannica.com/place/Numidia.

———, s.v. "The Post-Nicene Period. Patristic Literature." 2018. Accessed October 9, 2018. https://www.britannica.com/topic/patristic-literature/The-post-Nicene-period#ref8045.

Encyclopedia.com, s.v. "Christianity: Christianity in North Africa." Accessed October 12, 2018. https://www.encyclopedia.com/environment/encyclopedias-almanacs-transcripts-and-maps/christianity-christianity-north-africa.

Erskine, Steuart. *Vanished Cities of Northern Africa*. London: FB & Ltd, Dalton House, 2018.

Eternal Word Television Network. The New Evangelization: Building the Civilization of Love. " Africa: Evangelization of the Continent." Accessed April 8, 2017. http://www.ewtn.com/new_evangelization/africa/ history/continent.htm.

Faraji, Salim. *The Roots of Nubian Christianity Uncovered: The Triumph of the Last Pharaoh*. Trenton: Africa World Press, 2012.

Farmer, David. "Marian and James." In *The Oxford Dictionary of Saints*. Oxford University Press, 2011. https://www.oxfordreference.com/view/10.1093/acref/9780199596607.001.0001/acref-9780199596607-e-1085.

Ferguson, Everett. "Factors Leading to the Selection and Closure of the New Testament Canon." In *The Canon Debate*. Edited by L. M. McDonald & J. A. Sanders. Peabody, MA: Hendrickson Publisher, 2002.

Fitzhenry, James. "Saint Arcadius." Roman Catholic Saints. 2011. Accessed May 7, 2017. http://www.roman-catholic-saints.com/saint-arcadius.html.

Fourth Century Christianity. "Early Christian Councils." 2012. Accessed October 12, 2018. https://www.fourthcentury.com/councils-and-creeds/.

Foxe, John. *Foxe's Book of Martyrs*. Edited by John Bruno Hare. Internet Sacred Text Archive. 2010. Accessed May 7, 2017. http://www.sacred-texts.com/chr/martyrs/.

France in Ethiopia: Embassy of France in Addis Ababa. "Inauguration Ceremony of Abba Garima Museum – Adwa." June 6, 2012. Accessed April 28, 2019. https://et.ambafrance.org/Inauguration-ceremony-of-Abba.

Frank, Michael. "In Morocco, Exploring Remnants of Jewish History." *The New York Times*. May 30, 2015. Accessed February 9, 2019. https://www.nytimes.com/2015/05 /31/travel/in-morocco-exploring-remnants-of-jewish-history.html.

The Freeman Institute. "Ancient Nubia." Accessed October 9, 2018. http://www.freemaninstitute.com/Gallery/nubia.htm.

Fuller, J.M. "Caecilianus, Archdeacon and Bishop of Carthage." In *Dictionary of Christian Biography and Literature to the End of the Sixth Century A.D., with an Account of the Principal Sects and Heresies*. Edited by Henry Wace and William Piercy. Christian Classics Ethereal Library. July 13, 2005, http://www.ccel.org/ccel/wace /biodict.html?term=caecilianus%2C+archdeacon+and+bishop+of+carthage.

Gabra, Gawdat, and Hany Takla, eds. *Christianity and Monasticism in Aswan and Nubia*. New York: The American University of Cairo Press, 2016.

Galli, Mark, and Ted Olsen, eds. *131 Christians Everyone Should Know*. Nashville: Broadman & Holman, 2000.

Gascoigne, Bamber. "History of the Byzantine Empire." History World. 2001. Accessed April 5, 2017. http://www.historyworld.net/wrldhis/PlainTextHistories.asp ?groupid=2751&HistoryID=ac59&gtrack=pthc.

Gates, Henry L. "Great Ancient African Civilizations." VHS. Produced and Directed by Henry L. Gates. Arlington, VA: Public Broadcasting Service, 2017.

Gearon, Eamonn. "Arab Invasions: The First Islamic Empire." *History Today.* June 2011. Accessed April 17, 2019. https://www.historytoday.com/archive/arab-invasions-first-islamic-empire.

Gibbon, Edward. "Chapter XVI: Conduct Towards the Christians, From Nero to Constantine.—Part VI." In *History of the Decline and Fall of the Roman Empire.* Christian Classics Ethereal Library. 2005. Accessed May 22, 2017. http://www.ccel.org/ccel/gibbon/decline.iv.vi.html?highlight=marcellus,the,centurion#highlight.

Gilson, Etienne. *The Philosopher and Theology.* New York: Random House, 1962.

Gonzalez, Justo, L. *The Story of Christianity.* Vol. 1, *The Early Church to the Dawn of Reformation.* New York: HarperSanFrancisco, 1984.

Gottheil, Richard, and Samuel Krauss. "Jason of Cyrene." In *JewishEncyclopedia.com.* 2011. http://www.jewishencyclopedia.com /articles/8528-jason-of-cyrene.

Graham, Alexander. *Roman Africa: An Outline of the History of Roman Occupation of North Africa, Based Chiefly upon Inscriptions and Monumental Remains in That Country.* London: Longmans, Green, and Co., 1902.

Graves, Dan. "Cassian and Marcellus Beheaded for Their Bold Stand." *Christianity.com.* 2007. Accessed April 5, 2017. http://www.christianity.com/church/church-history /timeline/1-300/cassian-and-marcellus-beheaded-for-their-bold-stand-11629631.html.

Hartig, Otto. "Nubia." Catholic Answers. Accessed April 4, 2017. https://www.catholic.com /encyclopedia/nubia.

Haughton, Brian. "What Happened to the Great Library at Alexandria?" In *Ancient History Encyclopedia.* February 1, 2011. Accessed December 11, 2018. https://www.ancient.eu/article/207/what-happened-to-the-great-library-at-alexandria/.

Heaton, Chris. "Nero and the Christians." UNRV History. Accessed May 19, 2017. http://www.unrv.com/early-empire/nero-christians.php.

Houghton, H.A.G. "The Latin New Testament: A Guide to Its Early History, Texts, and Manuscripts." Oxford Scholarship Online. 2016. Accessed May 19, 2017. http://www.oxfordscholarship.com/view/10.1093/acprof:oso/9780198744733.001.0001/acprof-9780198744733-chapter-1.

Hyman, Mark. *Blacks Who Died for Jesus: A History Book.* Nashville: Winston-Derek Publishers, 1983.

Ibrahim, Medhat. "The History of the Coptic Church: St Mark, the Apostle and Beholder of God." *Mighty Arrows Magazine*, April 2003. Accessed April 4, 2017. http://www.suscopts.org/mightyarrows/vol3_no1/stmark.pdf.

Ignatius. "Ignatius to the Smyrnaeans." Translated by Lightfoot & Harmer. Early Christian Writings. 2017. Accessed May 22, 2017. http://www.earlychristianwritings.com/ text/ignatius-smyrnaeans-lightfoot.html.

Irvine, A. K. "Frumentius." In *Dictionary of African Christian Biography.* 1975. Accessed May 13, 2017. https://dacb.org/stories/ethiopia/frumentius/.

IWGIA. "Indigenous Peoples in Algeria." Accessed April 5, 2017. http://www.iwgia.org /regions/africa/algeria.

Jemaneh, Yohanes. "Ethiopia: Strengthening the Historical Tight Bond." *The Ethipoian Herald*, March 30, 2017. Accessed May 23, 2017. http://allafrica.com/stories/201703300590 .html.

Jerome. "The Principal Works of St. Jerome." Translated by W. H. Fremantle, G. Lewis, and W. G. Martley. In *A Select Library of the Nicene and Post-Nicene Fathers of the Christian Church*. Second Series. Vol. 6, *Jerome: Letters and Select Works*. Christian Classics Ethereal Library. 2005. Accessed May 27, 2017. http://www.ccel.org/ccel /schaff/npnf206.ii.html.

JesusCentral.com. "First Century Context of Palestine (Israel)." Accessed October 9, 2018. http://www.jesuscentral.com/ji/historical-jesus/jesus-firstcenturycontext.php ?show=Editor.

Josephus, Flavius. *The Works of Flavius Josephus*. Translated by William Whiston. Auburn and Buffalo. John E. Beardsley. 1895. http://www.perseus.tufts.edu/hopper/text?doc=urn:cts:greekLit:tlg0526.tlg004.perseus-eng1:6.9.2.

Kelley, Joseph T. *Saint Augustine of Hippo: Selections from Confessions and Other Essential Writings*. Woodstock, VT: SkyLight Paths Publishing, 2010. Kindle.

King, Noel Q. *Christian and Muslim in Africa*. New York: Harper & Row Publishers, 1971.

———, Review of *The Planting of Christianity in Africa*, by C.P. Groves. *The Journal of African History* 1, no. 1 (January 1960): 157-159. https://doi.org/10.1017/S0021853700001596.

Kirby, Peter. "Church Fathers." Early Christian Writings. Accessed April 28, 2017. http://www.earlychristianwritings.com/churchfathers.html.

Kreis, Steven. "The Church Fathers: St. Jerome and St. Augustine." The History Guide: Lectures on Ancient and Medieval European History. 2006. Accessed May 23, 2017. http://www.historyguide.org/ancient/lecture16b.html.

Lactantius. "Of the Manner in Which the Persecutors Died." In *The Ante-Nicene Fathers: Translations of the Writings of the Fathers Down to A.D. 325*. Vol. 7, *Fathers of the Third and Fourth Centuries*. Translated by Alexander Roberts and James Donaldson. Christian Classics Ethereal Library, 2005. Accessed May 31, 2017. http://www.ccel.org/ccel/schaff/anf07.iii.v.xliv.html.

Larson, Marisa. "Did You Know?" *National Geographic*. January 2005. Accessed April 5, 2017. http://ngm.nationalgeographic.com/ngm/0501/feature4/.

Lewis, Charlton T. *A Latin Dictionary Lewis and Short*, s.v. "Afer," Oxford University Press, New York, 1879, https://archive.org/details/in.ernet.dli.2015.147309/page/n79.

Linsley, Alice C. "Biblical Anthropology: The Nubian Context of YHWH." *Biblical Anthropology* (blog), September 7, 2013. Accessed April 5, 2017. http://biblicalanthropology.blogspot.com/2013/09/the-nubian-context-of-yhwh.html.

Lipinski, Edward. *Itineraria Phoenicia*. Leuven, Belgium: Peeters Publishers, 2004.

Lippold, Adolf. "Theodosius I: Roman Emperor." In *Encyclopaedia Britannica*. 2018. Accessed October 9, 2018. https://www.britannica.com/biography/Theodosius-I.

Lucian of Samosata, "The Passing of Peregrinus." Translated by Peter Kirby. Early Christian Writings, 2017. Accessed May 19, 2017. http://www.earlychristianwritings.com/text/peregrinus.html.

Mark, Joshua J. "Roman Empire." In *Ancient History Encyclopedia*, 2011. Accessed April 4, 2017. http://www.ancient.eu/Roman_Empire/.

Markoe, Glenn. *Phoenicians*. Berkley: University of California Press, 2000.

Marniche, Dana. "African Moors: The Appearance of the Original Berbers According to European Perceptions." *Rasta Livewire* (blog), September 12, 2008. Accessed April 4, 2017. http://www.africaresource.com/rasta/sesostris-the-great-the-egyptian-hercules/the-appearance-of-the-original-berbers-according-to-european-perceptions-by-dana-marniche/.

Martindale, John R. *The Prosopography of the Later Roman Empire*: Volume 2, AD 395-527. New York: Cambridge University Press, 2006.

Mathetes. "Epistle of Mathetes to Diognetus." Translated by Alexander Roberts and James Donaldson. Early Christian Writings, 2017. Accessed April 28, 2017. http://www.earlychristian writings.com/diognetus.html.

Matusiak, John. "Martyr Africanus and 40 Others, Beheaded at Carthage." Orthodox Church in America. 2017. Accessed April 4, 2017. https://oca.org/saints/lives /2017/04/10/101043-martyr-africanus-and-40-others-beheaded-at-carthage.

———. "Martyr Timothy the Reader and his wife in Egypt." Orthodox Church in America, 2017. Accessed April 4, 2017. https://oca.org/saints/lives/2011/05/03/101278-martyr-timothy-the-reader-and-his-wife-in-egypt.

Meinardus, Otto Friedrich August. *Monks and Monasteries of the Egyptian Deserts*. Cairo, Egypt: The American University in Cairo Press, 1989.

Merrills, Andrew. *Vandals, Romans and Berbers: New Perspectives on Late Antique North Africa*. New York: Routledge Publishing, 2017.

Merrills, Andrew, and Richard Miles. *The Vandals*. Chichester, UK: Wiley-Blackwell Publishers, 2010.

Metzger, Bruce. *The Canon of the New Testament: Its Origin, Development, and Significance*. London: Oxford University Press, 1987.

Miller, Catherine. s.v. "Nubien, berbère et beja : notes sur trois langues vernaculaires non arabes de l'Égypte contemporaine." Égypte/Monde arabe, Première série. 1996. Accessed November 11, 2019. https://journals.openedition.org/ema/ 1960#article-1960.

Moorhead, John, trans. *Victor of Vita: History of the Vandal Persecution*. Vol. 10, *Translated Texts for Historians*. Liverpool: Liverpool University Press, 2006. https://epdf.tips /queue/victor-of-vita-history-of-the-vandal-persecution.html.

Mullen, Roderic L. *The Expansion of Christianity: A Gazetteer of its First Three Centuries*. Boston: Brill Leiden, 2004.

Mutiso-Mbinda, J. "List of African Saints." Archdiocese of Baltimore. 1998. Accessed June 1, 2017. http://www.archbalt.org/wp-content/uploads/2017/05/List-of-African-Saints.pdf.

National Library of Sweden. Codex Gigas. "Translation of the Greek Text into Latin." 2015. Accessed May 25, 2017. http://www.kb.se/codex-gigas/eng/Long/texter /medeltida-bibel/translations/#Translation of the Greek text into Latin.

New World Encyclopedia. s.v. "Magi." Last modified August 7, 2018. Accessed December 17, 2018. http://www.newworldencyclopedia.org/entry/Magi.

Nova Roma. "Syncretism." 2009. Accessed October 9, 2018. http://www.novaroma.org/ nr/Syncretism.

Oden, Thomas C. *The African Memory of Mark: Reassessing Early Church Tradition*. Downers Grove, IL: InterVarsity Press, 2011.

———. *Early Libyan Christianity: Uncovering a North African Tradition*. Downers Grove, IL: InterVarsity Press, 2011.

———. *How Africa Shaped the Christian Mind: Rediscovering the African Seedbed of Western Christianity*. Downers Grove, IL: InterVarsity Press, 2007.

Oldest.org. "8 Oldest Books That Ever Existed." July 1, 2018. http://www.oldest.org/culture/books-ever-existed/.

Oliver, W.H., 'The Catechetical School in Alexandria', Verbum et Ecclesia 36(1), 2015, Accessed September 30, 2024. http://dx.doi.org/10.4102/ve.v36i1.1385.

Omer, Ibrahim M. "Investigating the Origin of the Ancient Jewish Community at Elephantine: A Review." *Ancient Sudan-Kush*, 2008. Accessed April 4, 2017. http://www.ancientsudan.org/articles_jewish_elephantine.html.

Originalpeople.org. "Arius: Libyan Christian Priest of Alexandria, Egypt and the Council of Nicaea." 2013. Accessed October 9, 2018. http://originalpeople.org/arius-libyan-christian-priest-alexandria-egypt-council-nicaea/.

OrthodoxWiki Contributors. "Main Page." *OrthodoxWiki*. https://orthodoxwiki.org/Main_Page.

Oshitelu, G.A. "Athanasius." In *Dictionary of African Christian Biography*, 2002. Accessed March 13, 2017. https://dacb.org/stories/egypt/athanasius.

———. "Cyprian." In *Dictionary of African Christian Biography*, 2002. Accessed April 6, 2017. http://www.dacb.org/stories/tunisia/cyprian.

———. "Origen of Alexandria." In *Dictionary of African Christian Biography*, 2002. Accessed April 6, 2017. http://www.dacb.org/stories/egypt/origen.

———. "Tertullian." In *Dictionary of African Christian Biography*, 2002. Accessed April 6, 2017. http://www.dacb.org/stories/tunisia/tertullian.

Pamphilius, Eusebius. "Those in the Palace." In *A Select Library of the Nicene and Post-Nicene Fathers of the Christian Church*. Second Series. Vol. 1, *Eusibius Pamphilius: The Church History of Eusebius*. Translated by Arthur Cushman McGiggert. Christian Classics Ethereal Library. 2005. Accessed May 22, 2017. http://www.ccel.org/ccel/schaff/npnf201.iii.xiii.vii.html.

Papal Encyclicals Online. "First Council of Nicaea – 325 AD." Accessed October 9, 2018. http://www.papalencyclicals.net/Councils/ecum01.htm.

"Paulist Fathers." *Catholic World*. Vols. 175-176, 1952.

Phillot, H.W. "Felix of Aptunga." In *Dictionary of Early Christian Biography and Literature to the End of the Sixth Century A.D., with an Account of the Principal Sects and Heresies*. Edited by Henry Wace and William Piercy. Christian Classics Ethereal Library. 2005. Accessed October 9, 2018. http://www.ccel.org/ccel/wace/biodict.html?term=Felix%20(26)%20I.,%20bp.%20of%20Aptunga.

Peiraeus Public Library. "Names of Libya (Africa)." Ancient Names Galleria. November 20, 2009. http://www.peiraeuspubliclibrary.com/names/libya.html.

Pick, Bernhard. *The Attack of Celsus on Christianity*. Oxford, UK: Oxford University Press, 1911.

Pliny the Younger. "Pliny the Younger to the Emperor Trajan." Translated by Peter Kirby. Early Christian Writings, 2017. Accessed May 19, 2017. http://www.earlychristianwritings.com/text/pliny.html.

Pontius the Deacon. "The Life and Passion of Cyprian, Bishop and Martyr." Translated by Ernest Wallis. In *Ante-Nicene Fathers*. Vol. 5, *Hippolytus, Cyprian, Caius, Novatian, Appendix*. Edited by Alexander Roberts and James Donaldson. Christian Classics Ethereal Library, 2005. Accessed May 20, 2017. Christian Classics Ethereal Library, 2005. Accessed May 21, 2017. http://www.ccel.org/ccel/schaff/anf05.iv.iii.html.

Powers, Tom. "A Second Look at the 'Alexander Son of Simon' Ossuary: Did It Hold Father and Son?" Biblical Archaeology Society. 2006. Accessed October 9, 2018. https://israelpalestineguide.files.wordpress.com/2010/06/alexander-simon-ossuary-a-second-look-from-bar.pdf.

Prengaman, Peter. "Morocco's Berbers Battle to Keep From Losing Their Culture / Arab Minority Forces Majority to Abandon Native Language." *San Francisco Chronicle*, March 16, 2001. Accessed April 5, 2017. http://www.sfgate.com/news/article/Morocco-s-Berbers-Battle-to-Keep-From-Losing-2941557.php.

Preobrazhenskoe. "King Ezana of Axum (Ethiopia)." *World Historia* (blog), March 15, 2007. Accessed April 6, 2017. http://archive.worldhistoria.com/king-ezana-of-axum-ethiopia_topic18570.html.

Press, Gerald A. *Development of the Idea of History in Antiquity*. Montreal: McGill-Queen's Press, 2003.

Race: Are We So Different? 2007. Accessed May 15, 2017. http://www.understandingrace.org/history/science/early_class.html.

Rashidi, Runoko. *Black Star: The African Presence in Early Europe*. London, UK: Books of Africa, 2011.

Rauh, Nicholas K. "The Rise of Christianity." *Culture and Society in Imperial Rome Preliminary Syllabus. Fall 2010. College of Liberal Arts, Purdue University. West Lafayette, IN*. Accessed April 6, 2017. http://web.ics.purdue.edu/~rauhn/Hist_416/hist420/RISE%20OF%20CHRISTIANITY.htm.

Reardon, JoHannah. "The Nicene and Apostles' Creeds." Christian Bible Studies, 2008. Accessed May 27, 2017. http://www.christianitytoday.com/biblestudies/articles/churchhomeleadership/nicene-apostles-creeds.html.

ReligionFacts: Just the Facts on Religion. "Persecution in the Early Church." 2016. Accessed May 19, 2017. http://www.religionfacts.com/persecution-early-church.

_____. "St. Anthony of Egypt." Accessed May 21, 2017. http://www.religionfacts.com/anthony-egypt.

Richardson, Ernest Cushing, trans. "Jerome and Gennadius, Lives of Illustrious Men." In *A Select Library of the Nicene and Post-Nicene Fathers of the Christian Church*. Second Series. Vol. 3, *Theodoret, Jerome, Gennadius, and Rufinus: Historical Writings*. Christian Classics Ethereal Library. 2005. Accessed May 22, 2017. http://www.ccel.org/ccel/schaff/npnf203.v.iii.lxxxii.html.

Rigney, Melanie. "Wednesday's Woman: St. Dionysia." *Faith, Saints and Life* (blog), December 2, 2015. Accessed April 4, 2017. http://melanierigney.com/blog/catholicism/4201/.

Roberts, Adrian. "The Nicene Creed." Church on the Net, 2017. Accessed May 27, 2017. http://www.church-on-the-net.com/reference/creed.aspx.

Roberts, Alexander, and James Donaldson, eds. *Ante-Nicene Christian Library: Translations of the Writings of the Fathers*. Vol. 19. Translated by Hamilton Bryce and Hugh Campbell. Edinburgh: T&T Clark, 1871.

———. *Ante-Nicene Christian Library: Translations of the Writings of the Fathers*. Vol 22. Translated by William Fletcher. Edinburgh: T&T. Clark, 1900.

Robertson, Archibald. *Select Writings and Letters of Athanasius, Bishop of Alexandria*. Northwestern Theological Seminary, 2006. Accessed May 27, 2017. http://www.ntslibrary.com/PDF%20Books/Athanasius%20Select%20Writtings%20and%20Letters.pdf.

Robertson, J.C. "Chapter XXI: St. Augustine (A.D. 354-430). In *Sketches of Church History: From AD 33 to the Reformation.*" Christian Classics Ethereal Library, June 1, 2005. Accessed October 9, 2018. https://www.ccel.org/ccel/robertson/history .iii.xxi.html.

Rodriguez, Tommy. "The World of the Ancient Carthaginians." The Ancient World. Accessed May 19, 2017. http://www.theancientworld.net/civ/carthage.html.

Rutherfurd, Andrew. *The Passion of the Scillitan Martyrs*. Translated by J. A. Robinson. Early Christian Writings, 2017. Accessed May 19, 2017. http://www.earlychristian writings.com/text/scillitan.html.

Saint Antonius Coptic Orthodox Church. "The Church of Martyrs." Accessed April 5, 2017. http://www.antonius.org/about/the-coptic-orthodox-church/.

Salih, Abu. *The Churches and Monasteries of Egypt and Some Neighboring Countries*. Translated by B.T.A. Evetts. Piscataway, NJ: Gorgias Press, 2002.

Sallust. *The Jugurthine War*. Edited by John S. Watson. New York: Harper & Brothers, 1899. http://www.perseus.tufts.edu/hopper/text?doc=Perseus%3Atext%3A1999 .02.0126%3Achapter%3D18.

Samaan, Moses. "The Origins of the Coptic Horologion (Agpeya)." Become Orthodox. 2019. http://becomeorthodox.org/prayer/the-origins-of-the-coptic-horologion-agpeya/.

Schaff, Philip. "The Edicts of Toleration. A.D. 311–313." In *History of the Christian Church*. Vol. 2, *Ante-Nicene Christianity*. Christian Classics Ethereal Library, 2005. Accessed April 28, 2017. http://www.ccel.org/ccel/schaff/hcc2.v.iv .xiv.html.

Schaff, Philip, and Henry Wace, eds. *The Canons of the 318 Holy Fathers Assembled in the City of Nice, in Bithynia*. In *A Select Library of the Nicene and Post Nicene Fathers of the Christian Church*. Vol. 14, *The Seven Ecumenical Councils*. Christian Classics Ethereal Library. 2005. Accessed May 27, 2017. https://www.ccel.org/ccel/schaff /npnf214.vii.vi.i.html.

_____. "Introductory Note." In *The Canons of the CCXVII Blessed Fathers Who Assembled at Carthage. Commonly Called the Code of Canons of the African Church*. In *A Select Library of the Nicene and Post Nicene Fathers of the Christian Church*. Vol. 14, *The Seven Ecumenical Councils*. Christian Classics Ethereal Library. 2005. Accessed May 23, 2017. https://www.ccel.org/ccel/schaff /npnf214.i.html.

Schneider, Wolfgang. "When Was the Book of Revelation Written?" BibelCenter. 2010. Accessed June 4, 2017. http://www.biblecenter.de/bibel/studien/e-std310.php.

Septuagint. "Septuagint and Reliability" 2016. Accessed on May 29, 2017. http://www.septuagint.net/.

Severus. "Life of the Apostle and Evangelist Mark." Translated by B.T.A. Evetts. Severus of Al-Ushmunain: History of the Patriarchs of the Coptic Church of Alexandria. The St. Pachomius Orthodox Library. 1996. Accessed April 5, 2017. http://www.voskrese.info/spl/patmark.html.

Shaw, Brent D. "Bad Boys: Circumcellions and Fictive Violence - Version 2.1." Princeton/Stanford Working Papers in Classics. February 3, 2006. Princeton, NJ. Accessed October 9, 2018. https://www.princeton.edu/~pswpc/pdfs/shaw /020603.pdf.

Shinnie, P.L. "Medieval Nubia." Sudan Antiquities Service. 1954. Accessed April 6, 2017. http://rumkatkilise.org/nubia.htm.

Shuma, Toni. "What are the Main Contributions of St. Augustine?" *Quora* (blog), January 5, 2013. Accessed October 12, 2018. https://www.quora.com/What-are-the-main-contributions-of-St-Augustine.

Slouschz, Nahum. *Travels in North Africa*. Philadelphia: The Jewish Publication Society of America, 1927.

Smith, Clyde C. "Speratus." In *Dictionary of African Christian Biography*. 2004. Accessed April 5, 2017. http://www.dacb.org/stories/tunisia/speratus.

Smitha Frank E. "Order under Diocletian, to Constantine." MacroHistory: WorldHistory. Accessed October 9, 2018. http://www.fsmitha.com/h1/rome22.htm.

Snowden, Frank M. *Before Color Prejudice*. Cambridge, MA: Harvard University Press, 1983.

Strand, Emily K. C. "Desert Fathers." Solitary Life. Solitaries of De Koven. 1995. Accessed May 23, 2017. http://www.solitariesofdekoven.org/articles.html.

Study.com. "The Phoenicians: History, Religion & Civilization." Chapter 1/Lesson 22, 2019, https://study.com/academy/lesson/the-phoenicians-history-religion-civilization.html.

Studzinski, Raymond. *Reading to Live: The Evolving Practice of Lectio Divina*. Trappist, KY: Liturgical Press, 2009.

Suetonius [C. Suetonius Tranquillus]. *Nero*. Edited by Alexander Thomson. Perseus Digital Library. Accessed May 19, 2017. http://www.perseus.tufts.edu/hopper/text?doc=Perseus:text:1999.02.0132:life=nero:chapter=16&highlight=superstition2Csuetonius2Cwicked.

A Survey of Church History: Part 1. Ligonier Ministries. CD. Produced and Directed by Ligonier Ministries. Ligonier Valley, PA: Ligonier Ministries, 2012.

Tacitus, Cornelius. *The Annals*. Edited by Alfred John Church, William Jackson Brodribb, and Sara Bryant. Perseus Digital Library. Accessed May 19, 2017. http://www.perseus.tufts.edu/hopper/text?doc=Perseus%3Atext%3A1999.02.0078%3Abook%3D15%3Achapter%3D44.

Teissier, Henri. "The African Roots of Latin Christianity." *30 Days in the Church and in the World*. 2004. Accessed April 24, 2017. http://www.30giorni.it/articoli_id_3553_l3 .htm?id=3553.

Tertullian. "An Answer to the Jews." Edited by Allan Menzies. Translated by S. Thelwall. In *Ante-Nicene Fathers*. Vol. 3, *Latin Christianity: Its Founder, Tertullian*. Christian Classics Ethereal Library. 2005. Accessed April 8, 2019. https://www.ccel.org/ccel /schaff/anf03.iv.ix.vii.html.

———. "The Apology." Edited by Allan Menzies. Translated by S. Thelwall. In *Ante-Nicene Fathers*. Vol. 3, *Latin Christianity: Its Founder, Tertullian*. Christian Classics Ethereal Library. 2005. Accessed May 27, 2017. http://www.ccel.org/ccel/schaff /anf03.iv.iii .i.html.

———. "Latin Christianity: Its Founder, Tertullian." Edited by Philip Schaff and Allan Menzies. In *Ante-Nicene Fathers*. Vol. 3. Christian Classics Ethereal Library. 2005. Accessed April 28, 2017. http://www.ccel.org/ccel/schaff/anf03.pdf.

———. "On the Pallium." Edited by Roger Pearse. Translated by S. Thelwall. The Tertullian Project, 1998. Accessed May 24, 2017. http://www.tertullian.org/anf/anf04 /anf04-03.htm#P128_5972.

———. *The Passion of Perpetua and Felicitas*. Translated by Peter Kirby. Early Christian Writings. 2017. Accessed May 19, 2017. http://www.earlychristianwritings.com/text/tertullian24.html.

———. "To Scapula." Translated by S. Thelwall. Early Christian Writings. 2017. Accessed April 28, 2017. http://www.earlychristianwritings.com/text/tertullian05.html.

Tilley, Maureen A. *The Bible in Christian North Africa: The Donatist World.* Minneapolis: Augsburg Fortress, 1997.

Toy, Crawford Howell, and Isaac Broydé. "Malchus (Cleodemus the Prophet)." In *JewishEncyclopedia.com.* 2011. http://www.jewishencyclopedia.com/articles/10328-malchus-cleodemus-the-prophet.

Tribunus. "Saint Maurice: Martyr, Black Saint, Knight Commander of the Theban Legion and Patron Saint of the Holy Roman Empire." *Roman Christendom* (blog), September 26, 2008. Accessed March 30, 2017. http://romanchristendom.blogspot.com/2008/09/saint-maurice-martyr-black-saint-and.html.

Unger, Merrill F., and William White Jr., eds. "Barbarian." In *Vine's Expository Dictionary of Biblical Words*, Nashville: Thomas Nelson, Inc., 1985.

Venter, Daniel Johannes, and E. W. Neuland. *NEPAD and the African Renaissance.* Johannesburg, South Africa: Richard Havenga & Associates, 2005.

Victor of Vita. *Victor of Vita: History of the Vandal Persecution.* Translated by John Moorhead. Liverpool: Liverpool University Press, 2006.

Weissenrieder, Annette. "Rethinking the Origins of the Gospel of Luke: The *Vetus Latina*." San Francisco Theological Seminary. 2016. Accessed May 26, 2017. http://sfts.edu/wp-content/uploads/2016/03/vetuslatina.pdf.

Wikipedia Contributors. *Wikipedia, The Free Encyclopedia.* https://en.wikipedia.org.

Wikisource Contributors. *The New International Encyclopedia.* https://en.wikisource.org/wiki.

Williams, Stephen. *Diocletian and the Roman Recovery.* New York: Routledge, 1997.

Windsor, Rudolph R. *From Babylon to Timbuktu.* Chicago: Lushena Books, 2003.

Woods, David. "St. Maximilian of Tebessa (BHL 5813)." The Military Martyrs. 2003. https://www.ucc.ie/archive/milmart/Maximilian.html#B.

WordSense.eu, s.v. "Maurus." Accessed April 7, 2019. https://www.wordsense.eu/Maurus/.

About the Author

Jimmie D. Compton, Jr. confessed faith in Jesus Christ at the age of twenty-eight. Many believers, pastors, and church leaders have been drawn into a more intimate relationship with Jesus Christ as a result of his pastoral gifts. Other books by him can be found on Amazon.

Pastor Compton is a biblically grounded pastor/teacher, author, expositor, servant-leader, licensed counselor, certified software engineer, and certified manager. He has a Bachelor of Arts in Sociology and Anthropology from Wayne State University, a Diploma in the Bible from Birmingham Bible Institute, and a Master of Arts in Pastoral Counseling from Ashland Theological Seminary. For thirty years he has founded and pastored Hope Bible Fellowship Church in Detroit. Pastor Compton is available to lecture on Early African Church History. Go to *www.onegodtvnetwork.com/early-african-church-history* to sample his lecture content.

His mitochondria DNA profile matches the Berber population in Africa's ancient Mauretania region (today's Morocco).

To purchase this survey or any book by Jimmie D. Compton, Jr. visit his author page at

lulu.com/spotlight/jcomptonjr or amazon.com/author/jimmiecompton
for coiled spine *for glued spine*

Surveying Christianity's African Roots

Contact us at theafricastop@gmail.com

- To send critiques, inquiries, suggestions, testimonies, or updates
- For information about direct purchases or volume discounts

www.ingramcontent.com/pod-product-compliance
Lightning Source LLC
Chambersburg PA
CBHW081223170426
43198CB00017B/2702